OXFORD MONOGRAPHS ON CRIMINAL LAW AND JUSTICE

This series aims to cover all aspects of criminal law and procedure including criminal evidence. The scope of this series is wide, encompassing both practical and theoretical works.

OTHER TITLES IN THIS SERIES

How Juries Work
And How They Could Work Better
Rebecca K Helm

Civil Recovery of Criminal Property
Colin King and Jennifer Hendry

The Insanity Defence
International and Comparative Perspectives
Ronnie Mackay and Warren Brookbanks

Justice In-Between
A Study of Intermediate Criminal Verdicts
Federico Picinali

Criminal Fraud and Election Disinformation
Law and Politics
Jeremy Horder

Policing the Borders Within
Ana Aliverti

Criminalizing Sex
A Unified Liberal Theory
Stuart P Green

Reasons to Doubt
Wrongful Convictions and the Criminal Cases Review Commission
Carolyn Hoyle and Mai Sato

Fitness to Plead
International and Comparative Perspectives
Ronnie Mackay and Warren Brookbanks

Criminal Misconducts in Office
Law and Politics
Jeremy Horder

The Preventive Turn in Criminal Law
Henrique Carvalho

Criminal Justice and Taxation
Peter Alldridge

In Search of Criminal Responsibility
Ideas, Interests, and Institutions
Nicola Lacey

Preventive Justice
Andrew Ashworth and Lucia Zedner

Character in the Criminal Trial
Mike Redmayne

Homicide and the Politics of Law Reform
Jeremy Horder

The Insecurity State
Vulnerable Autonomy and the Right to Security in the Criminal Law
Peter Ramsay

Manifest Madness
Mental Incapacity in the Criminal Law
Arlie Loughnan

The Ethics of Plea Bargaining
Richard L Lippke

Prosecuting Domestic Violence
A Philosophical Analysis
Michelle Madden Dempsey

Abuse of Process and Judicial Stays of Criminal Proceedings
Second Edition
Andrew L-T Choo

Victims as Agents of State Accountabilit

Victims as Agents of State Accountability

A Comparative and Normative Analysis

MARIE MANIKIS

Associate Professor and William Dawson Scholar, Faculty of Law, McGill University, Canada

OXFORD
UNIVERSITY PRESS

OXFORD
UNIVERSITY PRESS

Great Clarendon Street, Oxford, OX2 6DP,
United Kingdom

Oxford University Press is a department of the University of Oxford.
It furthers the University's objective of excellence in research, scholarship,
and education by publishing worldwide. Oxford is a registered trade mark of
Oxford University Press in the UK and in certain other countries.

Published in the United States of America by Oxford University Press
198 Madison Avenue, New York, NY 10016, United States of America.

British Library Cataloguing in Publication Data
Data available

Library of Congress Control Number: 2025948689

ISBN 9780198885313

DOI: 10.1093/9780191993947.001.0001

Printed and bound by
CPI Group (UK) Ltd., Croydon, CR0 4YY

The manufacturer's authorised representative in the EU for product safety is
Oxford University Press España S.A. of Parque Empresarial San Fernando de Henares,
Avenida de Castilla, 2 – 28830 Madrid (www.oup.es/en or product.safety@oup.com).
OUP España S.A. also acts as importer into Spain of products made by the manufacturer.

MIX
Paper | Supporting responsible forestry
FSC® C013604
FSC www.fsc.org

Acknowledgements

This monograph is the result of years of research, reflection, and dialogue, and I owe deep thanks to many individuals and institutions who helped shape its path.

I am profoundly grateful to my mentors, collaborators, and colleagues who have inspired and challenged me throughout this journey. I am particularly indebted to the following individuals, whose intellectual generosity and critical insights through seminars, comments, and conversations have strengthened components of this monograph: Antony Duff, Paul Cassell, Nicola Lacey, Lucia Zedner, Tatjana Hörnle, Jason Varuhas, Michelle Madden-Dempsey, Hadar Dancig-Rosenberg, Jo-Anne Wemmers, Meg Garvin, and Sandra Marshall. A heartfelt thank you to Julian V Roberts, Carolyn Hoyle, and Andrew Ashworth, whose initial guidance throughout my doctoral journey helped lay early foundations for this work.

I would also like to thank my wonderful research assistants who have contributed to the editorial and research process of this monograph. I am especially grateful to Sophia Rafuse, whose editing acumen, thoughtful insights, research skills, and dedication have made a significant contribution to this project from beginning to end. I also extend my sincere thanks to Marina Li-Pook, Anna Prykhodko, Audrey Matheson, Siobhan O'Connell, Charlotte Taylor-Baer, Gillian Smith, and Nicolas Kamran for their valuable assistance.

I am equally thankful for the support and encouragement of family and friends. Véronique Grenier, Irène Skyllas, Dimitri Manikis, and Antoine Manikis, your unconditional love, support, encouragement, sacrifices, and tireless devotion built the foundation and strength that made this work possible. Jonas-Sébastien Beaudry, Stefanie Carsley, Jeffrey Kennedy, Colleen Sheppard, Derek Jones, Alana Klein, Sarah Riley-Case, Noah Weisbord, Marion Vannier, Fernanda Fonseca-Rosenblatt, Carina Gallo, Daniel Pascoe, Daniel Alati, Julia Viebach, George Mawhinney, Ignacio Cofone, David LaChance, Eva Villalba, Rachel Jean-Pierre, Constanza Martinez, Ingrid de Rauglaudre, Cristiana Spinelli, Yassemine Khawajkie, and Déborah Grausem, who reminded me that scholarly work is sustained not only by ideas but also by supporting and caring communities.

Thank you all for reminding me of what matters beyond the page.

I extend my thanks to the William Dawson Scholarship, McGill University, and the Social Sciences and Humanities Research Council of Canada for their generous support, and to the scholars and staff at the Centre for Criminology at the University of Oxford, the Max Planck Institute for the Study of Crime, Security and Law, the Centre for the Study of Law and Society at UC Berkeley, and the National Crime Victim Law Institute. Your intellectual environments, reflections, and resources provided fertile ground for many parts of this monograph.

I would likewise offer my warm thanks to Fiona Briden, Kezia Johnson, Charlotte Kershaw, Titus Prathish, the anonymous reviewers, and the academic editors at Oxford University Press for their enthusiastic support and meticulous work in bringing this monograph to fruition.

Finally, I dedicate this book to those who continue to push for justice, substantive equality, accountability, and dignity within systems that too often fall short.

Contents

PART I

PRELIMINARY CONSIDERATIONS AND THE CONCEPTUALIZATION OF VICTIM PARTICIPATION

1
Introduction

In recent decades, one of the most significant developments in criminal justice has been the evolving role of the victim as a participant within criminal justice systems. Across common law jurisdictions, laws, regulations, and guidelines offer victims of crime various avenues of participation to engage and potentially influence the criminal justice process. These forms of participation vary in nature and in the degree of engagement offered to victims. For example, victims can request information on the development of the criminal justice process, confer with prosecutors during decision-making processes, seek to review certain state prosecutorial decisions, present victim impact statements at sentencing, and request redress when state actors fail to comply with their legal obligations.

An important, yet under-researched form of participation developed in this monograph is the role of victims in holding the prosecutorial state accountable for instances of state fallibility. This role is recognized in very few common law jurisdictions and enables victims to challenge state decision-making when failures occur. Illustrative examples include the initiation of private prosecutions when the state declines to act in England and Wales, the contestation of prosecution agreements in the United States, and the judicial review of prosecutorial decisions in England and Wales as well as in certain US states.

High-profile cases in which victims have challenged prosecutorial fallibilities illustrate the importance of this role. Victims of Jeffrey Epstein's sexual abuse fought in court[1] to overturn a secret non-prosecution agreement negotiated between the state prosecution and Epstein negotiated without their knowledge. The family of Tamir Rice, a twelve-year-old Black boy shot and killed by a white police officer, filed a motion supported by an affidavit[2]—enabling citizens to trigger the criminal process when prosecutors fail to act. In England and Wales, two women who worked as sex workers successfully brought a private prosecution after state prosecutors refused to press charges against an

[1] *In re Wild*, 955 F 3d 1269 (11th Cir 2020); *In re Wild*, 994 F 3d 1244 (11th Cir 2021) (en banc).
[2] *In re Affidavits Relating to Timothy Loehmann & Frank Garmback* (Cleveland Mun Ct 11 June 2015).

Victims as Agents of State Accountability. Marie Manikis, Oxford University Press. © Marie Manikis 2026.
DOI: 10.1093/9780191993947.003.0002

individual who was ultimately convicted of these sexual assaults.[3] Relatedly, victims of domestic, sexual, physical, and state violence[4] from marginalized groups have also successfully challenged decisions not to prosecute in cases where prosecutorial failures were rooted in substantive inequalities.

These cases, along with others examined in this monograph, illustrate the possibility that prosecutorial fallibilities may occur within the exercise of discretionary powers, as well as the potential for victims to hold the state accountable for these fallibilities. They also raise the broader questions animating this monograph: why, and in what ways, should victims be recognized as legitimate actors capable of holding the state accountable in instances of prosecutorial fallibility?

From the onset, the broader matter of victim participation in adversarial models of criminal justice raises contentious questions regarding its rationale, the types and extent of participation, and the relationship between public and private interests in a purportedly public state-driven process. Scholarship has primarily conceptualized victim participation as individual rights—understood as private entitlements and grounded in possessive individualism, which frame victims as bearers of distinct personal interests separable from those of the state and the accused.[5] This private conception has shaped both criticism and advocacy of victim participation. Critics worry that victim participation is changing the understanding of the state prosecutor's role, the concept of the public interest, and the broader criminal process by introducing a private dimension into what has traditionally been conceived as public—in ways that are perceived as conflicting with rights of the accused.[6] Advocates have also relied on this private conception to argue in favour of recognizing victim participation as a way to have victims needs and personal harms considered and redressed within the criminal process.

Far less attention, however, has been devoted to a public conception of victims, their role, and interests—as citizens[7] who contribute to deliberative

[3] English Collective of Prostitutes, 'Successful Private Prosecution of Serial Rapist—R v Davies' (*English Collective of Prostitutes*, 1 January 1996) <https://prostitutescollective.net/private-prosecution/> accessed 24 June 2023. Similarly, in *Moher v Moher* [2019] EWCA Civ 1482, a victim of domestic violence brought forward a successful private prosecution in a context where the state prosecution did not charge the offender.

[4] *R(B) v DPP* [2009] EWHC 106 (victim of assault was not perceived as credible on the basis of disability); *R v DPP Ex p Manning* [2001] QB 330; [2000] 3 WLR 463 (Black man who died in state custody following violence from prison officers successfully judicially reviewed the prosecution's decision not to charge).

[5] Douglas Beloof, 'The Third Wave of Crime Victims' Rights: Standing, Remedy, and Review' (2005) 2 BYU L Rev 255.

[6] Andrew Ashworth and Mike Redmayne, *The Criminal Process* (4th edn, OUP 2010).

[7] RA Duff and SE Marshall, 'Communicative Punishment and the Role of the Victim' (2004) 23(2) Crim Just Ethics 39; R Holder, *Just Interests: Victims, Citizens, and the Potential for Justice* (Elgar 2018);

practices and make claims in the public interest. This monograph develops precisely this public conception. Borrowing from the legal public–private spectrum[8] and the literature on citizenship and the public interest[9], it argues that victims should not only be understood as individuals with private interests but also as citizens capable of representing public interests.[10]

This conception is especially relevant for analysing—and further developing—the novel and evolving role of victims explored in this monograph: that of victims as agents of state accountability. This monograph advances the literature on victim participation by offering a comparative account of how victims in England and Wales and the United States have assumed participatory roles in holding the prosecutorial state accountable in the face of various forms of state failures. It explores the diverse dimensions of this role by examining the mechanisms through which it is exercised, as well as the impact of such engagement and the challenges to its recognition and implementation—especially for marginalized victims.

The importance of recognizing, analysing, and developing state accountability as a form of victim participation in criminal justice—with a focus on state prosecutions—stems from the fact that the state, including prosecutors, as part of a structure created and comprising humans, is fallible.[11] This is compounded by what political theorists have identified as an 'accountability deficit'[12] in modern liberal societies. Within the criminal justice context, this deficit is most acutely concentrated in the executive branch and is exemplified by the expansive and largely unchecked discretionary power wielded by state prosecutors over decisions relating to prosecutions.[13] As Angela J Davis observes, prosecutors are 'the most powerful officials in the system'[14], operating

Jeffrey Kennedy, 'The Citizen Victim: Reconciling the Public and Private in Criminal Sentencing' (2019) 13(1) Crim L & Phil 83.

[8] Anna Grear, 'Theorizing the Rainbow? The Puzzle of the Public-Private Divide' (2003) 9 Res Publica 169.

[9] Virginia Held, *The Public Interest and Individual Interests* (Basic Books 1970).

[10] Ian Edwards, 'An Ambiguous Participant: The Crime Victim and Criminal Justice Decision-Making' (2004) 44(6) Br J Criminol 967; Marie Manikis, 'Conceptualising the Victim in England and Wales and the United States within a Spectrum of Public and Private Interests' (2021) 41(1) OJLS 219.

[11] RA Duff, 'When Should We Plead Guilty' in Julian V Roberts and Jesper Ryberg (eds), *Pleading Guilty: Ethical Perspectives on Sentencing the Self-Convicted* (Hart 2023).

[12] Mark Bovens, Thomas Schillemans, and Paul T Hart, 'Does Public Accountability Work? An Assessment Tool?' (2008) 86(1) Public Adm 225, 229.

[13] Angela Davis, 'The Perils of Private Prosecutions' (2022) 13(7) Cal L Rev 7, 9; Jordan A Sklansky, 'The Nature and Function of Prosecutorial Power' (2016) 106(3) J Crim L Criminol 473.

[14] Davis (n 13); This is especially true of the American prosecutor who not only holds wide discretionary charging powers but also pleabargaining decisions—the latter being more widespread in the United States than England and Wales.

with vast discretion and minimal oversight—conditions ripe for decision-making errors, notably rooted in inequalities.[15]

Prosecutorial fallibilities can take many forms: errors of law or procedure, flawed credibility assessments, conflicts of interest, and over and under charging.[16] Indeed, discretionary decisions by prosecutors, which are at the heart of this monograph, include decisions as whether to charge, drop charges, engage in agreements with defendants, and assessments of credibility—and can be rooted in substantive inequalities that perpetuate under- or over-prosecution.[17] This is particularly prominent in cases marked by power asymmetries between victims and defendants. These dynamics are shaped by broader social inequalities related to race, class, gender, disability, and other intersecting axes of marginalization. Both England and Wales and the United States continue to experience state fallibilities and accountability deficits, albeit shaped by their respective socio-legal and historical contexts.

Moreover, the role of the prosecutorial state is expanding, particularly through the proliferation of prosecutorial agreements—such as plea bargains, deferred prosecution agreements, and non-prosecution agreements—which have become entrenched in the United States and are gaining increasing traction in England and Wales.[18] These developments have largely consolidated significant discretionary powers within prosecutorial authorities, rendering public trials exceptional, and raising critical questions regarding substantive equality and power dynamics, transparency, public accountability, and the extent to which victims are legitimate actors in holding the state accountable for undertaking such agreements. As prosecutorial discretion shapes assessments about responsibility and the public interest behind closed doors, reflecting on the role of victims in ensuring state accountability in this regard becomes all the more urgent.

Accountability in matters of state prosecutions was not always as important in common law, as citizens historically held more control over criminal prosecutions. Specifically, within the early common law tradition, crime was viewed as a public wrong against 'any one of the public'.[19] As such, criminal prosecutions, referred to as private prosecutions, were considered a public responsibility in the public interest—shared between citizens (including

[15] Angela J Davis, *Arbitrary Justice: The Power of the American Prosecutor* (OUP 2007).

[16] See eg Robert J Smith and Justin D Levinson, 'The Impact of Implicit Racial Bias on the Exercise of Prosecutorial Discretion' (2012) 35 Seattle U L Rev 795, 797.

[17] Bennett Capers, 'Against Prosecutors' (2020) 105 Cornell L Rev 1561; Davis (n 13).

[18] Mary E Vogel, 'Plea Bargaining Under the Common Law' in Darryl K. Brown, Jenia Iontcheva Turner, and Bettina Weisser (eds), *Oxford Handbook of Criminal Process* (OUP 2018).

[19] Frederic W Maitland, *Justice and Police* (MacMillan and Co 1885) 141.

victims) and, to a lesser extent, the executive. Tensions involving accountability within public prosecutions were present but were more focused on the powers of private prosecutors. The rise of the nation-state—particularly in imperial England—and the expansion of criminal law as a tool of governance across its colonies contributed to the emergence of a conception of the state as the representative of the public interest. This shift brought with it an increasing state control over public prosecutions, especially in colonial contexts such as the United States.

The consolidation of state powers over the public interest, combined with accountability deficits in prosecutorial decision-making in instances of state failures, created tensions over public prosecutions. In response, both England and Wales and the United States developed various legal mechanisms of accountability enabling citizens and victims to hold the state accountable. Out of this dynamic has emerged a novel and evolving role for victims: that of agents of state accountability. This monograph theorizes and critically explores this role, situating it within a broader framework of private–public interests, deliberative democratic participation, state legitimacy, and the pursuit of democratic values, such as substantive equality in criminal law.

The monograph analytically compares this role undertaken by victims, focusing on their engagement with the legal mechanisms available to them as individuals and citizens in England and Wales and the United States. It examines how these mechanisms have conceptualized victims across a public–private spectrum and enabled them to respond to various forms of state failures—particularly in prosecutorial decision-making.[20] These developments raise important questions about the ways victims' interests are understood within the public criminal prosecutorial process and how such understandings have shaped their role as agents of state accountability, particularly in cases of prosecutorial fallibilities.

The comparative literature suggests that, for the purposes of comparing jurisdictions, certain places are more relevant than others in clarifying issues in specific areas of criminal justice.[21] England and Wales and the United States were selected for having enacted policy changes aimed at making the prosecutorial state more transparent and accountable in criminal justice, including in

[20] As outlined in Michelle Madden Dempsey, *Prosecuting Domestic Violence* (OUP 2009) 53, 'prosecutorial actions come in two flavours: pursuit and non-pursuit'. Acts of prosecutorial pursuit are those which initiate criminal cases and move them towards conviction, while acts of prosecutorial non-pursuit prevent the initiation of criminal cases and impede conviction. These distinctions are relevant since prosecutorial actions are not only made when prosecutors decide to prosecute but also when they decide to use other means or outright retreat from prosecutions.

[21] David Nelken, *Comparative Criminal Justice: Making Sense of Difference* (Sage 2010) 28.

relation to victims. These include common law private prosecutions in England and Wales,[22] administrative and common law judicial review in England and Wales,[23] vestiges of English common law private prosecutions and judicial review retained in some American states,[24] along with a novel approach under the federal *Crime Victims' Rights Act* in the United States,[25] which serves as a model to several other states within the United States.

Such mechanisms remain largely inexistent and unavailable in other common law jurisdictions, and the ones in the jurisdictions under analysis remain underexplored in the criminal justice literature. Importantly, from a policy perspective, reflections on matters of prosecutorial accountability—including recent discussions about the role of private prosecutions in England and Wales and the under- and over-prosecution of certain groups in society[26]—remain very topical and therefore analysing developments from a comparative perspective within the common law is relevant to ground and inform upcoming and future reforms.

Finally, these jurisdictions share historical roots in the common law and a current state-driven adversarial system. Since the common law originated in England, comparing its approach to criminal prosecutions with that of a former colony—namely, the United States—offers valuable insights into how prosecutorial powers, citizen participation, and state accountability have developed, been interpreted, and could potentially evolve within different common law traditions.

The methodology employed to undertake this analysis includes an examination of case law, complemented by motions filed in court cases, administrative decisions, as well as policy and prosecutorial guidelines to understand the

[22] Prosecution of Offences Act 1985.

[23] See prosecutorial guidelines that include guidance on the administrative review enacted by the CPS, 'Victims' Right to Review Scheme' (*CPS*, May 2021) https://www.cps.gov.uk/legal-guidance/victims-right-review-scheme accessed 1 May 2023, as well as guidance relating to judicial reviews of prosecutorial decisions about whether to prosecute, CPS, 'Appeals: Judicial Review of CPS Prosecuting Decisions' (*CPS*, September 2019) <https://www.cps.gov.uk/legal-guidance/appeals-judicial-review-cps-prosecuting-decisions> accessed 1 May 2023.

[24] These include mechanisms available in some states that enable victims as citizens to empanel or have access to grand juries.

[25] *Crime Victims' Rights Act* 18 USC (2004). This includes the potential for victim standing in court proceedings to present motions in criminal proceedings and mandamus reviews.

[26] See eg recent government consultations relating to private prosecutions in England and Wales, Ministry of Justice, *Consultation on the Oversight and Regulation of Private Prosecutors in the Criminal Justice System* (CPd 43/2025, March 2025) <https://assets.publishing.service.gov.uk/media/67c57c4f72e83aab48866ce8/oversight-regulation-private-prosecutors-consultation.pdf> accessed 7 June 2025. In the United States, the recent Boeing case discussed in this monograph raises ongoing policy debates around the role of victims in holding the state accountable: Clifford Krauss and Gregory Wallace, 'DOJ Drops Boeing Criminal Charge over 737 Max Crashes' *CNN* (30 May 2025) <https://www.cnn.com/2025/05/30/business/boeing-criminal-charge-dropped> accessed 28 June 2025.

functioning and implementation of the victim's role as agents of state accountability in the context of criminal justice. Moreover, extra-legal sources—such as media sources and public statements made by victims—were relevant to the analysis, as they offer contextual insights into the lived experience of the crime and criminal legal mechanisms, as well as their perceptions of state fallibilities that are often absent from formal legal documents. It also includes close engagement with various theoretical frameworks within public law, criminal law, and political theory to develop a deeper interdisciplinary understanding and development of the role of accountability across the public–private spectrum.

The monograph makes both comparative and normative contributions to the existing literature in law and criminal justice. The comparative analysis reveals significant differences in how the victim's role as an agent for state accountability is conceptualized, implemented, and evolving over time in England and Wales and the United States.

Mechanisms of state accountability in England and Wales have tended to conceive of victims and their interests closer to the public end of the private–public spectrum, while those in the United States situate the victim and their interests closer to the private end of the spectrum. These differences have contributed to the development of more substantive forms of accountability in England and Wales, allowing victims to challenge the substance of prosecutorial decisions, including those rooted in inequalities relating to gender, race, and disability. However, several developments, including the recent Victims' Right to Review Scheme (VRRS), have directed victims and their interests closer to the private end of the spectrum. This shift has had an impact on other mechanisms of state accountability, notably judicial review, increasingly placing wider limits to the potential for substantive accountability.

In the United States, more procedural forms of accountability have taken shape, under which victims can merely challenge process-related decisions rather than their substance. Nevertheless, in some American states that have held on to vestiges of private prosecutions and judicial review, case law has shown that victims have, to a limited extent, used these mechanisms to hold the state accountable in more substantive ways. This has included bringing forward wider discussions about systemic racism in the context of prosecutorial decisions about whether to prosecute.

Moreover, situating victim interests across the private–public spectrum has important implications for how victims are conceptually defined. In contexts that view victims as part of the broader citizenry and potential bearers of public interests, definitions of 'victim' and rules of standing tend to be broader than in contexts where victims are viewed as individuals that hold private interests.

In such contexts, the monograph will generally use the language of 'citizen-victims', which is distinct to a conception of victims rooted in a framing that perceive their interests as private.

As the analysis shows, the types of victims engaging these mechanisms have evolved over time and vary between the jurisdictions, while presenting certain commonalities. In both jurisdictions, victims—including those from disadvantaged and marginalized groups—have experienced prosecutorial state failures and used available mechanisms to signal these failures and hold the state accountable. It is worth highlighting that in some cases of prosecutorial failures, discussed in the monograph, it may be that victims may not always see themselves as undertaking a public role or a role as agents of state accountability. Even in cases where at times they may be unconscious of their role, they may still be bringing forward arguments and perspectives that have the effect of holding the prosecutorial state accountable in practice. The nature of these failings and the corresponding forms of accountability differ between the two jurisdictions. While mechanisms of state accountability in England and Wales have mainly enabled victims to substantively challenge flawed decisions in relation to decisions about whether to prosecute, the ones available in the United States have primarily addressed procedural breaches by prosecutors of victims' participatory rights in criminal proceedings—in instances where victims were not given a chance to participate. In recent years, some of these mechanisms, particularly in England and Wales, have enabled victims from disadvantaged groups to challenge decisions that are rooted in systemic inequalities, including those relating to race, gender, class, and disability in prosecutorial decision-making.

Building on these comparative distinctions, the monograph offers a normative contribution to the scholarship in criminal justice by proposing a framework to further develop the victim's role as agents of state accountability. This framework is grounded in a citizenship-based, public, and deliberative democratic understanding of victims and their interests. It conceptualizes victims as members of the broader citizenry who are capable of directly and substantively engaging with state assessments and the public interest to contribute to holding the state accountable for individual and systemic failures within prosecutorial decision-making. An important dimension of this approach is the linkage between public interest and substantive equality, as well as the integration of social sciences and experiential knowledge—enabling victims to hold the state accountable for various failures, including those that stem from structural inequalities. This foundation is important for providing a legitimizing basis to advance governance and promote state accountability in criminal justice.

Importantly, this conception challenges scholarly accounts that portray victim participation as inherently punitive and in tension with defendants' rights. Instead, it advances a participatory model rooted in public citizenship and accountability—one that recognizes victims, communities, and defendants, particularly within marginalized groups, as citizens with shared interests in state governance and accountability. Such an understanding enables the development of an expanded notion of criminal responsibility—one that incorporates broader elements of social context inequalities and incorporates relational forms of responsibility,[27] including the role of state failures throughout prosecutorial decision-making and the wider criminal process. This broader vision of the public and their common interests offers a more accurate and equitable assessment of criminal responsibility that fosters more sustainable and less criminogenic responses to harm.

The monograph is divided into three parts: preliminary considerations and the conceptualization of victim participation, followed by comparative perspectives of victims as agents of state accountability, and ending with the development of a normative framework. The monograph begins with this introduction as Chapter 1 and comprises seven additional chapters and a conclusion. Chapter 2 contributes to the existing literature by suggesting that the various types of victim participation can be understood differently depending on how victim interests are positioned along the public–private spectrum. It argues that existing scholarship on victim participation has developed a typology of victim participation, which includes control, consultation, information provision, and expression,[28] and emphasizes how this typology has generally framed victims as actors with individualized and private interests. The chapter contends that reconceiving the victim's interest along the public end of the spectrum can enrich this typology by offering a more nuanced understanding of rights and duties, and by recognizing additional participatory roles in the criminal justice process. The chapter proceeds by examining how these various types of participation can be conceived across the public end of the spectrum. It lays essential groundwork for the novel idea of the victim as an agent of state accountability—a form of participation, which can be meaningfully advanced and understood through the application of the public–private framework.

[27] Marie Manikis, 'Recognising State Blame in Sentencing: A Communicative and Relational Framework' (2022) 81(2) CLJ 294.
[28] Edwards (n 10) 975.

Chapter 3 expands the typology of victim participation by introducing and conceptualizing a novel type of participation: the role of victims as agents of state accountability within the criminal justice process. It identifies specific types of state failures—including individual and systemic—for which victims can hold the state accountable and outlines the different ways in which accountability can be understood. This is done by drawing on a range of frameworks from public law and public accountability literature. In particular, the chapter distinguishes between normative and descriptive conceptions of accountability, contrasts red light and green light functions of accountability, and situates accountability across both the public–private and substantive–procedural spectra. These diverse frameworks provide conceptual tools to analyse and compare how victims participate as agents of state accountability in the jurisdictions analysed in the following chapters.

Chapters 4 and 5 apply these frameworks to examine the development and implementation of accountability mechanisms available to victims in England and Wales, with a focus on state prosecutions. These mechanisms include private prosecutions, judicial review of prosecutorial decisions, mandamus actions, and administrative prosecutorial review processes. The analysis reveals how victims, their interests, and their role as agents of state accountability have been understood in England and Wales. Chapter 4 argues that victim interests have historically been—and to some extent continue to be—conceived predominantly within a public framework, with the potential to substantively review prosecutorial state failures in this jurisdiction. Nevertheless, this conception has increasingly shifted over time, with an increasingly private conception of victims' interests, including in traditional common law mechanisms (private prosecutions and judicial review), as discussed in Chapter 4, as well as the VRRS as a new mechanism of accountability, as discussed in Chapter 5. The implementation of the VRRS, in particular, reflects a partial shift towards victims' interests understood as increasingly private with a more limited form of accountability. This has contributed to a portrayal of victims and their interests closer to what is found in the United States, discussed in Chapter 6.

Chapter 6 discusses the evolution of the role of victims as agents of state accountability in the United States and highlights that their approach has parted quite rapidly and nearly completely from many of the English common law public conceptions of victim interests and practices relating to prosecutions. While some vestiges of the English common law remain in some states, including direct access to the grand jury and rare instances of judicial review, they have also been permeated by an increasingly privatizing approach that conceptualizes victims as holders of private interests. This, in turn, translates in them having less legitimacy in holding the prosecutorial state substantively accountable in decisions about prosecutions. Nevertheless, some of these mechanisms have created space for raising issues regarding state accountability in relation to systemic inequalities and injustices, including racial and gender inequalities—particularly in the context of movements such as Black Lives Matter and #MeToo.

Chapter 7 argues that recent victim participatory mechanisms of state accountability in the United States, particularly motions in criminal proceedings and mandamus under the federal Crime Victims' Rights Act, have also contributed to reinforcing a private conception of victim interests—understood as rights grounded in possessive individualism. This has given rise to a primarily procedural/process-based form of prosecutorial accountability. This type of accountability has generally enabled victims to participate in processes to provide their personal views but not challenge or shape the rationales or content of prosecutorial decisions. As such, the victim's role as an agent of state accountability in the United States has largely been limited to holding the state accountable for procedural shortcomings related to victim participation, rather than for the substantive content of its decisions.

Building on the comparative analysis in the four preceding chapters, Chapter 8 examines the limitations of anchoring state accountability within a private conception. It highlights the normative importance of grounding the victim's role as an agent of state accountability within a public conception—one that envisions victims as citizens with legitimacy of holding the state to account and contributing directly to discussions about the public interest. The chapter argues that a public conception, rooted in deliberate democratic values, including substantive equality, can foster more robust and meaningful forms of state accountability, since it frames the victim's participatory role as a legitimate civic duty within a public process, which recognizes the need for a substantive engagement with decisions made by state actors regarding the public interest.

Further embedding accountability within a public conception of the victim enables the development of a broader understanding of state responsibility—one that supports challenges to, and contributions towards, a more systemic conception of accountability that can enable more accurate assessments of responsibility when those made by the state are rooted in inequalities. Chapter 8 also engages with potential objections and limitations to this proposed role, both theoretical and practical.

Rooting the victim's role within a predominantly public framework also allows to rethink the relationship between victims and the accused in criminal proceedings. Existing literature often characterizes this relationship as inherently oppositional, framed in terms of a 'balance' between the rights of victims and those of the accused. This new framework introduces important nuance by arguing that victim participation need not conflict with the rights of the accused. Both theoretically and empirically, it may in fact promote shared interests in the criminal justice process. In this light, Chapter 8 suggests that certain policies could be reconsidered or expanded to support a reimagined role for victims—one more closely aligned with a broader engagement in the public interest.

Finally, the concluding chapter advances the monograph's arguments in four key ways. First, it offers comparative reflections on how victims are conceptualized in both jurisdictions and their contributions to the criminal justice process. Second, it evaluates the significance and limitations of the comparative and normative analyses, identifying key questions for future research on victim participation and conceptualization. Third, it outlines conclusions relevant to practitioners, policymakers, and citizens who seek to advance a more accountable state. Lastly, it addresses the broader implications of this work for criminal justice scholarship and public administration—particularly regarding the nature, role, and legitimacy of legal processes designed to enhance public accountability and state governance.

2

A Typology of Victim Participation Across Private–Public Conceptions

1. Introduction

In recent years, the victim literature has developed a typology of victim participation to make sense of the role of victims and their relationship with state decision-makers within the criminal process. This literature has generally conceptualized the victim as an actor with predominantly private interests in the criminal justice process. This chapter outlines the typology of participation developed in the literature and suggests that a framework which conceives of the victim across a private and public spectrum can provide complementary and additional understanding of various types of victim participation. Specifically, recognizing that victim interests and roles can be understood as not merely personal or private but also across a private–public spectrum, that can also conceive them as holding public roles and interests, adds nuance to the existing categories and accounts of victim participation. This conception also allows for a more comprehensive discussion and identification of victims' rights and obligations.

The chapter is divided into four parts. First, it draws out the debates around the private and public divide in the legal literature and presents a framework found in public law that conceives of public and private interests across a spectrum. This spectrum-based framework is a key part of this chapter, and of this monograph, since it provides several nuances to our understanding of victims and their interests in the criminal legal process. Second, this chapter highlights how the literature on victim participation has predominantly conceptualized victims as bearers of private interests, with a specific focus on Edwards' typology of victim participation. The chapter proceeds by infusing Edwards' typology with a complementary predominantly public conception of the victim, developing our understanding of the relationship between victims and criminal justice agencies. Furthermore, the chapter engages with the

Victims as Agents of State Accountability. Marie Manikis, Oxford University Press. © Marie Manikis 2026.
DOI: 10.1093/9780191993947.003.0003

potential rights and duties victims hold, along with those held by criminal justice decision-makers.

2. Conceiving of Interests Across a Public–Private Spectrum and Within Aggregate and Unitary Theories of the Public Interest

The relevance of distinguishing between the public and private has given rise to much debate across literature.[1] In law, Oliver suggests that the distinction should be abandoned in favour of a fusion known as a commonality.[2] She highlights that the conceptual distinction between public and private law is pedagogically convenient, but not conceptually compelling, because in practice the two cannot be separated.[3] One aspect of commonality is the common function served by public and private law, characterized as orderings concerned with the control of power and the protection of interests against abuses of state and private power in the shared democratic context. Oliver suggests that an additional commonality between public and private law emerges from the five key values they share: dignity, autonomy, respect, status, and security—which support paramount values of democracy, citizenship, and participation.

Grear argues that both attempting to obliterate the private–public distinction and maintaining a rigid distinction are conceptually problematic approaches.[4] Her theorization of the private and public divide partly relies on Teubner's notion of 'polycontexturality',[5] which contends that the public–private relationship is multilayered. However, she adds that a polycontextural reconceptualization of the private–public relationship should explicitly acknowledge the archetypal conceptual paradigms in both public and private law. These paradigms are important because they exist in the history, philosophical foundations, and contemporary cognitive structure of the law. For instance,

[1] Understandings and references to the private–public divide vary widely depending on context. For instance, Tracy E Higgins, 'Reviving the Public/Private Distinction in Feminist Theorizing' (2000) 75 Chicago-Kent L Rev 847 and Ruth Gavison, 'Feminism and the Public/Private Distinction' (1992) 45 Stan L Rev 1 discuss the divide in feminist theory. Derek McKee, 'The Public/Private Distinction in Roncarelli v. Duplessis' (2010) 55 McGill LJ 461 challenges the distinction between State and civil society. In this chapter, the private–public divide refers to the division between civil and criminal process (systemic), as well as the conception of the victim.

[2] Dawn Oliver, *Common Values and the Public/Private Divide* (Butterworths 1999).

[3] ibid 14.

[4] Anna Grear, 'Theorizing the Rainbow? The Puzzle of the Public-Private Divide' (2003) 9 Res Publica 169, 172.

[5] Gunther Teubner, 'After Privatisation: The Many Autonomies of Private Law' (1998) 51 CLP 393. This term rejects fusion between the private and public and argues for the replacement of the distinction with a concept capturing the multidimensional complexity of law in multiple social contexts.

individualized relations of private law contrast strongly with the unilateral institutionalized power of public law. The starting point of private law is the primacy of self-regarding behaviour, while public law departs from the primacy of public-regarding (or other-regarding) behaviour. Similarly, archetypal conceptions of public and private interests exist across many legal traditions even if some cases do not neatly fit into either end of the spectrum. Hence, the difficulty in classifying some cases as public or private does not justify the inference that the conceptual distinction between the categories is unsound.

In this sense, Grear's theory recognizes that traditional conceptions of the private and public remain present but are now engaged in increasingly complex interactions with other conceptions, reflecting social, economic, and political evolution. As such, Grear's thesis rejects monolithic and rigid binary concepts. Instead, she argues that 'the relationships between public and private law are to be seen as existing on a spectrum, or even an overarching meta-spectrum, in which the existence of distinctive "archetypal conceptual paradigms" influence as "meta-spectrum extremities"'.[6] This theory provides a convincing response to calls to abandon the public–private divide. It proposes a dynamic use of the public and private, which recognizes the pertinence of referring to the distinctive 'archetypal conceptual paradigms' while considering them as meta-spectrum extremities to avoid occluding important distinctions and nuances. Grear suggests that while a rigid binary distinction is unsustainable, some distinction remains analytically important. This analytical framework embraces an understanding of law as complex, dynamic, and multidimensional. Although this theory refers to the private and public divide in law, it remains helpful for understanding complex and multidimensional conceptualizations of the role of actors and various interests within legal processes.

This framework is particularly relevant at a time when public law is becoming increasingly multidimensional by including various subfields, notably regulatory fields such as the ombudspersons, human rights law, and common law judicial review. As will be seen in greater depth in Chapter 3, human rights law and the common law of judicial review rest on different underpinnings and serve different functions that can be understood by looking at public–private interests across a spectrum.

A framework that places the public and private along a spectrum is useful in understanding the role and interests of the victim who has historically been present as an actor of the criminal process, and has also seen her role and interests change, re-emerge, and be redefined across history and common

[6] Grear (n 4) 171.

law systems. The following discussion compares the conception of victims in England and Wales and the United States by analysing the ways their role and interests have been constructed across time and within different mechanisms of participation. As will be seen, the victim's conception within the criminal process does not neatly fit within a rigid public–private divide. Instead, it oscillates within these categories, sensitive to contexts and jurisdictions. This resonates with scholarship that has argued in favour of a dynamic private–public framework in criminal justice to account for the nuances that exist when thinking about the roles of private actors and interests in criminal justice systems.[7]

This monograph argues that, in England and Wales, victims have been traditionally conceived as citizens with predominantly public interests, but those interests can also be aligned with their private interests. Thus, victims can be situated within Grear's mid-spectrum area, but closer to the public end. Though victims in the United States also rest within the mid-spectrum area, since they are participants in a public process, they have nevertheless been conceived for a longer time as individuals with *predominantly* private interests—placing them closer to the private end than the traditional common law of England places. Despite these conceptualizations, nuances are accounted for and discussed due to the rise in the privatization and individualization of victim interests even in settings that had recognized their public interests.

In addition, the literature on the public interest offers a complementary framework to understand the relationship between individual citizens, private and public interests. In particular, Virginia Held has discussed archetypal paradigms of private and public interests and has classified theories of the public interest into categories.[8] These categories are useful tools for making sense of public and private interests, and in turn understanding how the victim's role is conceived in relation to those interests.

The first category regroups preponderance (or *aggregate*) theories of the public interest. These theories conceive the public interest as a summing up or aggregation of various magnitudes or orderings numerically representable.

[7] See Stephen Riley, 'The Public-Private Divide: Which Side is Criminal Justice On?' in Malcolm Cowburn and others (eds), *Values in Criminology and Community Justice* (Policy Press 2013), which suggests that the public–private divide is always dynamic since it depends upon social and political values that relate to the limitations of governmental power in a liberal state. This gives rise to complexities, since there are no simple ways to evaluate the rights and responsibilities of private actors within a criminal justice system; Marie Manikis, 'Conceptualizing the Victim within Criminal Justice Processes in Common Law Tradition' in Darryl K Brown, Jenia I Turner, and Bettina Weisser (eds), *The Oxford Handbook of Criminal Process* (OUP 2019) also discusses the public–private dimensions of the role of victims and challenges the predominant view that victims solely represent private interests. See, eg, Helen Fenwick, 'Procedural "Rights" of Victims of Crime: Public or Private Ordering of the Criminal Justice Process?' (1997) 60 MLR 317.

[8] Virginia Held, *The Public Interest and Individual Interests* (Basic Books 1970).

According to this conception, there may be justifiable conflicts between individual or group interests, but a preponderance can be identified in different ways. Some theories in this group base preponderance upon a greater amount of power, on the votes of a majority, on the forces of contending interest groups, and on calculations of preference or utility.[9]

Preponderance theories generally rely on a classical Hobbesian distinction between public and private interests. These theories see private interest as what is desired by individuals—which can be instrumental, personally satisfying, and, at times, erroneous. The private interest includes a restless desire for power, which is found in the state of nature, and thus must be limited to escape conditions of conflicts and wars that inevitably come from unconstrained private interests. Private interests come prior to any others, but the public interest is necessary to limit the conflictual state of nature. The public interest is also seen as justifiable because it is conceived as the preponderance of individual interests. Within this theory, when enough decisions claimed by the sovereign to be in the public interest are not in the interests of enough individual members of a commonwealth, the existence of the sovereign's power can cease to be in the public interest.[10] In such instances, individual interest might instead find legitimacy and a claim to be in the public interest. Similarly, for Bentham, the preponderance upon which the public interest rests is utility. In order to calculate the preponderance of interests, he offers a procedure which highlights that 'for every action under consideration as being in or not in the public interest, account should be taken of the numbers of persons affected, and of the way they are affected'.[11]

The second category refers to theories of *unitary* conception, which are underpinned by a single ordered and consistent value scheme. This conception highlights the importance of identifying and developing a core meaning to the public interest, rooted in normative content, beyond mere economic aspects. Such a core meaning would limit its vulnerability to annexation or colonization by those who exercise power in society. This framing suggests the public interest should have a degree of conceptual independence and be ascertainable beyond an empirical basis understood as the sum of existing individual interests. A unitary conception includes a normative framework rooted in deliberative justice and communitarian theories that recognize that citizens

[9] Preponderance theories of the public interest are discussed by Held, including those of Hobbes, Hume, and Bentham.

[10] Thomas Hobbes, *Leviathan* (first published 1651, EP Dutton & Co 1947) 98.

[11] Held (n 8) 65.

share common values and are able to represent and frame the public interest.[12] Feintuck developed a unitary account rooted in deliberative justice that addresses the public interest in the context of regulations. He conceives individuals as citizens—part of a collective—embodying community values and as representatives of the public interest that take part in a wider deliberative process 'while simultaneously requiring the accountability of those who exercise such power'.[13]

Applying the concept of public interest this way should facilitate that regulatory and decision-making processes fulfil their potential as a locus of deliberation and encourage courts to support and enforce citizen deliberation. Such deliberative processes are meant to serve accountability in a way that goes beyond a 'Red Light' function of stopping excesses of power or jurisdiction to develop a 'Green Light' function of encouraging good administration.[14] Within a unitary framing of the public interest, citizens have legitimated and direct access in defining the public interest, in more than aggregate ways. Their participation in this endeavour limits state monopoly and serves good governance and public accountability.

This unitary conception of the public interest can be rooted in an egalitarian and democratic view of citizenship[15] that weighs citizenship values in the face of market forces. This aims to avoid problems of majoritarianism associated with other theories of the public interest, by going beyond the mere aggregation of individual or group interests.

Similarly, Marshall's political citizenship theory of criminal law can also be seen as a unitary theory of the public interest, since it considers individuals as citizens that are 'part of a collective defined in terms of a shared identity, shared values, mutual concert and shared dangers that threaten them'.[16] Accordingly, this vision considers that a wrong done to one is a wrong done to all. In other words, an attack on a member of the group, as a fellow citizen, provides the legitimacy and duty for citizens, including the victim, to participate actively in

[12] Jeffrey Kennedy, 'The Citizen Victim: Reconciling the Public and Private in Criminal Sentencing' (2019) 13(1) Crim L & Phil 83 explores the ways in which a deliberative democratic framework can justify direct participation of victims as citizens in the public criminal process, namely by recognizing that victims can provide justifications for public action that others could accept as rational rather than simply pressing one's own preferences. In turn, Sandra E Marshall, 'Victims of Crime: Their Station and Its Duties' (2004) 7(2) CRISPP 104 explores the ways in which a communitarian theory of public wrongs can shape the victim's position within the criminal process as a member of the wider citizenry that has been wronged and thus represents the rest of citizens.

[13] Mike Feintuck, *'The Public Interest' in Regulation* (OUP 2004).

[14] Carol Harlow and Richard Rawlings, *Law and Administration* (2nd edn, Butterworths 1997).

[15] ibid.

[16] Marshall (n 12) 110.

Figure 2.1 Spectrum of private-public interests. Source: Author's drawing.

the criminal justice process. The victim therefore 'stands not just for herself but for all'.[17]

These theories of the public interest and their relationship with victims can in turn be situated within Grear's public–private spectrum. Unitary communitarian and deliberative models of the public interest are situated closer to the public end of Grear's spectrum. Indeed, they conceive victims as citizens that bring forward shared values and interests with a community, in order to shape and represent the public interest. Preponderance models conceive victims as individuals closer to the private end of the spectrum than the unitary models, since they consider victims as bringing their own private preferences and interests, which can come into conflict with other individual and private interests in forming an overall public interest.

The public–private spectrum along with understandings of the public interest provide relevant frameworks that will be applied throughout this monograph to make sense of the various ways victims have participated in the criminal legal process. Moreover, these frameworks will also be helpful in developing a normative framework that legitimizes the victim's role in holding the state accountable.

3. A Predominantly Private Conception of the Victim Within the Wider Literature on Victim Participation

To date, the scholarship on victim participation in the criminal process has mainly focused on a private conception of the victim, underpinned by possessive individualism—as bearers of individual rights and interests—with much less focus on a public conception of the victim, underpinned by deliberative and communitarian-liberal frameworks,[18] as a citizen representing wider

[17] ibid 110.

[18] RA Duff and SE Marshall, 'Communicative Punishment and the Role of the Victim' (2004) 23(2) Crim Justice Ethics 39; Kennedy (n 12).

public interests, who has historically and continuously taken an active and public role in the common law tradition.

Indeed, scholars, activists, and policymakers that have written on victim participation—whether to question the victim's greater participatory role in criminal justice decision-making processes or to argue in favour of greater participation—have primarily focused on a private conception of the victim, thrusting new obligations upon criminal justice agencies to account for victims' personal needs and interests. These obligations can conflict with state and public interests, as well as those of the accused.

In both the United Kingdom and the United States, the literature on victim participation has articulated arguments in favour of or against victims' greater involvement, the extent of their participation, the nature of rights and remedies, as well as the relationship between public and private actors in a purported public process by predominantly conceptualizing the victim as an actor with private interests in a public process.

Proponents of greater victim participation in criminal processes have articulated this role by acknowledging the independence of personal individual rights and remedies in court from state interests. The recognition of individual enforceable rights possessed by victims is considered to be, within that literature, a robust means to bring about the necessary changes to the culture within the state-based criminal justice process, in addition to adequately representing individual interests.[19] Indeed, a substantive portion of this literature equates victim participatory 'rights' with human rights, utilizing a normative view that they must be, like defendants' rights, legally robust and enforceable.

Similarly, opponents of victim participation in the criminal process have also relied on a conception of victims that conceives them as bringing forward predominantly private interests in the criminal justice process to depict them as lacking the legitimacy of decision-making in such public processes that

[19] Douglas E Beloof, 'The Third Wave of Crime Victims' Rights: Standing, Remedy, and Review' (2005) 2 BYU L Rev 255; David E Aaronson, 'New Rights and Remedies: The Federal Crime Victims' Rights Act of 2004' (2008) 28 Pace L Rev 623; Douglas E Beloof, Paul G Cassell, and Steven J Twist, *Victims in Criminal Procedure* (3rd edn, Carolina Academic Press 2010); Erin C Blondel, 'Victims' Rights in an Adversary System' (2008) 58 Duke LJ 237; Paul G Cassell, 'Protecting Crime Victims in Federal Appellate Courts: The Need to Broadly Construe the Crime Victims' Rights Act's Mandamus Provisions' (2010) 87 Denv U L Rev 599; Matthew Hall, *Victims and Policy Making: A Comparative Perspective* (1st edn, Willan Publishing 2010); Jonathan Doak, *Victims' Rights, Human Rights and Criminal Justice: Reconceiving the Role of Third Parties* (1st edn, Hart Publishing 2008); Jonathan Doak, 'The Victim and the Criminal Process: An Analysis of Recent Trends in Regional and International Tribunals' (2003) 23 LS 1; Fenwick (n 7); Helen Fenwick, 'Rights of Victims in the Criminal Justice System: Rhetoric or Reality?' (1995) Crim LR 843.

need to maintain the state's monopoly over the public interest.[20] Opponents have also relied on this private conception to suggest that victim participation would introduce partiality and subjectivism into the process, distorting an otherwise impartial process that is meant to be oriented towards the common good.[21] Indeed, within this literature, there is also a sense that victims' participative rights and remedies are changing the understanding of the public prosecutor's role, the public interest, and the wider public process by thrusting a private dimension into the latter, which is often perceived as conflicting with the public process' role as well as with defendants' rights.[22]

These predominantly private conceptions can be understood within the spectrum discussed above, specifically rooted in possessive individualism and aggregate theories of the public interest that recognize that victims can indeed contribute to the public interest, but to a lesser degree because they are perceived as bringing forward their personal interests and views as part of the public interest.

A predominant focus on a private conception occludes the degree to which the victim has and can continue to play an important public role as a citizen directly shaping the public interest. As highlighted above, closer to the public end of the public–private spectrum are unitary theories of the public interest, which include liberal communitarian and deliberative frameworks that conceive of victims as citizens that share values and can represent, frame, and directly contribute to discussions about the public interest.

The next section presents a typology of victim participation proposed by Edwards and suggests that a predominantly private conception of the victim is also present within this typology. The section then proceeds by infusing a public conception into Edwards' typology to provide different, more comprehensive ways to understand and conceptualize victim participation.

[20] Erin Ann O'Hara, 'Victim Participation in the Criminal Process' (2005) 13 JL & Pol'y 229. Erez also notes fears about reforms by highlighting that allowing for victim input might 'shift the primary goal of criminal justice administration from meeting the concerns of the state to meeting the concerns of the private individual'. Edna Erez, 'Victim Participation in Sentencing: And the Debate Goes On . . . ' (1994) 3 IRV 17.

[21] Paul H Robinson, 'Should the Victims' Rights Movement Have Influence Over Criminal Law Formulation and Adjudication?' (2002) 33 McGeorge L Rev 749; Donald J Hall, 'Victims' Voices in Criminal Court: The Need for Restraint' (1991) 28 Am Crim L Rev 233.

[22] Andrew Ashworth and Mike Redmayne, *The Criminal Process* (4th edn, OUP 2010).

Table 2.1 Four different participatory roles for victims

	Participation Type	Obligation on Criminal Justice Decision-Maker	Obligation on Victim
Dispositive	Control	To seek and apply victim preference	Non-optional supply of preference Victim is the decision-maker
Non-Dispositive	Consultation	To seek and consider victim preference	Optional supply of preference
	Information-Provision	To seek and consider victim information	Non-optional supply of information
	Expression	To allow victim expression	Optional supply of information and/or expression of emotion

4. Edwards' Typology of Victim Participation as Predominantly Rooted Within a Private Conception

Edwards' typology of victim participation has been a seminal development in the literature on victim participation. Influenced by Arnstein's 'ladder of participation',[23] which outlines an eight-level gradation of involvement, Edwards' typology highlights eight main types of victim participation in the criminal process. These types mean to expose the different forms that participation can take, and the different ways in which participation may or may not affect outcomes. Table 2.1[24] presents an overview of this typology, which can be regrouped into two categories: dispositive and non-dispositive. Within these categories, there are four corresponding forms of participation: control, consultation, information-provision, and expression. Dispositive participation suggests that the victim is the decision-maker while non-dispositive participation entails that the decision rests on someone else, but the victim's input might in some way influence the decision.

[23] Sherry R Arnstein, *A Ladder of Citizen Participation in the USA* (Royal Town Planning Institute 1971) 176.

[24] Figure reproduced from Ian Edwards, 'An Ambiguous Participant: The Crime Victim and Criminal Justice Decision-Making' (2004) 44 Brit J Criminol 967, 975.

When analysing this typology more closely, there are underlying assumptions about the role of victims that feature in this categorization. Like most of the literature on victim participation discussed in the previous section, most types of participation described by Edwards, namely control, consultation, and expression, conceive the victim within a predominantly private conception. Only information-provision considers the victim closer towards the public end of the spectrum.

Types of participation rooted within a predominantly private conception: control, consultation, and expression

This section discusses the three types of participation described by Edwards that appear to be rooted primarily within a private conception of the victim: control, consultation, and expression.

The first type of participation is *control*. Edwards describes this type of participation as offering victims a decisional veto. It is also understood as giving rise to an obligation on their part to supply their 'preference'. In turn, criminal justice actors are under an obligation to ascertain and 'apply the victim's preference' in a given case.[25] The language of the victim's 'preference', used by Edwards to describe the victim's contribution, points towards the inherently personal dimension of this decision, which can be understood within the realm of subjectivity and is thus closer to a private conception. Moreover, describing the victim's contribution as a preference suggests that the decision does not need to respect certain more objective standards. Examples provided by Edwards to illustrate this form of participation further substantiate this more private conception. He refers to mechanisms of victim participation within Islamic law, making it very clear that 'control' as a type of participation exists in that tradition, but not in common law. This distinction is important as the common law is rooted in the premise that decisions need to respect certain predetermined standards of rationality and objectivity to ensure that decisions in public processes do not strictly rely on mere preferences. For these reasons, as highlighted above, Edwards' description of this type of participation seems to conceptualize the victim and their contribution, including their role and interest, towards the private end of the public–private spectrum.

[25] It is not entirely clear whether this provides victims with a veto or whether there is any potential for review by authorities if certain standards are not met.

The second type of privately rooted participation in Edwards' model is *consultation*, understood as a non-dispositive form of participation. Similar to control, Edwards employs the language of victim 'preference' and provides examples that also presuppose a personal dimension, rather than conceiving of victims' role and interests within a predominantly public conception. Nevertheless, Edwards' examples of consultation seem to consider victims as possible contributors to the public interest. However, this contribution is aggregate, understood as victims bringing forward their own personal and private interests to constitute the wider public interest. For instance, examples offered by Edwards include contributions to decisions about public prosecutions under the *Victim's Charter* (currently referred to as the Code), as well as under the *Code of Crown Prosecutors* which offers participatory possibilities to victims by requiring prosecutors to take into account their views as part of the test of whether prosecution is in the public interest. This is also the case in the context of domestic violence where prosecutors must take into account their consultation with victims in assessing the suitability and desirability of arresting and prosecuting suspected offenders. These aspects suppose an aggregate understanding of the victim's contribution to the public interest, which conceptualizes their interests as closer towards the private end of the spectrum and the state prosecutor as a representative of the public interest.

Another type of participation described by Edwards which also seems to rest within a primarily private conception of the victim is *expression*. He distinguishes this type of participation from *information-provision* by highlighting that instead of the decision-maker needing information from or about the victim, expression takes the form of the victim wanting to provide information or communicate their feelings to the decision-maker. Within this participation type, Edwards highlights that the criminal justice system would need to allow an opportunity for the victim to emote. To some extent, this form of participation seems to be the closest to the private end of the public–private spectrum, since victims can present 'emotional, subjective' aspects and express a range of emotions 'simply for their own benefit'.[26] Indeed, this seems closer to the private end of the spectrum than consultation, since there is no engagement or contribution in shaping the public interest in this form of participation.

Having argued that some types of participation developed by Edwards seem to be rooted within a predominantly private conception of the victim, the following discussion suggests that *information-provision* is predominantly rooted within a public conception. Indeed, contrary to the types of participation

[26] Edwards (n 24) 976.

discussed above, Edwards uses a terminology that does not refer to the victim's preferences, but rather to information. This difference seems to suggest that this type of participation is not about victims providing their preferences, but rather about a more objective metric that needs to meet certain standards. Indeed, Edwards specifies that this type of participation by victims needs to be accurate. Further, an essential characteristic of this form of participation is that the victim's participation is contingent on the decision-maker's need for such involvement, and therefore their participation is required only to the extent that they can provide useful elements to the decision-maker. This form of participation conceives of victims closer to the public end of the spectrum. Yet, victims are not as actively and directly involved in decision-making, contrary to the previous forms of participation seen above. To illustrate this form of participation, Edwards provides examples in England and Wales where victims are considered witnesses to the prosecution. Edwards highlights that this is the level at which victims are 'typically and historically involved, merely as "evidentiary fodder" (much to the chagrin of many victim campaigners)'.[27] Indeed, while this form of participation is present across the common law world, Chapter 4 highlights that the victim's role in common law was historically much more active and, especially in England and Wales, closer to a public conception of actively engaged forms of participation, such as control.

Having presented these four types of participation, Edwards highlights that it is useful to distinguish between these types and a form of non-participation: *receiving information*. According to Edwards, a victim who merely receives information 'lacks the essential characteristic of a participatory act'.[28] In this sense, the victim is considered a 'passive recipient' of information and does not provide any input into the decision-making process.[29] Accordingly, within Edwards' framework, receiving information is seen as passive and his typology includes active forms of participation. It is only if the victim responds to this that the relationship between the victim and the decision-maker can become active and take the form of one of the four participatory types discussed. While this might be the case in conceptions of the victim that are predominantly private, when victims are conceived more towards the public end of the spectrum within unitary theories of the public interest, the reception of information is not passive, since it allows victims to take part in a deliberative process that consists of listening to others, weighing certain considerations, and giving

[27] ibid 976.
[28] ibid 976–77.
[29] ibid 977.

reasons, all of which are relevant in forming a decision, either as control or consultation.

Finally, in recent years, a complementary type of participation was added to Edwards' typology, referred to as *accountability*.[30] This book develops this type of victim participation more thoroughly in the following chapters and specifically engages with its various underpinnings and forms on a public–private spectrum, as well as its implications.

As will be discussed in the next section, while important and useful, this typology also needs to be complemented and expanded to conceptualize victims as closer to the predominantly public end of the spectrum.

5. Expanding Edwards' Framework by Rooting Certain Types of Participation Within a Predominantly Public Conception

Conceptualizing the victim closer to the private end of the spectrum is useful and relevant in a descriptive sense since it accurately depicts and provides an understanding of some types of participation in the criminal process. Nevertheless, the sole emphasis on a private conception for certain types of participation—namely, control, consultation, expression, and information-reception—can limit the development of additional types of participation that conceive victims towards the public end of the spectrum. Moreover, as will be discussed in Chapter 8, this framing can also have repercussions in a more normative sense since it can hinder possibilities of conceptualizing the victim closer to the public end of the spectrum. The following section highlights the ways that some of Edwards' typologies—namely, control, consultation, and expression—can be rooted in a predominantly public conception of the victim, to expand and complement this typology.

First, conceiving of victims closer to the public end of the spectrum, as understood within unitary theories of the public interest, discussed in Chapter 3, can provide a different and additional understanding of *control* as a type of participation. This suggests that control as a dispositive decision would require victims to not solely rely on their own personal preferences but on certain standards rooted in common values, found within deliberative democratic frameworks[31] and what Duff and Marshall refer to as 'the values of the polity'.[32]

[30] Marie Manikis, 'Expanding Participation: Victims as Agents of Accountability in the Criminal Justice Process' (2017) 1 PL 63.
[31] Kennedy (n 12).
[32] Duff and Marshall (n 18) 41.

In this sense, victims as citizens within a public underlying framework, such as deliberative democracy, would provide reasons for their perspective and would also be capable of self-restraint while holding a civic-minded attitude. This framing would recognize the victim's ability to reason publicly with careful consideration and reason while holding a veto for certain decisions.

While victims in common law jurisdictions may not have control within Edwards' private conception, they did have decision-making abilities and roles, particularly in decisions that related to prosecutions. Historically, as will be seen in Chapter 4, victims in England and Wales had the ability to decide whether they would start a private prosecution. This example relies on a different framing than Edwards' notion of control because such decisions are, in theory, not based on mere preferences. Indeed, these decisions must meet certain public values and standards of reasoning, including a public interest analysis, in order to be successful.[33] In this sense, it would be useful to complement Edwards' dispositive and control forms of participation with a public conception of the victim underpinned by unitary conceptions of the public interest, in order to account for and expand this typology of victim participation.

Second, a complementary and additional way of framing *consultation* as a form of participation would be by conceiving the victim as a consultant within a public unitary lens of citizen participation vis à vis the public interest. Framing the victim in those terms would allow for more nuance within Edwards' typology since consultations would not be exclusively about victim preferences but also about bringing forward their perspectives and analyses that directly engage with criteria considered relevant to decisions, such as the public interest. In this sense, the views and perspectives of victims as consultants would not refer to merely personal preferences but would also include a reflected analysis that takes into account the weighing of various considerations in this decision. Within this conception, victims would be seen as capable of reasoning publicly. This added approach to the typology would arguably give rise to a more dynamic, direct, and evolving understanding of victim participation towards the public interest, which is rooted within unitary conceptions, seen in this chapter, that include communitarian and deliberative democratic frameworks.

[33] Although formally the Crown Prosecution Service code does not apply to private prosecutions, there is a requirement that decisions be made in the public interest. Therefore, in practice, these standards are also meant to guide private prosecutors.

Third, a conception of victims closer to the public end of the spectrum would also complement Edwards' *expression* category by suggesting that victims are not sharing emotions simply for their own personal benefit, therapeutic or other, but also for the public, such as others in the process. Perhaps methods exist within this framework to circumscribe the ways emotions are conveyed and their role within a public process. One can imagine this form of participation within a communicative approach to sentencing[34] that recognizes the relevance of victim participation with emotion to the public process, rather than merely to meet victims' personal needs.

One noteworthy consequence of developing expression by rooting it within a public conception of victims would be that the line between information and expression might become less clear since, according to Edwards' framework, information is distinct from expression, based on who needs this information, and *information-provision* by victims is more objective than expression. Arguably, an emotion and expression needed within the public process can be considered information rather than expression, even if provided in expressive terms. Moreover, in terms of *information-provision*, Edwards' typology seems to root this type of participation within a public conception of the victim.

Finally, infusing a public conception of the victim would also enrich *information-reception* as a form of participation. As highlighted in the previous section, within Edwards' typology, receiving information is considered a passive state and therefore is not understood as an active form of participation to add to the typology. Accordingly, it is only if the victim responds to this information-reception that the relationship between the victim and the decision-maker can become active and take the form of one of the four participatory types discussed. While this might be the case in conceptions of the victim that are predominantly private, when victims are conceived as closer to the public end of the spectrum (namely, within unitary theories of the public interest), the reception of information is not passive, since it allows victims to take part in a deliberative process that consists of listening to others, weighing certain considerations, and giving reasons, all of which are relevant in forming a decision, either as control or consultation.

[34] Duff and Marshall (n 18) 41; Julian V Roberts and Edna Erez, 'Communication in Sentencing: Exploring the Expressive Function of Victim Impact Statements' (2004) 10 IRV 223; Marie Manikis, 'Victim Impact Statements at Sentencing: Towards a Clearer Understanding of Their Aims' (2015) 65 UTLJ 85.

6. Obligations Held by Victims and State Decision-Makers Within Edwards' Typology of Victim Participation

A framework that is attentive to a conception of the victim across a public–private spectrum can be useful to frame victim participation as a duty or a right. This is particularly important when examining the relationship between victims and decision-makers and in considering their wider mutual obligations.

In his typology, Edwards engages, to some extent, with some of these dimensions. His typology distinguishes between forms of participation that create obligations for victims and those that create them for state decision-makers. Indeed, as will be shown below, since Edwards' typology seems to predominantly conceive the victim as a bearer of individual and personal interests in the criminal process, this conception inevitably affects the obligations that victims and the criminal justice system have towards one another.

Participatory obligations held by victims within Edwards' typology

While certain types of participation are understood as providing victims with participatory choices ('optional supply'), other types of participation compel victim participation ('non-optional supply'), particularly when their participation is useful to the state or system. Specifically, if the victim is understood primarily within a private conception, their participation within a public process will be different, as well as their obligations and rights. In this regard, Edwards highlights that some types of victim participation, including *consultation* and *expression*, are optional. Indeed, when the participant's private interests are predominantly at play, it seems conceivable to offer them a choice to take part in this participation. Nevertheless, it remains curious to see that Edwards considers *control* as being non-optional, since he describes this type of participation as a 'preference', the same way he uses this private and subjective understanding in *consultation* and *expression*. Arguably, if victims are to be provided *control* in supplying their preference, and this control is rooted in preferences held by victims, they should also have the ability to decide whether to participate in this endeavour. Finally, *information-provision* as a type of participation is understood as an obligation for victims to provide information needed by the state as a decision-maker. This indeed corresponds to Edwards rooting this type of participation within a predominantly public conception, as further discussed below.

State decision-makers and their obligations towards victims within Edwards' typology

According to Edwards, all types of participation create some obligation on the part of state decision-makers. This obligation, however, varies in nature and in the level of discretion provided to the decision-maker. Indeed, Edwards distinguishes between obligations to 'seek and apply', 'seek and consider', or to 'allow' the various participatory contributions of victims. A commonality between most of these obligations is that state decision-makers generally need to 'seek' or 'allow' the victim's contribution, terms that seem to be equivalent. This can be understood as a procedural obligation, further discussed in Chapter 3, since they need to invite or allow participation. Some types of participation are understood as requiring a further step on the part of state decision-makers and include additional more substantive obligations to 'consider' victim preferences or 'apply' these preferences. While 'consideration' still allows some discretion on the part of state decision-makers, a duty to apply these preferences does not and makes this obligation more robust.

Rooting participation and these obligations within the public–private conception is useful since it allows us to make sense of these state obligations differently. As highlighted above, Edwards generally conceives of the victim in a predominantly private manner, which can have an impact on the corollary obligations possessed by criminal justice state decision-makers. The following analysis examines the types of participation rooted within this private conception, including 'control', 'consultation', and 'expression', and the way the corollary obligations of decision-makers are understood and relate to victim participation.

First, under Edwards' typology, when victims conceived within a private framework engage in 'control' types of participation, the state decision-maker has an obligation to seek and apply the victim's preference. Accordingly, the criminal justice system has an obligation to incorporate the victim's subjective and personal interests. The private dimension of these interests can explain why Edwards makes clear that this type of participation and its corollary obligations are not present in common law systems. Indeed, it would be antithetical to the notion of a public process to oblige the application of private and subjective preferences—typically more relevant within private law.

Second, 'consultation' is also understood within a predominantly private conception of the victim and recognizes that state decision-makers have obligations to seek and 'consider' the victim's preference. This suggests that there is some discretion embedded in the ways preferences shared by victims are considered substantively by decision-makers. Arguably, if the victim's contribution is understood as subjective and related to their personal interests, there is a serious possibility that this contribution may have a limited impact and may be considered less legitimate in decisions that are seen as part of the wider public interest.

Similarly, 'information-provision' also gives rise to the same obligations on the part of decision-makers, namely, the duty 'to seek and consider victim information'. Considering that victims within this role contribute in a way that is considered more objective and rational, as 'information' rather than as a preference, decision-makers might take this contribution more seriously and grant it more weight in their decision.

Finally, 'expression' is also a type of participation that Edwards conceives of as bringing forward subjective preferences and emotions. In this sense, while decision-makers have a duty to allow expression by victims, they do not have any duty to consider it relevant in decision-making, since this type of participation is considered purely self-interested and aiming at a self-therapeutic dimension.

7. Obligations Held by Victims and State Decision-Makers Within a Predominantly Public Conception and Typology of Victim Participation

As seen above, a framework that conceives the victim across a public–private spectrum adds to and complements Edwards' typology, which is predominantly rooted in a private conception of the victim, by developing a predominantly public conception of victims. This development adds important nuances and reflections about the mutual obligations held by victims and decision-makers in relation to victim participation in the criminal justice process.

Obligations held by victims within a predominantly public conception

Conceptualizing the victim within a predominantly public conception allows us to frame victims' participatory obligations differently than when the victim is conceived within a predominantly private conception. The following analysis begins by discussing the frameworks that underpin victims within a predominantly public conception and discusses the ways these frameworks may understand victim participatory obligations. It then proceeds by complementing Edwards' typology, which is underpinned by a private conception of the victim, by examining how these types of participation might conceive of obligations held by victims differently when rooted within a predominantly public conception.

Conceiving the victim predominantly within a public lens would recognize victims' obligation to participate, but their nature and conceptualization would depend on the underlying theory that supports this public form of participation discussed above. For instance, under a liberal communitarian approach, victims are considered not only as individuals but also as members of a broader community that was also wronged, thus sharing identity and having certain responsibilities to their fellow citizens.[35] These responsibilities may indeed create duties towards them. Similarly, as part of this framework and in light of this understanding of public wrongs as shared wrongs, the victim acts as a 'representative of the public, the "we" who calls the offender to account'.[36] The criminal law is their law as citizens of the polity. Therefore, they have a civic responsibility to assist the criminal law's enterprise, which includes contributing to or preserving the public interest when it is challenged by the state, as will be discussed in Chapter 4.

Similarly, under a deliberative democratic approach, the legitimacy of public decisions rests upon participation that offers public reasoning among equals. In this sense, citizens are tasked with offering and reflecting on public, mutually acceptable and justified reasons, rather than simply offering their own preferences, to arrive at and shape binding decisions.[37] Decisions within this framework are linked to persuasive reasons through a deliberative process that allows for equal participation and reflexivity, with various views from those affected by the decision. In this sense, citizenship is in great part a way of co-governing and contributing to the public interest and wider public governance. Accordingly, there is a general sense that victim participation should be considered a duty that victims as citizens have towards the wider polity, since it contributes to decisions that are more reflective and comprehensively representative of the public interest.

[35] According to Marshall (n 12), these duties include reporting crimes, bearing witness to the crime in support of the community's collective norms, and contributing to providing statements. A parallel can be made between the duty of the police to maintain the Queen's peace that is 'owed to members of the public at large' according to *Michael v Chief Constable South Wales* [2015] UKSC 2 [343], [33], [35], [37], [120], [191].

[36] Claes Lernestedt, 'Victim and Society: Sharing Wrongs, but in Which Roles?' (2014) 8 Crim L & Phil 187, 191.

[37] Kennedy (n 12).

The nature of these duties, however, would not be legal but rather civic, owed to the polity.[38] Duff distinguishes between the two, highlighting that civic responsibilities lack the force of law and are enforceable only by informal persuasion from our fellows. In this sense, if a victim does not participate, they would not be considered as committing an offence because there are many reasons including personal safety that might militate against recognizing this duty as legal. These would be primarily grounded in the responsibilities that victims hold in a decent society, as owing to fellow citizens assistance in the enterprise of the criminal law and doing so honestly.

Participative duties by type of participation

Having examined the types of contexts and participative duties that can be held by victims within a public framework vis à vis the polity, this section builds on Edwards' typology to highlight the ways such duties would be understood when they relate to specific types of participation.

'Control' as a type of participation would be conceived of as an obligation held by victims to participate, since their contribution would be essential to the functioning of the public process. Indeed, whether rooted within a communitarian or deliberative conception, this type of victim participation would consider that, as a final arbiter of certain decisions, victims have a duty towards their fellow citizens to participate in this way. An example of this may include private prosecutions that must be made in the public interest, which requires the same standards as public prosecutions.

'Consultation' would also create duties to participate if the victim is understood as essential in shaping the public interest. Indeed, instead of merely offering preferences as part of the consultative process, victims would be providing perspectives that are legitimized and framed in a way society has established would serve the public interest. For instance, this can include conferring with prosecutors or with sentencing courts as part of victim personal statements to bring forward fleshed out arguments about decisions to prosecute as well as sentences that are based on the same standards that legal actors must follow.

Finally, 'expression' may also be rooted within a perspective that conceives of the victim and their contribution as public. As highlighted above, this would

[38] RA Duff, 'When Should We Plead Guilty?' in Julian V Roberts and Jesper Ryberg (eds), *Sentencing the Self-Convicted: The Ethics of Pleading Guilty* (Hart Publishing 2023).

be the case in societies that do not place emotions in a purely subjective and self-serving account and can recognize the value of emotions in public processes as communicative and towards broader reconciliatory aims.

Obligations held by state criminal justice decision-makers within a predominantly public conception

Conceiving the victim within a predominantly public lens would recognize that state decision-makers would be under a *duty* to allow the victim's decision or to seek and consider the victim's contributions and perspectives, since these contributions would be seen as relevant to the public interest, rather than merely personal.

Contrary to the way 'control' is presented by Edwards, a complementary understanding of 'control' that is rooted within a predominantly public framework of the victim would see the victim as a direct public contributor to the public process that makes decisions and holds ultimate control (veto) over those decisions. As highlighted above, an example of this can be found in the participatory mechanism of private prosecutions as they existed historically when victims were considered as directly contributing to the public interest and had the monopoly over these decisions.

Under 'consultation', victims would be considered legitimate consultants capable of providing relevant information on the public interest to state decision-makers. State decision-makers within the criminal justice system would not only have a duty to seek this consultation but also to apply it in their decisions, since they would be necessary and complementary to their own assessment of the public interest. Under a deliberative democratic framework, the rational engagement between victims and state decision-makers about public values would further the development of a consultative relationship that would advance public decision-making. Similar to 'information provision', victim participation would be considered relevant and not predominantly representing victims' personal individual interests. Although victim roles as consultants and information provisions would be public and enable a say on dimensions relevant to the public interest, the duties of state decision-makers towards victims would slightly differ between these two roles. The former would require state decision-makers to treat the victim as a consultant on the public interest and their perspective on the public interest would need to be rooted within a principled framework at the same level and

Table 2.2 Expanded participatory types for victims

	Participation Type	Obligation on Criminal Justice Decision-Maker	Obligation on Victim
Dispositive	Control	To seek and apply victim's reasoned decision	Non-optional supply of reasoned decision Victim is the decision-maker
Non-Dispositive	Consultation	To seek and consider victim's reasoned perspective	Non-optional supply of reasoned perspective
	Information-Provision	To seek and consider victim information	Non-optional supply of information
	Expression	To seek and consider victim expression	Non-optional supply of expressive information

with the same legitimacy as state decision-makers. Victims as information providers, however, would have less of an equivalent status with decision-makers and would strictly be providing relevant information about specific events in the public interest, rather than making representations about the public interest.

Finally, the duties of state decision-makers in the context of 'expression' as participation would require them to allow this form of expression, not just for the victim's own personal therapeutic welfare but within a view that considers this expression as relevant to the public interest and values. As highlighted above, this can perhaps be justified under an expressive model of criminal justice as understood in some sentencing processes.

Table 2.2 summarizes the typology, which is rooted within a predominantly public conception of the victim. This complements and adds to Edwards' typology, which is predominantly grounded within a private conception.

8. The Relationship Between Victim Participation and Victim Rights

The terminology of 'rights' has often been used widely and indiscriminately within the victims' literature to refer to victim participation in the criminal justice process. This terminology is often used without much attention paid to the underlying conceptions of victim participation and rights. There is surprisingly little theoretical engagement with the potential interests (or potential rights) that are held by victims and their relationship to the wider underpinnings of participation. These limitations are also present in the victims' literature that uses the language of rights without discussing the nature of the rights and duties in common law. This resonates with Varuhas' analysis, which pointed to the lack of analysis of the nature of rights under the HRA 1998 in England and Wales.[39]

As highlighted in the previous section, there are various types of participation that should be informed by the different conceptions of victims across the public–private spectrum. Referring to this typology can be useful to determine whether participation can be conceptualized as a right. Similarly, the concept of rights can also be understood in different ways within the vast literature on rights. For these reasons, it is important to refrain from automatically equating victim participation to rights without having a clear sense of their conceptual underpinning.

Within a traditional understanding, rights are meant to protect private and personal interests held by individuals that are deemed inherently important. As highlighted by Varuhas, 'the very gist of human rights law is generally understood to be individual protection'.[40] Accordingly, rights are meant to 'protect basic interests from outside interference, to maintain those interests inviolate, and affirm and reinforce their importance and that they ought to be held in the utmost respect'.[41] This conception of rights rooted in possessive individualism is much closer to an understanding of participation that is predominantly rooted within a private conception of the victim, since victims possess their own private and personal interests that they bring forward in the process. Examples of such types of participation that are equivalent to rights in the traditional sense include 'expression' as well as 'control', which predominantly consider the victim as bringing forward their own predominantly private 'preferences' or personal interests to be considered in criminal justice.

This conception is quite different from an understanding of victim participation that conceptualizes victims, including their role and interests, as predominantly public by considering them as citizens who can represent the

[39] Jason NE Varuhas, *Damages and Human Rights* (Hart Publishing 2016) 204. Varuhas pointed out that some commentators considered the 'rights' under the HRA 1998 in England and Wales to be generalized standards or principles of legality or, more amorphously, values, as opposed to genuine individual rights (often analogizing them with common law grounds of review).

[40] ibid 203.

[41] ibid 345.

polity and their shared values from a deliberative democratic perspective and thus are considered relevant to directly discuss and shape the public interest. Forms of participation rooted in these underpinnings would not be considered rights in the traditional sense, since victims would not predominantly bring forward their own private and personal interests.

This public conception rooted in a deliberative democratic framework has several differences from a traditional framework in public common law that posits that in public law, citizens are private individuals who do not possess rights, only the ability to enforce duties owed to the public. The public common law framework is rooted in the notion that wrongs within common law review are not individual, as breaches of individual rights, but rather public wrongs, that is, breaches of duties owed to the public as a whole. Within this common law review approach, good public administration is required to consider the legitimate interests of individual citizens. Nevertheless, in judging the relevance of an individual interest, however legitimate, regard must be had as to the purpose of the administrative process concerned. In other words, individual interests, but only those deemed legitimate as part of the administrative process concerned, may be relevant to the remedial inquiry as an aspect of good administration (rather than because they are inherently important). In this sense, their relevance and weight are contingent on the public purposes for which power is conferred.[42] This view is closer to an aggregate conception of the victim, which understands the victim as having the potential to contribute to the public interest but, from a predominantly private interest standpoint, only when this interest aligns with the broader aims of the public process.

These traditional frameworks of rights and citizen contribution within public common law have been challenged over the years, particularly with the rise of human rights as part of a public law framework. Indeed, as highlighted by Varuhas, possessive rights stemming from a private dimension have been incorporated into public common law approaches, which have tended to diminish the private underpinning of these rights.[43] Similarly, the wider literature on rights has also seen a development by which certain rights have increasingly been discussed within a collective conception rather than one that is primarily focused on the individual.[44]

[42] ibid 195.

[43] Jason NE Varuhas, 'Against Unification' in Hanna Wilberg and Mark Elliot (eds), *The Scope and Intensity of Substantive Review* (Hart Publishing 2015) 91; Mary Liston, 'Expanding the Parameters of Participatory Public Law: A Democratic Right to Public Participation and the State's Duty of Public Consultation' (2017) 63 McGill LJ 375.

[44] Leslie Green, 'Two Views of Collective Rights' (1991) 4 CJLJ 315; Peter Jones, 'Group Rights' in Edward N Zalta (ed), *The Stanford Encyclopedia of Philosophy* (Stanford 2016).

The distinct frameworks that underpin the conceptions of rights and participation discussed in this section highlight the importance for the scholarship that engages with victim participation and rights to carefully consider and articulate their chosen underpinnings. To date, the scholarship has relied on certain assumptions that tend to equate victim participation to human rights. Such generalizations should be avoided by clearly articulating the underpinning of the victim's interests and version of rights it alludes to. In this sense, when victim participation is framed within a human rights perspective, it would be important to be clear about whether they rely on the idea that victims' rights need to be protected by the state and are considered personal and a central concern for protection of individual interests or whether they rely on another framing of rights within a more collective and public understanding.

9. Conclusion

Conceptions of the victim and their interests across the public–private spectrum are fundamental aspects to consider when developing a typology of victim participation. Infusing Edwards' existing typology with these different underpinnings allows for a complementary and additional typology that enables more thoroughness and nuances. This in turn enables a greater theoretical, comparative, and practical understanding of the various roles victims can or have taken on within the public criminal justice process. Further, it infuses the existing typology—predominantly focused on a private framing of the victim—with a complementary predominantly public conception, which is useful to understand certain roles taken on by victims in the criminal process. Finally, this analysis and complementary typology enables to make greater distinctions between the potential duties and rights held by victims, as well as the potential duties held by criminal justice decision-makers.

3

An Additional Role for Victims

Conceptualizing State Fallibilities and Accountability

1. Introduction

A complementary role for victims in Edwards' typology consists of holding the state accountable in instances of state failures. Although scholarship has started discussing this form of participation,[1] it remains underdeveloped. This chapter, along with the rest of the book, provides a novel contribution to the field by developing analytical tools to examine accountability and analysing this complementary role undertaken by victims within the criminal legal process. While this chapter highlights some of the conceptual frameworks around accountability, the next chapters will explore, from a comparative perspective, the development and analysis of this role on the ground by focusing on the role of victims as state prosecutorial accountability.

This chapter begins by classifying the different types of state failures and forms of accountability by referring to scholarship in criminal legal theory, public law, and public accountability.[2] These conceptions of accountability will enrich our understanding of this role by offering frameworks to understand and compare the different ways victims engage in legal processes as agents of accountability in both jurisdictions discussed in Chapters 4–7. Moreover, the various dimensions of accountability will also be useful for developing normative grounds of the ways victims should engage as such agents in the criminal legal process in Chapter 8.

This chapter is divided into two sections. The first section develops this additional form of victim participation by providing conceptual and contextual distinctions between the various forms of state fallibilities. These distinctions are useful to understand the rationale of this role. The second section draws

[1] Marie Manikis, 'Expanding Participation: A Comparative Approach to Victims as Agents of Accountability in the Criminal Justice Process' (2017) 1 PL 63.

[2] Marcus Bovens, Robert Goodin, and Thomas Schillemans, *The Oxford Handbook of Public Accountability* (OUP 2014).

Victims as Agents of State Accountability. Marie Manikis, Oxford University Press. © Marie Manikis 2026.
DOI: 10.1093/9780191993947.003.0004

on the various conceptions of accountability developed in the public law and accountability literature to provide frameworks for analysing this role and its evolution within the jurisdictions under analysis. Forms of accountability include differences depending on whether victim interests are conceived as predominantly public or private within the public criminal legal process. They also include normative and descriptive conceptions, green light and red light functions, as well as substantive and procedural forms of accountability.

2. State Fallibilities

The premise of this type of participation stems from the recognition that the state, as part of a structure created and comprising humans, is fallible and therefore can fail its duties in different ways.[3] In the context of criminal justice, the state and its agents—notably police, prosecutors, and the judiciary—are not flawless. These failures range from procedural, technical, and substantive legal mistakes to deeper patterns of bias, abuse of discretion, and misuse of power.

For the purposes of this monograph, state fallibilities are classified into two principal categories: individual and systemic. This distinction provides a conceptual framework for understanding the nature of failures within the criminal legal system—particularly within prosecutorial decision-making and broader state accountability.

Individual fallibilities refer to errors, omissions, or misconduct that can be attributed to a particular person or small group of individuals within the legal process and are not necessarily symptomatic of a broader institutional or structural problem. They can be described as anomalies capable of individual corrections. Examples include overlooking key evidence, misunderstanding legal standards, or misapplying the law in a specific case when those errors are not rooted in broader social inequalities or institutional practices.

Systemic fallibilities are rooted in structural and institutional deficiencies that create patterns of failure, often affecting multiple individuals or groups and reproducing harm over time. They are often rooted in broader, at times more insidious, forms of patterns and thus can be conscious or unconscious. They include forms of self-interested private-based failures that can be rooted

[3] RA Duff, 'When Should We Plead Guilty' in Julian V Roberts and Jesper Ryberg (eds), *Pleading Guilty: Ethical Perspectives on Sentencing the Self-Convicted* (Hart 2023).

Table 3.1 Characteristics of state fallibilities

Characteristics	Individual Fallibilities	Systemic Fallibilities
Source	One or a few actors	Structural or institutional-wide practices
Scope	Case-specific, isolated, rare	Widespread, recurring, patterned
Visibility	Often more visible	May be obscured or normalized
Accountability	Focus on the fallible actor(s)	Broader state or institutional responsibility

in entrenched norms and hierarchical/organizational pressures[4] or as part of biases rooted in social inequalities—such as racial, gendered, ableism, or class-based stereotypes in decision-making.[5] Within the criminal legal system, the disproportionate non-prosecution and prosecution of marginalized individuals and groups are part of these realities and several other examples, which will be discussed throughout this monograph.

While it is important to categorize these failures to better understand their distinct manifestations, as illustrated in Table 3.1, individual and systemic fallibilities frequently intersect and mutually reinforce one another within state decision-making processes.[6]

State fallibilities within social context

Duff's framework on utopias and relative eutopias/dystopias[7] is enlightening in this regard as it allows to bring forward the two main forms of state fallibilities within a broader social context. These forms of errors can coexist and intertwine but it is worth distinguishing them to understand the various facets of state failures towards victims. While Duff's framework focuses on failures vis-à-vis the accused, this section expands and adapts this framework to include state failures vis-à-vis victims. These failures can heavily affect the various

[4] Bruce A Green and Rebecca Roiphe, 'Rethinking Prosecutors' Conflicts of Interest' (2017) 58 BCL Rev 463; Sara Sun Beale, 'Rethinking the Identity and Role of United States Attorneys' (2005) 6 Ohio St J Crim L 369, which explores how personal and institutional incentives affect prosecutorial decisions; Bruce A Green, 'Why Should Prosecutors "Seek Justice"?' (1999) 26(3) Fordham Urb LJ 607, discussing the ethical obligations of prosecutors and failures of individual discretion.

[5] Kimberlé Crenshaw, 'Mapping the Margins: Intersectionality, Identity Politics, and Violence against Women of Color' (1991) 43 Stanford L Rev 1241, which is seen as a foundational article outlining how systems fail to account for intersectional vulnerabilities.

[6] ibid.

[7] ibid.

assessments in criminal legal decision-making and therefore there is an important need for accountability mechanisms that can bring those dimensions forward and require individual and systemic responses, discussed in greater depth in Chapter 8.

Quasi-eutopias and predominant individual state failures

Duff distinguishes between two scenarios that lie near opposite ends of a spectrum, ranging from a quasi-eutopia to a quasi-dystopia. The first scenario, referred to as a quasi-eutopia, describes the context of a decent democratic republic in which liberty, equality, and respect are values to which its citizens and government are genuinely committed to.[8] This treatment entails a context in which criminal laws are democratically validated and legitimate in their scope; one whose criminal process respects the rights associated with due process and treats defendants with substantive equality and respect. Punishments in this context are moderate in their severity and constructive in their intent. Their impact does not entail the loss of dignity. An underlying value within this scenario includes the prevention of oppression towards individuals, through which charges of wrongdoing are tested in a way that protects citizens from potential oppression and injustice. Duff highlights that a relative eutopia can be understood in a context of a decent polity, in which defendants are treated (by their fellow citizens and by the state) with equal concern and respect.

Adding to Duff's framework, this scenario would also apply to victims, who would be treated with the same level of concern as other citizens. In turn, victims would extend the same level of respect and commitment for equality and liberty to their fellow citizens. Processes that relate to prosecutions and determination of responsibility would therefore treat victims and defendants with respect, namely, with a presumption of honesty, good faith, and free from stereotypes rooted in systemic inequalities. Additionally, these processes would pursue this wider assessment for determining the truth about the public wrong that would merit accurate censure.

Made this way, decisions would need to be made in the public interest rather than in ways that advance purely private interests that may be tied to self-serving and professional relationships and personal financial interests, as well as those that may be tied to personal beliefs and biases that undermine the prosecutor's ability to pursue justice in pursuit of broader public values.

According to Duff, even in a quasi-eutopia, the state can commit wrongdoing. He highlights that 'even in our eutopia, protections against various kinds

[8] Ronald Dworkin, *A Matter of Principle* (OUP 1986) 190.

of potential state oppression are important: it is a society of fallible human beings, including fallible officials and institutions."[9] In this context, the state, including its prosecutors and its representatives, would recognize that a system run by humans can be fallible, which can relate to its own processes and decisions, and therefore would enable citizens (dissenting or not) to guard against its own fallibility. Specifically, this recognition would entail processes by which citizens, including victims, could bring forward instances of state fallibilities in various decisions as part of checks and balances in the process. Conversely, citizens, including victims, would also be understood as fallible—highlighting the importance of a system of accountability in which power would not be held as a monopoly or quasi-monopoly.

Importantly, within this quasi-eutopian scenario, most instances of state fallibility would be predominantly *individual* failures by state actors, as opposed to decision-making flaws rooted in wider systemic failures. This would be the case, since within this scenario, values of liberty, respect, and substantive equality are for the most part respected and therefore, flaws rooted in systemic failures would not be frequent.

Individual errors by state actors in such contexts would typically include instances such as good faith misinterpretations or misunderstandings of laws and policies, or errors in accounting for certain facts, which are not rooted in substantive inequalities. These can take place in various decisions, including in prosecutorial decisions as part of assessing the standard of evidence required or facts related to the evidence. In sentencing, they may also include an erroneous failure of considering a mitigating factor as relevant.

Quasi dystopias and predominant state systemic failures

The second scenario, referred by Duff as a quasi-dystopia, envisages a polity (and system) that is significantly dystopian, although not to the extent that law is nothing more than empty rhetoric. Within this scenario, in addition to potential individual errors by state actors, most instances of state fallibilities would be underpinned by flaws rooted in systemic failures. Indeed, in such polity, values of liberty, equality, and fraternity, of equal concern and respect for all, still have *some* purchase within the social fabric, though as much by their absence as by their presence. While these values inform the polity's institutions and its life, Duff suggests that they function more prominently as ideals that the polity radically fails to achieve—or even to pursue with serious commitment. Significant groups within this society are excluded from its rights

[9] Duff (n 3) 19.

and benefits—and thus from the status of citizenship. While the law can claim to have some authority, its application is substantively unequal and disproportionately used towards these groups. This results in the over- and under-criminalization of groups based on power dynamics.

Relatedly, Lacey's typology of social injustices is particularly useful in conceptualizing these different forms of systemic state failures present within quasi-dystopias.[10] She distinguishes between material injustices, epistemic injustices, and injustices of standing. Material injustices refer to the unjust distribution of access to public goods, opportunities, and material resources, which are known to be criminogenic. An upshot of this distributive injustice includes epistemic injustice, understood as the way knowledge is shaped, received, and validated, rendering certain claims as less valid and less audible. This can be rooted in material injustices, but also more subtly flow from factors such as implicit biases, for example in how veracity and credibility are assessed. Finally, closely related to epistemic injustice lies the notion of injustices of standing, referring to the basic level of participation or status within a political community, meant to be marked by reciprocity and the minimal level of respect warranted to participate in such processes. Indeed, this form of injustice can be seen at a more basic level than epistemic injustices.

Within such scenarios, some individuals would be considered less credible and respected as their existence and voices would be perceived as illegitimate due to stereotypes and biases towards them. As will be seen, this can include state prosecutorial flaws that consider victims as inherently less credible due to their belonging to certain groups.

Adding to Duff's second scenario of quasi-dystopias, it would make sense that in such contexts the state would resist initiatives that aim to offer possibilities for citizens to critically examine state actions/decisions. As explained by MacCormick, the aims of modern criminal law are broader in scope than simply the justification of punishment. They include the monopolization and control by the state over disputes by articulating a narrative that suggests 'ending forms of private vengeance and blood feuds and securing a state monopoly over the legitimate use of violence, further institutionalized through the development of a specialized body of criminal law and agencies to enforce it'.[11] As such, within a quasi-dystopian scenario, state monopoly would

[10] Nicola Lacey, 'Criminal Justice and Social (In)Justice' in Virginia Mantouvalou and Jonathan Wolff (eds), *Structural Injustice and the Law* (UCL Press 2024).

[11] Neil MacCormick, *Institutions of Law: An Essay in Legal Theory* (OUP 2007) 207–09.

be preserved by limiting oversight of state decisions. Indeed, state processes/decisions, which include prosecutorial decisions, would be less transparent and could not be substantively engaged with. This resistance would be made explicit by the state in its discourse or implicit through its implementation. Explicit resistance refers to a form of state resistance that is overtly narrated in state discourse by relying on ideals about the state being a rational, objective, and independent entity that holds the monopoly of the public interest and operates in a quasi-eutopian assumption that presupposes substantive equality between its citizens. It also stems from the idea that the state is the only entity that can make objective and independent decisions, promote public values, and protect the public interest in a way that does not seek to advance private or personal interests. Implicit resistance also relies on the same underpinnings, but their manifestation is more subtle since the state would offer certain mechanisms of accountability to citizens, though with substantial limitations that render their use eutopian.

Understanding state failures as ranging from individualized to systemic in nature is particularly relevant to the analysis of victims' roles as agents of state accountability. These distinctions are useful for comparing the various mechanisms available to victims across the jurisdictions under analysis, and for assessing the extent to which those mechanisms can address systemic fallibilities. This classification will also serve as an important foundation for the penultimate chapter, which proposes a normative framework for recognizing the victim's role as an agent of accountability—one that is responsive not only to individual errors but also to broader systemic failures.

3. Conceptions of Accountability

The development and analysis of an additional role for victims as agents of state accountability necessitates a closer examination of the concept of accountability itself. Widely invoked in policy and public discourse—often as a symbol of transparency, legitimacy, and institutional trust—accountability is a multifaceted and context-dependent concept. In legal, political, and administrative theory, accountability is not a singular notion but encompasses various forms, including legal, political, administrative, social, and professional accountability. Marcus Bovens has defined accountability as 'a relationship between an actor and a forum, in which the actor has an obligation to explain and justify his or her conduct, the forum can pose questions and pass judgment, and the actor may face consequences'.[12] This conception highlights the procedural and relational aspects of accountability while allowing for variation across settings.

Furthermore, scholars such as Dubnick and Frederickson[13] have emphasized the normative and aspirational elements of accountability, distinguishing between accountability as a mechanism of constraint (often ex post, reactive, etc.) and as a tool for learning, deliberation, and democratic renewal. This latter 'deliberative' form of accountability resonates with communitarian and participatory democratic theories that view accountability not only as a retrospective judgement of performance but also as a forward-looking process of civic engagement and public justification.

In this context, understanding accountability is essential for situating the role of victims within the prosecutorial process. Drawing from the theoretical frameworks discussed in this section, this monograph considers multifaceted dimensions of accountability and examines how victims' rights and participation mechanisms across jurisdictions align with—or fall short of—addressing systemic fallibilities.

Normative and descriptive conceptions

Bovens and others have also examined some of the reasons for this conceptual ambiguity and multiplicity of meanings.[14] They argue that one of the reasons is that 'accountability' is an Anglo-Norman concept, which has no semantic equivalents on the European continent.[15] Another reason provided by these authors is that within Anglo-American political and scholarly discourse, the concept seems to be ever-expanding with certain patterns.

Within American academic and political discourse, accountability is used predominantly as a normative concept, as a set of standards for the evaluation of the behaviour of public actors. In this sense, being accountable is considered

[12] Marcus Bovens, 'Analysing and Assessing Accountability: A Conceptual Framework' (2007) 13(4) Eur LJ 447, 450.

[13] Melvin J Dubnick and H George Frederickson, 'Accountable Agents: Federal Performance Measurement and Third-Party Government' (2011) 40(2) J Pub Adm Res Theory 437.

[14] Marcus Bovens, Thomas Schillemans, and Paul Hart, 'Does Public Accountability Work? An Assessment Tool' (2008) 86 Public Admin 225.

[15] Accordingly, languages such as French, Portuguese, Spanish, German, and Dutch have no exact equivalent and do not (yet) distinguish semantically between 'responsibility' and 'accountability'. See Carol Harlow, *Accountability in the European Union* (OUP 2002) 14–15; Melvin J Dubnick, 'Accountability and the Promise of Performance: In Search of the Mechanisms' (2005) 28(3) Public Perform & Manag Rev 376; Richard Mulgan, *Holding Power to Account: Accountability in Modern Democracies* (Palgrave 2003).

a virtue, a positive quality of organizations or officials. Within this understanding, accountability has a broad meaning and is used to 'positively qualify a state of affairs or the performance of an actor'[16]. In this sense, it is considered a contested and contestable concept, because there is no general consensus about the standards for accountable behaviour and it can differ within each context, including time, place, or actors involved.

In British, Australian, and continental scholarly debates, the concept of accountability is often used in a much more descriptive and narrow sense—understood as a social 'mechanism', as an institutional relation or arrangement in which an actor can be held to account by a forum.[17] The focus of this concept is not whether the agents have acted in an accountable way by looking at the behaviour of public agents, but rather the way in which these institutional arrangements operate and 'whether they are or can be held accountable *ex post facto* by accountability forums' (emphasis in original). In this sense, Bovens has defined accountability as 'a relationship between an actor and a forum, in which the actor has an obligation to explain and justify his or her conduct, the forum can pose questions and pass judgment, and the actor may face consequences'.[18]

Both conceptions are relevant to governance, including the broad one where accountability is seen as a state of being or organizational value and the narrow one in which accountability is understood as a social mechanism. However, the typology of victims as agents of accountability in this chapter and throughout this book has mainly developed in the more descriptive sense. Indeed, this chapter analyses the relationships between state actors in the criminal justice process and victims who are engaging and given space *ex post facto* within the various forums/mechanisms to enable state accountability. However, a broader understanding of accountability is also discussed in the penultimate chapter of this monograph.

Within this conception, accountability as a process can emanate and be triggered by different actors involved in the process. This project seeks to understand, compare, and analyse the ways that victims of crime can and have contributed to state accountability—with a focus on prosecutorial state accountability—within the state's initial decisions relating to prosecutions in the context of criminal justice. By focusing on victims and their relationship

[16] Bovens, Schillemans, and Hart (n 14) 227.

[17] Patricia Day and Rudolph Klein, *Accountabilities: Five Public Services* (Tavistock 1987); Mulgan (n 15).

[18] Marcus Bovens, 'Analysing and Assessing Public Accountability: A Conceptual Model' (European Governance Papers (EUROGOV) C-06-01, 16 January 2006) 227.

to state accountability, accountability is understood in part as operating from a bottom-up perspective—where victims are bringing forward prosecutorial errors either on their own, through NGOs, community organizations, or pro-bono lawyers. However, some of the forums employed by victims—such as courts—can complement the bottom-up initiative and oscillate towards a more top-down perspective. Top-down accountability follows a hierarchical structure, whereas bottom-up accountability allows grassroots action to hold power wielders accountable for their actions.[19] The literature on accountability also recognizes social accountability, which acknowledges the interplay between bottom-up and top-down accountability and views these concepts as complementary.[20] Social accountability implies that grassroots action—including citizen participation by way of pro bono lawyering, NGOs, civil society organizations, and communities—can be used to hold the state accountable, particularly when the formal state system is failing.[21] Specifically, it can be defined as follows:

> the broad range of actions and mechanisms (beyond voting) that citizens, communities, civil society organizations (CSOs) and independent media can use to hold public officials and servants accountable. Traditionally, these have included a variety of citizen or civil society-led actions such as public demonstrations, protests, advocacy campaigns, investigative journalism and public interest lawsuits.... They also include efforts to enhance citizen knowledge and use of conventional mechanisms of accountability (for example, through public education about legal rights and available services) and/or efforts to improve the effectiveness of 'internal' accountability mechanisms, for example, through citizen involvement in public commissions and hearings, citizen advisory boards and oversight committees.[22]

[19] See Edith Brown Weiss, 'Bottom Up Accountability' (2007) 37 Environ Policy L 259. See also Lisa Yarwood, *State Accountability under International Law: Holding States Accountable for Breach of Jus Cogens Norms* (Routledge 2011) 620; Derick W Brinkerhoff and Anna Wetterberg, 'Gauging the Effects of Social Accountability on Services, Governance, and Citizen Empowerment' (2016) 76(2) Public Admin Rev 274, 275; and Bovens (n 18) 20–21.

[20] Carmen Malena, Reiner Forster, and Janmejay Singh, 'Social Accountability: An Introduction to the Concept and Emerging Practice' (Social Development Papers: Participation and Civic Engagement, Paper No 76, The World Bank 2004) 3–4.

[21] Anuradha Joshi and Peter P Houtzager, 'Widgets or Watchdogs?: Conceptual Explorations in Social Accountability' (2012) 14(2) Public Manag Rev 145, 154. Joshi and Houtzager argue that social accountability is too focused on the state. While we agree that their argument has value, the fact that this study is centred on police misconduct requires focusing on state actors; Malena, Forster, and Singh (n 20) 4.

[22] Malena, Forster, and Singh (n 20) 3–4. See also Brinkerhoff and Wetterberg (n 19) and Malena, Forster, and Singh (n 20) 7.

This definition is quite broad and includes a wide variety of actions and contexts.[23] For the purposes of this monograph, the focus is circumscribed on the ways victims and their representatives, which have included citizens, NGOs, pro bono lawyers, and civil society organizations, can and have engaged specific mechanisms within prosecutorial processes and the courts—in the context of criminal justice to hold the prosecutorial state accountable. These mechanisms are predominantly state-based and include the use of courts as well as internal state prosecutorial reviewing processes to enable state accountability.

Accountability within red light and green light frameworks

The literature on accountability is also informed by certain legal and political constitutional frameworks that can be referred to as 'red light' and 'green light' theories.[24] These frameworks rely on a normative theory of the state that tends to have specific assumptions and views on accountability. Indeed, Harlow and Rawlings refer to 'red light' and 'green light' theories as 'loosely-defined camps, some of the distinctions between which broadly echo the divisions between legal and political constitutionalism'.[25]

Specifically, constitutionalist Adam Tomkins characterizes 'red light' theories as rooted in the following ideas:

> (1) the law is autonomous to and superior over politics; (2) that the administrative state is something which needs to be kept in check by the law; (3) that the preferred way of doing this is through rule-based adjudication in courts'; and (4) that the goal of this project should be to enhance individual liberty where liberty is conceived as being the right to be left alone, the absence of external constraints—an idea of liberty which is best realized by having small government.[26]

Accordingly, the paradigmatic example of this framework in practice can be the classic instance of illegality, whereby the executive decision-maker exceeds in powers provided by the legislature. Subsequently, this decision is challenged

[23] Joshi and Houtzager (n 21) 151. Bovens also highlights the lack of sanctioning capacity of actors within social accountability mechanisms. See Bovens (n 18) 17–18.

[24] Nicholas Bamforth, 'Accountability of and to the Legislature' in Nicholas Bamforth and Peter Leyland (eds), *Accountability in the Contemporary Constitution* (OUP 2013) 258.

[25] Carol Harlow and Richard Rawlings, *Law and Administration* (3rd edn, CUP 2009) ch 1.

[26] Adam Tomkins, 'In Defence of the Political Constitution' (2002) 22 OJLS 157, 158. See also Martin Loughlin, *Public Law and Political Theory* (OUP 1992) 60–61.

by way of judicial review, which results in the court invalidating the decision because it was not authorized by the legislature.

By contrast, 'green light' theories are underpinned by the following idea:

> (1) that law is nothing more than a sophisticated (or elitist) discourse of politics and is neither autonomous from politics nor superior to administration; (2) that public administration is not a necessary evil to be tolerated, but a positive attribute to be welcomed; (3) that the objective of administrative law and regulation is not merely to stop bad administrative practices, but to encourage and facilitate good administrative practices—to control administration by channelling and guiding—and that the best people to do this will not necessarily be professional lawyers, that the best institutions in which to achieve these aims will not necessarily be courts, and that the best vehicle through which to realize these objectives will not necessarily be rule-based adjudication; and (4) that the goal of this project should be to enhance individual and collective liberty where liberty is conceived of as something which is, if not constituted by the state, then is at least facilitated by it, and is certainly not necessarily threatened by it. Thus, the goal of the state might be to house the homeless, to feed the hungry, to care for the sick, to educate the young, and so on, and the role of the administrative law is to help the state perform these tasks well, to distinguish between good and bad administrative practices, and to encourage and facilitate the former as well as to minimize the latter.[27]

While both theories value accountability, they differ in the processes through which it is pursued. Red light theory typically prioritizes courts as the primary forum for accountability, whereas green light theory emphasizes democratic or political institutions as the appropriate arenas for holding the state to account.[28]

These dimensions of accountability will serve as valuable tools for analysing the victim's role as an agent of state accountability in the jurisdictions under review, and for developing a normative conception of this role—one that can be advanced in courts while grounded in a deliberative democratic framework. As explored in Chapters 4–7, although victims have primarily engaged in 'red light' accountability functions in the jurisdictions studied, a public conception

[27] Tomkins (n 26) 158–59. See also Loughlin (n 26) 60–61.
[28] Harlow and Rawlings (n 25) 38.

of victims rooted in deliberative democratic theory offers the potential to enhance their role with stronger 'green light' accountability dimensions.

Accountability tied to conceptions of interests across the public/private spectrum

Similar to other types of victim participation discussed in the previous chapter, accountability as a type of victim participation can differ depending on whether victim interests are conceived within a predominantly public or private framework. Accordingly, Grear's spectrum coupled with Held's classification of private and public interests, discussed in Chapter 2, are relevant underpinnings that allow a clearer and more nuanced articulation of accountability as a complementary form of victim participation.

Table 3.2 below complements Table 2.1 about participation discussed in the previous chapter. It highlights the various forms accountability can take depending on whether victims and their interests are rooted predominantly within the public or private end of the spectrum. This conceptual distinction between the underpinnings of accountability is important since it can shape the duties of criminal justice decision-makers and of victims within the criminal legal process. Moreover, depending on the underpinnings of accountability, this distinction can affect notions of standing and remedies within the criminal legal process. The various distinctions are summarized in Table 3.2.

Table 3.2 Accountability distinctions across private–public interests

	Participation Type	Obligation on Criminal Justice Decision-Maker	Obligation on Victim
Non-dispositive	**Accountability** (predominantly **private** conception of victim interest)	To consider victim request to review	Optional supply of request to review if failure has been identified
	(predominantly **public** conception of victim interests)	To consider victim request to review	Non-optional (civic) supply of request to review if failure has been identified

Accountability by victims as bearers of predominantly private interests in a public process

As discussed in Chapter 2, when victims are conceived as entities that hold predominantly private interests, their participation in the public criminal legal process is generally understood as bringing forward their individual and personal interests in the process. The predominant justifying basis of this conception rests in liberal individualism rather than civic republicanism or deliberative democratic frameworks. This conception is often framed in the language of human rights,[29] individual human dignity, and humanness, as well as the importance of being attentive to victims' individual needs.[30] Rationales that support this conception highlight that when the state fails its duty to prevent, investigate, or prosecute crime, it has not upheld its duty to protect individuals, and that this failure justifies the recognition of procedural and participatory rights.[31] From this also stems an expectation that modern legal procedures ought to treat victims with sensitivity and respect in part due to the suffering they have endured and the important systemic service they are providing.[32] Finally, conceptions viewing victims as bearers of individual interests can be found in frameworks that consider victim participation as having personal therapeutic and cathartic value for victims.[33]

Relatedly, when victims are conceived as holders of private interests, their specific role as agents of state accountability would be understood as safeguarding and vindicating their fundamental individual, personal interests in instances of state failures. Consequently, victims ensure that their private interests are accounted for and respected by the state in a public process. This would mean that the relevant mechanisms of accountability conferred to victims would be tailored to enforce and respond to these predominantly private interests within a public process. Their role as agents of state accountability and related mechanisms would, therefore, be more aligned with those found

[29] Kent Roach, *Due Process and Victims' Rights: The New Law and Politics of Criminal Justice* (UP of Toronto 1999); Jonathan Doak, *Victims' Rights, Human Rights and Criminal Justice: Reconceiving the Role of Third Parties* (Hart Publishing 2008); Jo-Anne M Wemmers, 'Victims' Rights Are Human Rights: The Importance of Recognizing Victims as Persons' (2012) 19(2) Temida 71.

[30] Robert S Summers, 'Evaluating and Improving Legal Processes: A Plea for "Process Values" ' (1974) 60(1) Cornell L Rev 1.

[31] Sandra Walklate and Kate Fitz-Gibbon, 'The Evolving Place of Victims Within the Penal Landscape: The Case of England and Wales' (2019) 28(2) Soc & Leg Stud 181; Doak (n 29).

[32] Tom R Tyler, 'Procedural Justice and the Courts' (2003) 44(4) Court Rev 26.

[33] Dean G Kilpatrick and Randy K Otto, 'Constitutionally Guaranteed Participation in Criminal Proceedings for Victims: Potential Effects of Psychological Functioning' (1987) 34 Wayne L Rev 7; Edna Erez, 'Who's Afraid of the Big Bad Victim? Victim Impact Statements as Victim Empowerment and Enhancement of Justice' (1999) Crim LR 545.

in cases where private interests are at stake, providing specific forms of redress tailored to respond to individual interests and needs.

A similar accountability role also arises in situations where the public interest is understood under an aggregate conception, as discussed in Chapter 2. In this framework, victims are seen as presenting their own preferences, personal opinions, and perspectives to defend their private interests, which constitute one interest among several others that together form the public interest. Under this account, victims can hold the state accountable for failing to consider their private interests, which are regarded as one relevant component in shaping the public interest. As seen, majoritarian and aggregate perspectives of citizen input are premised on the notion that the various competing private preferences or interests of individual citizens are given equal weight and aggregated to produce a decision that reflects the quantitative distinction of those preferences or interests. This form of accountability does not extend to allowing victims to make direct substantive arguments about the public interest itself, since victims in this conception are limited to advancing their personal interests rather than unitary visions on the public interest.

Public law scholarship has also provided relevant insights into the relationship between private and public interest frameworks within public processes. Proponents of the bifurcation approach in public law argue for a distinction between areas of public law that engage with predominantly private interests and functions, and those that primarily engage the public interest and public functions.[34] In particular, Jason Varuhas has argued that certain areas of public law, such as those relating to human rights, are meant to predominantly afford strong protections and vindication of fundamental individual interests, akin to tort law. Accordingly, he suggests that these areas should be treated differently from areas like common law judicial review, which directly and predominantly engage with the public interest.

This analysis is relevant for the development of frameworks that conceptualize victims as agents of state accountability. The nature of the interests attributed to victims—whether predominantly private or public—can inform the appropriate approach within public law. Where victims are understood as individual rights-holders seeking to vindicate private interests, their role in accountability may align more closely with principles and frameworks drawn from private law, even when exercised within public legal processes.[35] In such

[34] Jason Varuhas, 'Against Unification' in Hanna Wilberg and Mark Elliott (eds), *The Scope and Intensity of Substantive Review: Traversing Taggart's Rainbow* (Hart Publishing 2015) 91; Michael Taggart, 'Proportionality, Deference, Wednesbury' (2008) 18 New Zealand L Rev 423.

[35] Varuhas (n 34).

contexts, public law doctrines may justifiably reflect private law reasoning to accommodate the protection of individual interests within the broader machinery of the state.

One such doctrine relates to standing and highlights that, when interests are understood as private, standing must be recognized for the specific individuals whose personal interests are at stake. Accordingly, remedies for state fallibilities that implicate private interests would need to be tailored to uphold those individual interests, consistent with private law logic. This approach influences both the discretionary nature and the types of remedies available. Notably, the discretionary character of public law remedies is significantly constrained when individual rights and interests are engaged, driven by a normative commitment to ensuring their robust protection.[36] Moreover, remedies traditionally associated with private law—such as damages—become particularly salient, offering meaningful redress and serving to vindicate rights and hold state actors accountable for their violation within a public process.[37] In particular, monetary compensation provides an additional layer of protection to these underlying private interests, reinforcing an individualistic conception.[38]

In the context of victim participation in criminal justice processes, this conception of accountability applies where victim interests are framed as predominantly private. In such cases, mechanisms of accountability available to victims would recognize them as rights-bearing individuals with standing to bring forward claims affecting their personal interests. Accordingly, state failures would need to be understood as failures towards the individual victim, and the forms of redress would have to be tailored to those private harms. Typically, this would include compensatory damages and other mechanisms that serve to vindicate the victim's interests.

Importantly, because this role is grounded in the protection of private interests, it should not be understood as imposing a duty on victims to pursue state accountability. Rather, the exercise of such a role remains a matter of individual choice. The closer the role aligns with private dimensions, the more discretion victims should be afforded in deciding whether to initiate accountability claims. Even within an aggregate conception of the public interest, it may be tempting to argue that victims have a civic duty to contribute to public accountability. However, where victims act based solely on their personal interests, they should retain the option not to participate. Framing such participation as

[36] ibid; Sir Tom H Bingham, 'Should Public Law Remedies Be Discretionary?' (1991) PL 64, 69.
[37] Varuhas (n 34) 97.
[38] ibid.

voluntary better respects the nature of private interests, recognizing that individuals ought not to be compelled to advance claims rooted in their personal experiences if they prefer not to do so.

Accountability by victims as bearers of predominantly public interests in a public process

Conversely, when victims are conceived as citizens whose interests are situated closer to the public end of the private–public spectrum, their role as agents of state accountability is understood differently. In such contexts, victims are seen as holding legitimate participatory claims over the public interest. As discussed in Chapter 2, within Grear's unitary theories of the public interest, victims are viewed as citizens who can directly articulate public claims and engage with the public interest. These claims are grounded in civic republicanism and liberal democratic understandings of citizenship, where the citizen plays an active role in holding the state to account. Under this conception, victims' standing and access to remedies shift accordingly—becoming aligned more closely with traditional frameworks and principles of public law.[39]

Within these frameworks, both the state and victims are understood as having public duties towards the polity. More specifically, the duties owed by the state to victims, in their capacity as citizens, are conceptualized as duties owed to the public at large. Breaches of these duties are therefore public in nature. On this understanding, state accountability is aimed primarily at ensuring the lawful and proper exercise of public power, rather than the strong protection or vindication of individual interests. As highlighted in the public law scholarship, such conceptions of accountability are embedded in public law mechanisms designed to ensure that 'public powers are exercised properly—that is, in accordance with axiomatic ideas of good administration—and in the public interest . . . to ensure public power is not misused or abused'.[40] Varuhas adds that when public powers confer benefits on individuals, this is a 'subsidiary' rather than a 'primary' function of public law.[41] Rock further notes that 'the relevant standards that are enforced via public law are not determined primarily by the failure to respect or protect individual rights and interests but

[39] ibid.
[40] ibid 101.
[41] Jason NE Varuhas, *Damages and Human Rights* (Hart Publishing 2016) 38.

relate more generally to proper administration of public power'.[42] Mechanisms that fall within this public-facing model of accountability include traditional forms such as common law judicial review, as well as newer structures like ombudsperson processes and public inquiries.

Understanding accountability and victims as serving public interests also shapes the doctrinal landscape, particularly in relation to standing and remedies. Indeed, in matters understood as closer to the public end of the spectrum of interests, notably traditional public law mechanisms of review, the public law scholarship suggests that 'remedies could be granted even to a stranger',[43] but the 'more direct the applicant's injury the greater his chances of obtaining discretionary relief'.[44] Historically, remedies in public law—especially in judicial review—have been discretionary, and the nature of the interests involved across the public–private spectrum has influenced whether relief is granted.[45] Nonetheless, there is an increasing judicial reluctance to exercise remedial discretion in a way that denies relief entirely. Indeed, in traditional fields of public law, namely, the common law of review, courts have had the ultimate discretion over whether to grant relief in matters of unlawful state practices. This shift is premised on the growing consensus that 'public life ought to be conducted lawfully'[46], rather than on ensuring strong protection of individual rights and interests. This is an important element to highlight in developing a participatory approach to accountability, which is rooted in a predominantly public conception of victim interests. Indeed, in such contexts, victims would have an important claim towards seeking remedies on the basis that public life ought to be conducted lawfully.

Within remedies that predominantly address public interests, variations exist between traditional mechanisms—such as common law judicial review—and more recent public law mechanisms, such as ombudspersons processes. As Rock explains, in the context of common law judicial review, 'the true character

[42] Ellen Rock, 'Fault and Accountability in Public Law' in Michael Elliot, Jason Varuhas, and Shona W Stark (eds), *The Unity of Public Law* (Hart Publishing 2018) 171, 184; see also Ellen Rock, *Making Sense of the Public Law/Private Law Divide* (Federation Press 2020) 9.

[43] Bingham (n 36) 69.

[44] ibid; see also Paul Craig, *Administrative Law* (9th edn, OUP 2021) 800.

[45] Varuhas (n 34) highlights that it was not uncommon for courts to declare administrative action unlawful but leave it intact to avoid undermining public interests in administrative certainty and finality. Similarly, relief has already been denied on the basis of public interest concerns. Some public law remedies, however—such as habeas corpus, which are legally and historically the most important of the prerogative writs—are not discretionary. Sir Bingham defines discretion here related to the remedy, 'it is only when he reaches the stage of asking himself what is the fair and just thing to do or order in the instant case that he embarks on the exercise of a discretion' (Bingham (n 36) 186). This can include different courses of action: namely, orders, penalties, or remedies.

[46] Varuhas (n 34) 12; Bingham (n 36) 187.

of the remedy is to contain public power within defined limits, and therefore redress within judicial review is limited in its contribution to accountability'.[47] However, as will be discussed in Chapter 4, in the context of victim participation in relation to prosecutorial discretion, judicial review has evolved to encompass more substantive engagement with prosecutorial decision-making, thereby expanding its accountability potential that can be part of structural reform.

Newer governance mechanisms such as ombudspersons—also situated closer to the public end of the interest spectrum—have introduced greater flexibility. These mechanisms are designed to accommodate both individual and systemic concerns. They provide a combination of remedies, including compensation for individuals and broader recommendations aimed at structural reform. However, in the context of state accountability vis-à-vis victims in criminal prosecutions, ombudsperson mechanisms generally refrain from engaging with the substance of prosecutorial decision-making. Instead, they are confined to addressing governance and service failures.

As will be elaborated in Chapter 8, the normative framework proposed incorporates systemic redress with a public-oriented model of state accountability. Victims within this framework and type of participation would be considered as having duties towards the wider polity to ensure that the public interest and other related public standards are respected by the state. More specifically, this framework includes obligations to hold the state accountable when it fails its own duties towards the polity, such as failing to act in the public interest, or meeting minimal standards of decision-making relating to good governance and accurate assessments.

As discussed in Chapter 2, however, these duties should be understood as civic in nature and thus should not be legally enforceable against victims. The expectation that victims hold the state accountable must remain non-compulsory as discussed in greater depth in Chapter 8. Moreover, the nature and extent of this civic duty may be informed by the broader socio-contextual factors, particularly the degree of dystopia or social injustice within the political system. Situating society along Duff's eutopia–dystopia spectrum helps illustrate the variability in institutional fallibilities, which in turn impacts victims' duties as citizens. As Duff argues, the more dystopian a society is or becomes, the more citizens may reasonably prioritize self-preservation over engagement in collective civic duties.[48]

[47] Rock, 'Fault and Accountability' (n 42) 175.
[48] Duff (n 3) 29.

The degree of dystopia in a society thus has an important impact for the scope of victims' civic duties towards the polity of pursue state accountability. Additionally, the availability and efficacy of accountability mechanisms also play important roles. The greater the dystopia and the state's failure in pursuing public aims (scenario 2), the least mechanisms of accountability within the state will be available for victims to employ. In such circumstances, victims may have to rely on external of informal mechanisms to hold the state to account. This places a substantial burden on victims, often requiring levels of mobilization and advocacy that may be unrealistic or unsustainable, particularly in the face of systemic breakdown or repression.

Accountability understood across a substantive and procedural spectrum

Another important distinction in developing a typology of victim-centred accountability relates to the divide between substantive and procedural forms of accountability. Although these dimensions often intertwine and have evolved over time, they provide a useful conceptual lens for comparing the ways in which victims can hold the state accountable.

Aronson articulates this distinction by suggesting that substantive accountability concerns *how well* something was done by the state, whereas procedural accountability is more narrowly concerned with *whether* something was done.[49] Similarly, Dawson and Maricut-Akbik[50] apply this distinction across different accountability forums—such as courts conducting judicial review and ombuds institutions undertaking administrative oversight. For these authors, substantive accountability refers to assessments of the merits or substantive worth of the decision. In contrast, procedural accountability focuses on whether appropriate processes were followed in making or implementing that decision.

Although these categories are useful, Aronson cautions against rigid binaries. He proposes instead that substantive and procedural accountability exist along a continuum claiming that it is impossible to draw a hard-and-fast distinction between procedure and substance.[51] He refines his analysis and

[49] Mark Aronson, 'The Growth of Substantive Review: The Changes, Their Causes and Their Consequences' in Jason NE Varuhas and others (eds), *Public Law Adjudication in Common Law Systems: Process and Substance* (Hart Publishing 2016).

[50] Mark Dawson and Adina Maricut-Akbik, 'Procedural vs Substantive Accountability in EMU Governance: Between Payoffs and Trade-offs' (2021) 28(11) J Eur Public Policy 1707, 1715.

[51] Aronson (n 49) 114.

proposes that substantive assessments move 'beyond checking both that the administrators stayed within the four corners of their powers and mechanistically ticked all the requisite boxes, and also ask how well they performed their tasks'.[52] Substance can be understood across a spectrum, whereby towards the end of the substantive spectrum, more space is afforded to assess the merits and reasoning of a decision. This includes cases involving factual errors, irrational or unreasonable reasoning, or decisions producing unreasonable outcomes. Less to that end of the spectrum, but still considered predominantly substantive assessments according to Aronson, are instances involving fundamental misunderstandings of an applicant's case and instances where evidence is overlooked.

In contrast, procedural accountability focuses on *whether* something was done as part of failures to observe procedural norms that regulate processes. These also include violations of procedural justice, such as excluding parties from processes that they are meant to be part of, as well as jurisdictional errors. This form of accountability is more concerned with the integrity of the process than with the substance of the decision itself.

As explained by Aronson, these distinctions can have blurred edges and are best understood as part of a continuum, which can at times intertwine.[53] Further, the terminology's meaning may not be fixed in time. For instance, it has been argued that in some jurisdictions, including England and Wales, there has been an expansion of substantive assessments in judicial review disguised as procedural fairness, even when they apparently lack in procedural content.[54] This suggests that the terminology might also refer to different meanings across time and jurisdictions. For these reasons, when analysing mechanisms of accountability using these frameworks, particularly in comparative contexts, it is useful to pay close attention and understand context, including historical and evolving purposes behind the analysis of specific mechanisms.

Despite the malleability of this divide, this substantive–procedural distinction remains a useful analytical framework—especially in comparative contexts. Mapping accountability along this continuum allows for a nuanced understanding of how accountability mechanisms are structured and the types of challenges that may be involved within the jurisdictions under analysis. This is particularly relevant in analysing how victims as agents of state accountability have been developed and understood in the various legal mechanisms.

[52] ibid 115.
[53] ibid 114.
[54] ibid.

4. Conclusion

The various conceptions of accountability in public law and accountability literature provide essential tools for analysing and comparing how accountability is constructed in specific legal and institutional contexts. These classifications are especially relevant to the comparative analysis in the chapters that follow, which examine the evolving roles of accountability attributed to victims in criminal legal systems in England and Wales and the United States. They enable a more nuanced understanding of what it means for victims to act as agents of state accountability, including the mechanisms through which such accountability is sought.

The following chapters will rely on some of these frameworks to analyse and compare the ways this novel type of participation, which recognizes victims as agents of state accountability, has developed and evolved in both jurisdictions. Finally, these frameworks for analysing accountability will also be useful in the penultimate chapter, which develops a normative model for recognizing victims as agents of state accountability—with a focus on state prosecutorial accountability in the context of the criminal legal process.

PART II

COMPARATIVE PERSPECTIVES: VICTIMS AS AGENTS OF STATE ACCOUNTABILITY

4

A Predominantly Public and Evolving Conception in the English Common Law Tradition

1. Introduction

This chapter analyses and compares the main mechanisms that enable victims to undertake a participative role as agents of state accountability within the criminal process in England and Wales—focusing on prosecutorial decisions. In this jurisdiction, such mechanisms that enable victims to hold the prosecutorial state accountable mainly relate to decisions about whether or not to prosecute and do not extend to decisions relating to plea agreements or other stages of the criminal legal process. This delimitation can be partially explained by the long-standing historical grounding of victim participation in the English common law tradition, wherein victims, as citizens, have been understood to possess a legitimate role and public interests in prosecution. The mechanisms analysed in this chapter—namely, private prosecutions and judicial review—are both rooted in that tradition and have historically conceptualized victims as potential bearers of public interest. The next chapter turns to the Victims' Right to Review Scheme (VRRS), a more recent mechanism of prosecutorial accountability that, unlike the others, is not grounded in traditional common law.

Building on the theoretical frameworks and characteristics of state accountability discussed in Chapter 2, this chapter analyses some of the dimensions that characterize accountability in England and Wales, as well as their development across time. Indeed, this chapter highlights the nuances in accountability by situating victims' interests across Anna Grear's public–private spectrum, examining their relationship to the public interest, and conducting substantive–procedural assessments.[1] This analysis simultaneously examines some of the limitations of each accountability mechanism.

[1] Anna Grear, 'Theorizing the Rainbow? The Puzzle of the Public-Private Divide' (2003) 9 Res Publica 169.

Victims as Agents of State Accountability. Marie Manikis, Oxford University Press. © Marie Manikis 2026.
DOI: 10.1093/9780191993947.003.0006

Specifically, this chapter illustrates how the role of victims as agents of state accountability in England and Wales has been primarily rooted within a public interest conception of the victim (as citizens and members of the public) and their interests. This conception has been important in giving rise to a more substantive conception of accountability that relates to prosecutorial decisions/discretion. In contrast, the following chapters highlight the ways that victim participatory mechanisms of state accountability which operate within a private conception of victim interests, as is prominent in the United States and increasingly so in England and Wales, have primarily recognized a procedural form of accountability.

Despite these broader trends, the current chapter and the following ones also highlight that these mechanisms of state accountability have evolved throughout the years. Thus, they also account for the nuances and variations that have changed conceptions of the victim in the jurisdictions under analysis. Specifically, England and Wales has recently seen a partial shift towards a private conceptualization of the victim and their interests, particularly with respect to private prosecutions and the development of the VRRS by the Crown Prosecution Service (CPS). This closely aligns with a phenomenon encountered much earlier on within criminal processes in the United States.

2. The Rise of State Accountability by Citizen-Victims in England and Wales

Before focusing on accountability as a form of victim participation, it is worth highlighting that the types of participation previously discussed in Chapter 3 have evolved considerably across time. Accountability is a relatively recent form of participation within the common law. Rather, 'control' followed by 'information-provision' have been the most prominent types of participation within the common law.

In Anglo-Saxon medieval times, victims held an important role in the administration of prosecutions as private prosecutors, which was primarily understood as 'control' over the prosecution. Prior to the King's Peace, in early societies based on kinship ties and tribal organizations, the concept of public wrong did not exist. Instead, crime was a private wrong limited to the interest of individuals and families involved.[2] Victims and their kin dealt with wrongs privately by carrying out blood

[2] Stephen Schafer, *Victimology: The Victim and His Criminal* (Reston Publishing Company 1977).

feuds.[3] With the rise of feudalism in England, between 700 and 1066, lords and bishops gradually replaced kinship groups as recipients of compensation, as some acts were considered wrongs against the fiefdom and morality.

During the King's Peace, wrongs began to be conceived of differently. 'Crime' emerged as a framework to consider harms and interests beyond those of victims and families involved and was increasingly conceived as a wrong against the monarch, the kingdom, as well as 'any one of the public'[4] sharing an interest in contributing to the King's Peace. Accordingly, it was 'not only the privilege but the duty of the private citizen to preserve the King's Peace and bring offenders to justice'.[5] As highlighted by Emma Kaufman, historically, as part of the common law, criminal law adopted a more capacious and wider notion of standing where anyone could lay claim in criminal proceedings on the conception that all are interested in the preservation of public order.[6] This conceptualization of victims as citizen-victims recognized their standing and legitimacy to represent and make decisions in the public interest.

Indeed as highlighted by Joseph Chitty, 'Criminal Prosecutions are carried on in the name of the King, and have for their principal object the security and happiness of the people in general, and not mere private redress.'[7] Despite these public conceptions of crime and the citizen's role and interests, he specifies that, in practice, 'as offences, for the most part, more immediately affect a particular individual, it is not usual for any other person to interfere'.[8] Hence, victims in England remained in charge of most aspects of the administration of criminal law, including apprehension, investigations, and prosecutions, well into the eighteenth century.[9]

Thus, the King's Peace indicated a pivotal moment in the reconceptualization of the victim's role. Following this era, victims were considered part of a wider citizenry, and their role was reconceptualized: they were no longer considered

[3] ibid; John Hagan, *Victims Before the Law: The Organizational Domination of Criminal Law* (Butterworths 1983).

[4] Frederic W Maitland, *Justice and Police* (MacMillan and Co. 1885) 141.

[5] Peter Burns, 'Private Prosecutions in Canada: The Law and a Proposal for Change' (1975) 21 McGill LJ 269, 271. See also Bernard M Dickens, 'Control of Prosecutions in the United Kingdom' (1973) 22 ICLQ 1, 2 and Sir Carleton Kemp Allen, *The Queen's Peace* (Stevens and Sons Ltd 1953).

[6] Emma Kaufman, 'The Past and Persistence of Private Prosecution' (2024) 173(1) Univ Pa L Rev 89, 93.

[7] Joseph Chitty, *Practical Treatise on the Criminal Law* (AJ Volpy 1816) vol I, 1.

[8] ibid.

[9] Douglas Hay and Francis Snyder (eds), *Policing and Prosecution in Britain 1750–1850* (Clarendon Press 1989); John H Langbein, 'The Criminal Trial Before the Lawyers' (1978) 45 U Chi L Rev 263; John H Langbein, *Prosecuting Crime in the Renaissance: England, Germany, France* (Harvard UP 1974). The Attorney General intervened exceptionally in very serious or notorious cases and has had a long-standing prerogative to halt any prosecution in a court of record by entering a nolle prosequi, of which in modern times is very rarely used in instances where the defendant is unfit to plead.

the sole entities harmed by the offence, and their participation was not seen as merely serving their own needs and interests with personal remedies for harm. Put otherwise, victims were conceptualized as *citizens*,[10] who occupied an important role in preserving the King's Peace by administrating criminal justice. Accordingly, citizens, including victims, were considered as having a 'sense of public duty'[11] and 'interested in the maintenance of law and order'[12] by bringing offenders to justice. In this sense, contrary to modern assumptions, criminal law was long understood as a public matter that conferred on every citizen the right to initiate prosecutions in the public interest.

The subsequent rise of the state-driven public prosecutor was an important development, albeit in different periods and intensities, in both England and Wales and the United States that resulted in the evolving role of victims. While private prosecutions as a mechanism and 'control' as a type of victim participation were more quickly limited and abandoned in the United States, England retained this role, albeit with some limitations, which evolved to a great extent as a role of accountability. In this sense, accountability took a different shape in these jurisdictions as will be seen in the following chapters.

Over time, the idea that the Sovereign had direct stakes in certain proceedings developed, and the Crown developed a limited prosecutorial role through the *attornatus regis* (Attorney General), counsel appointed to protect royal interests in select proceedings.[13] The *attornatus regis* carried certain powers that appear originate in the Crown's prerogative, namely,

1. *nolle prosequi*, that is, the discretionary power to stay criminal proceedings or, more generally, to intervene in and take over the conduct of criminal proceedings, and
2. the discretionary power to prefer indictments and control the mode of trial.[14]

In practice, however, *nolle prosequi* was rarely exercised and required the private prosecutor's consent.[15] As highlighted by Douglas Hay, 'it was a practical nullity in day-to-day prosecutions. The protection of the innocent was instead

[10] Hay and Snyder (n 9).
[11] John Llewelyn Jones Edwards, *The Law Officers of the Crown* (Sweet & Maxwell 1964).
[12] Patrick Devlin, *The Criminal Prosecution in England* (OUP 1960) 16–17.
[13] Hugh HL Bellot, 'Origin of the Attorney-General' (1909) 25(4) L Q Rev 400, 407.
[14] *R v Hauser*, 1979 CanLII 13 (SCC) at 1011–12.
[15] Philip C Stenning, *Appearing for the Crown: A Legal and Historical Review of Criminal Prosecutorial Authority in Canada* (Brown Legal Publications 1986) 30–31.

confided in the main to the grand jury, and properly so, in the view of contemporary [seventeenth-century] opinion.'[16]

Private prosecutions thus started to hold an accountability role in convention, particularly following the abuses of the Star Chamber during Stuart rule in the seventeenth century.[17] This was reflective of a widespread mistrust of executive power and a belief that the executive had the potential to be the most dangerous of oppressors. The idea that the Attorney General, an executive officer representing the King, could represent the public interest in criminal law was, at the time, untenable. Consequently, prosecutors were typically victims of crime or their representatives—as citizens—with only cases believed to be directly against the Sovereign—like those involving treason or seditious libel—brought by the Attorney General.[18]

In England, victim control over prosecutions slowly diminished by the nineteenth century. This evolution began with the sharing of this role with the newly constituted police forces in 1829. This was considered a partial loss of agency, particularly for victims to decide *not* to prosecute, since police in some instances would oblige victims who had no intention to pursue charges to participate in prosecutions.[19] Thus, it became increasingly difficult to know the actual prosecutor was and whose interests prosecutions represent, resulting in criticisms that gave rise to increased calls for a professionalized public prosecutor.

The creation in 1879 and the eventual rise of a national system of public prosecutions with the Director of Public Prosecutions (DPP), under the direction of the Attorney General, further diminished the victim's role of 'control' over prosecutions.[20] However, contrary to other common law jurisdictions, including the United States, the DPP was small, had strictly limited powers, and was responsible for prosecuting only the most serious cases—thus remaining exceptional.[21] This development gave rise to a distinction between 'private

[16] Douglas Hay, 'Controlling the English Prosecutor' (1983) 21(2) Osgoode Hall LJ 165, 171.

[17] This royal court was known for its arbitrary and cruel punishments, particularly for those who were seen as disloyal or went against the King's authority. It was thus associated with sovereign abuse of power.

[18] Hay (n 16) 167.

[19] This relates to the victim's loss of control in decisions not to prosecute, since in some instances, police would bring victims with no intention of prosecuting before a court, thereby obliging them to prosecute. This gave rise to mounting criticisms towards private prosecutions, particularly the police, which increased calls for a professional public prosecutor in England. See Hay and Snyder (n 9).

[20] In England, since the reign of Henry VIII, attempts were made to create a national system of public prosecutions, which was only accomplished in 1879 with the DPP.

[21] Burns (n 5); Hay and Snyder (n 9). Part 7 of the Prosecution of Offences Act 1879 (42 & 43 Vict c 22) read that 'nothing in this Act shall interfere with the right of any person to institute, undertake, or carry on any criminal proceeding', which was later repealed in 1908.

prosecutions' by members of the citizenry, including victims and police,[22] and 'public prosecutions' referring to a professionalized body of prosecutors representing the state.

Despite this difference in appellation, which can be seen as a misnomer, Frederic Maitland captures aptly the public interest dimension to private prosecutions:

> To speak of the English system as one of private prosecutions is misleading. It is we who have *public* prosecutions, for any one of the public may prosecute; abroad they have *state* prosecutions or *official* prosecutions (emphasis in original).[23]

Nevertheless, in contrast to the United States,[24] and despite the rise of professionalized public prosecutions, England held on to its tradition of private prosecutions. This was attributed in part to concerns that a public prosecutor would be given, or would acquire, a monopoly over proceedings.[25] Indeed, in England, there was a concern of a complete shift of power and veto from individual citizens to central government, which was seen to result in an increasing loss of citizen control, freedoms,[26] and inequalities among social classes.[27] As will be seen in Chapter 6, in the United States, different rationales, including the belief that a public prosecutor would curb abuses such as malicious proceedings linked to private prosecutions, contributed to the more rapid abandonment of private prosecutions, which in turn had an important effect on a different form of victims' accountability role.

These concerns regarding public/state prosecutors positioned the role of the English private prosecutor as an important constitutional safeguard

[22] In 1879, the police became convenient substitutes for private prosecutors who would not or could not go to the trouble or expense of proceeding. See Hay and Snyder (n 9).

[23] Maitland (n 4).

[24] In the nineteenth century, detailed bills providing for a new system with extensive evidence gathered from the United States, Scotland, Ireland, and France where public prosecution was long established. All of them failed and even the creation of the office of the DPP in 1879 was hardly what the name implied since it had very limited powers over the vast majority of prosecutions that remained private. See Hay (n 16).

[25] Hay and Snyder (n 9).

[26] First, there was a perception that the state persecuted the accused, and 'in every country where it has been introduced, confidence in the proper administration of justice has been destroyed'. HC, 1855, vol 136, cols 1654–55. Further, it was feared that the public prosecutor would risk refusing to proceed in cases where parties thought there ought to be a prosecution, and this power might (and particularly in cases of political excitement) cause a denial of justice. There was indeed a lack of confidence in public prosecutors, who by malice, caprice, and thus to appease their own private interests were thought to potentially refuse to proceed, leaving individuals who sustained injury with no remedies.

[27] James A Calaico, *James Fitzjames Stephen and the Crisis of Victorian Thought* (Palgrave Macmillan 1983) 3–4.

against the tyranny and rise of the executive.[28] During the nineteenth century, these discourses shaped the participative role of victims as agents of state accountability—for the public good—expressed before the Criminal Law Commissioners in the following terms:

> In this country any man has a right to indict any other man upon any charge. We are so accustomed to this right, and are so completely free from trammels to interfere with it, that it is no wonder if, having often to consider the unavoidable trouble of the duty, we are not always alive to the advantages of the right. This right, when exercised, is not without its responsibilities; another part of the law has wisely taken care of that; but it is a most valuable right, and perhaps next only to that of being fairly tried when we are ourselves indicted. Set up the 'public prosecutor', and then you have, at once, a power of veto against every man's prosecution; and the great offender, with great interest, may be allowed to escape by this new-fangled authority, without even the intervention of a Grand Jury's 'ignoramus'. If we absolutely prohibit the common law prosecutor, that is, the party injured or complaining, from taking legal steps, this is the result which will happen to a certainty... I repeat that you have no right to deprive the subject of his liberty, so long enjoyed, and with such good effects, by preferring a criminal charge against others who may have at once done him and his country a wrong, to strip him of the power of enforcing that redress, and making that example which the law requires for the good of both.[29]

As public/state prosecutions expanded in England and Wales in the twentieth century, private prosecutions remained available but with increasing limitations.[30] Most notably, the Prosecutions of Offences Act of 1908 enabled the DPP to assume a private prosecution and then drop it, with no recourse for the private prosecutor. This was described by John Llewelyn Jones Edwards as a 'significant blow to a constitutionally significant right',[31] who in turn called

[28] England increasingly conceived private prosecutions as an important constitutional safeguard against the tyrannical kings and any increasing power of the executive. Even the Attorney General was not seen as the protector of the ordinary citizen from oppressive prosecutions.

[29] *Royal Commission on Criminal Law, Eighth Report* (C 656, 1845) 295–96.

[30] While all the bills for the creation of a public system introduced in Parliament in the nineteenth century had some limitations, they specifically protected the right of the private prosecutor, including the Prosecution of Offences Acts 1879 and 1884. Limitations became more substantial at the start of the twentieth century. See, eg, Hay (n 16) 177–79.

[31] Edwards (n 11) 364.

for a re-enactment of a form of judicial review that existed in the previous act.[32]

Despite these changes, private prosecutions in England continued to be recognized as necessary for the victim's evolving public interest participatory role as agents of state accountability—specifically to a safeguard and '[stimulate] the public prosecutor into action where he is disposed to be remiss in his duty'.[33] Accordingly, Lord Diplock in *Gouriet* affirmed that it 'remains a valuable constitutional safeguard against inertia or partiality on the part of the authority'.[34] This suggests that the participatory role of victims as private prosecutors evolved from citizens with control over private prosecutions to citizens engaging in state accountability.[35]

This participatory role of state accountability has continued to evolve in England and Wales with the expansion of the administrative state and as will be discussed below the increasing privatization and corporatization of interests within mechanisms of state accountability. This evolution has taken different forms, as illustrated by various mechanisms of accountability available for victims. These mechanisms, analysed in greater depth below and in Chapter 5, include the varying iterations of private prosecutions, judicial review, and extra-judicial channels within prosecutorial departments, namely, the VRRS.

3. Victims as Citizens: Mechanisms Holding the State Predominantly Substantively Accountable in the Public Interest

As highlighted above, since the King's Peace, victims in England were and continue to be primarily conceived as members of the citizenry that hold private but also predominantly public interests within the criminal justice process. Rather than merely serving their own needs and interests with personal remedies for harm, victims as citizens have occupied important predominantly public roles and were conceptualized as serving public interests in preserving the King's Peace in the administration of criminal justice. They remained in

[32] Under the Prosecutions of Offences Act 1879 Act, if the DPP withdrew a prosecution, the original prosecutor had a right to apply to a judge of the High Court to have the prosecution reinstituted and continued either by the Director or by the private prosecutor himself.

[33] Edwards (n 11) 345.

[34] *Gouriet v Union of Post Office Workers* [1978] AC 435, 498.

[35] It is worth highlighting that this evolutive role also included information. This evolution is much more documented in the literature, but for the purposes of this book, the focus will be on the victim's role as agents of accountability.

charge of most aspects of criminal justice administration well into the eighteenth century as private prosecutors,[36] which as discussed in the previous section eventually evolved from a mechanism of prosecutorial control to one of accountability.

This wider move towards state accountability began with the rise of the state's role in public prosecutions, with the creation of the DPP, and evolved with the development of review mechanisms for holding state agencies accountable for various forms of fallibilities, including failures to act according to recognized duties, decision-making error, and biases relating to prosecutions. These various conceptions of accountability present in the various mechanisms can be analysed across the public–private spectrum of interests served as well as the substance–process spectrum of the assessment.

Despite these predominant conceptual trends, the relatively recent centralization of prosecutions with the creation and involvement of the CPS in 1985 has contributed to a narrative that increasingly suggests that victims should be conceived of as entities with private interests and the public state prosecutor as holding the primary legitimacy to speak in the public interest. This recent development can be seen in the way the VRRS was developed by the CPS, which further infuses an individual conception of the victim as holding predominantly private interests in the public process. This is an important development since as further developed in Chapter 5, this framing is used to reduce the victim's legitimacy in the public prosecutorial process.

This section compares the ways victims' participative roles as agents of state accountability are understood by analysing the main legal mechanisms of prosecutorial state accountability available for victims of crime in England and Wales. In particular, this chapter focuses on private prosecutions and common law judicial review. Other mechanisms available to victims to act as agents of state accountability include administrative channels, including the VRRS, discussed in Chapter 5.

This analysis uses public law frameworks, discussed in Chapters 2 and 3, to situate mechanisms across two spectrums. First, this chapter conceptualizes victims' interests and roles across the private–public spectrum. Second, it considers the implementation of accountability across the substantive–procedural spectrum. Particular attention is given to the relationship of accountability between the victim and the public–state prosecution, since the

[36] Indeed, the right to prosecute was also seen as a liberty that empowered an individual to obtain redress for a wrong 'once done to him and his country... making that example which the law requires for the good of both' (Her Majesty's Commissioners on Criminal Law, Eighth Report of Her Majesty's Commissioners on Criminal Law (1845), p. 296).

latter is understood to represent the state in criminal justice and make crucial decisions about prosecutions. Ultimately, the following discussion suggests that victims as citizens/public in England and Wales have had a long-standing role as agents of accountability—as potential holders of public interests—and thus can focus on substantive assessments of prosecutorial decisions that relate to the public interest.

Over the years, however, as will be discussed in this chapter and in Chapter 5, the role of victims as agents of accountability has increasingly started to be conceptualized closer to the private end of the spectrum, as an aggregate contribution to the public interest, which is in some ways closer to its American counterpart, discussed in Chapters 6 and 7.

Private prosecutions

The victim's accountability role rooted in the public interest

As discussed, the role of the victim as an agent of state accountability in England and Wales began with the rise of private prosecutions, which were considered constitutional safeguards against state failures in exercising public prosecutorial duties owed to its citizens.[37] In this sense, they were described as protecting 'against the inaction of authorities',[38] particularly in contexts where the state was called to prosecute members of its own establishment, including politicians and police officers.

Accordingly, within private prosecutions, victims have been entrusted with public prosecutorial duties[39] to safeguard the public interest against these forms of state failures. This suggests that under this mechanism, victims are understood as holding interests closer to the public end of the spectrum.[40] In this sense, victims can also hold private interests, as long as they remain compatible to the advancement of public interests, which victims are seen as capable and justified in bringing forward. As highlighted by the Supreme Court in *Gujra*,[41] a case relating to the power of the DPP to take over private prosecutions,

[37] *Gouriet* (n 34).

[38] HMSO, *Report of the Royal Commission on Criminal Procedure* (Cmnd 8092-I and II, 1981) para 7.47.

[39] The evidential threshold for obtaining a summons as a private prosecutor requires that the magistrate ascertain whether the allegation is an offence known to the law, and if so whether the essential ingredients of the offence are prima facie present; that the offence alleged is not time-barred; that the court has jurisdiction; and whether the informant has the necessary authority to prosecute. See *R (Kay) v Leeds Magistrates' Court* [2018] EWHC 1233 (Admin) [22].

[40] Marie Manikis, 'Conceptualising the Victim in England and Wales and the United States Within a Spectrum of Public and Private Interests' (2021) 41(1) OJLS 219.

[41] *R (on the application of Gujra) (FC) v CPS*, [2012] UKSC 52, 132.

private prosecutions remain virtually unlimited and those meeting the evidential standard and public interest tests are allowed to continue, save where there is a 'particular need' for the DPP to take over. Hence this case reaffirms the constitutional importance of private prosecutions and as specified by Lady Hale in her dissenting judgment in *Gujra*, the private prosecutorial role has also traditionally included safeguarding the public value of equality in evidential assessments, where prosecutorial decision-making marginalizes certain victims due to biases or stereotyping.

This public role undertaken by marginalized victims, in response to the state's equality-related failures, was particularly prevalent at a time before state prosecutors had the power to take over and dismiss prosecutions. As will be discussed in the next section, the new criteria that relates to the DPP's power to take over and discontinue a private prosecution has expanded the state prosecution's role and has reduced the potential for private prosecutions as mechanisms to hold the state accountable, contributing to an increasingly privatized role for victims in private prosecutions.

Towards substantive and systemic forms of state accountability

On the surface, private prosecutions allow victims to participate in a form of procedural accountability. In this sense, accountability is engaged by focusing on 'whether something was done' by the members of the state and, in turn, holding the state accountable for reluctance or unwillingness to prosecute. However, in its implementation, private prosecutions have also given rise in some contexts to substantive assessments. This resonates with the administrative literature that discusses the expansion of substantive assessments related to state powers in England and Wales, even if at times framed as procedural.[42] More specifically, this has been seen in contexts where victims as private prosecutors have challenged substantive elements of state prosecutorial decisions, notably by proposing different evidentiary or public interest interpretations.

Lady Hale's dissenting speech in *Gujra* has captured this role by highlighting that private prosecutions can be useful, and even more effective than judicial reviews—which require a more deferential standard of review,[43] to hold the state accountable in contexts where it has failed certain victims 'who have traditionally had such difficulty in getting their voices heard or, if heard, believed'.[44]

[42] Mark Aronson, 'The Growth of Substantive Review: The Changes, their Causes, and Their Consequences' in John Bell and others (eds), *Public Law Adjudication in Common Law Systems: Process and Substance* (Bloomsbury Publishing 2016) 113–43.
[43] *Gujra* (n 41) 132.
[44] ibid 124.

Indeed, she highlights that there is more than one view of how the evidential stage is supposed to work and suggests that when assessing the realistic prospect of conviction, private prosecutions may integrate an approach that takes into account an objective, impartial, and reasonable jury or judge rather than a bookmaker's approach, which incorporates decision-making biases based on stereotypes in deciding whether there is a reasonable prospect of conviction. This relates to importance of enabling a prosecutorial process which infuses a substantive equality dimension within the prosecutorial assessment since, at times, 'credible complaints have not been taken further because of so-called "lack of evidence"',[45] which according to Lady Hale would potentially involve a violation of the victim's rights under section 8 (privacy) or, in extreme cases, section 3 (torture) of the European Convention on Human Rights.[46] This critique seems to suggest that the state, including its prosecutors, can hold biases and thus make errors when accepting and interpreting testimonial evidence. It further suggests that these errors can be addressed through private prosecution, which enables procedural and substantive forms of accountability that would need to meet a lower standard of evidentiary assessment. Specifically, where complainants have not been provided the opportunity to be heard at all by prosecutors, aspects of procedural accountability are engaged via private prosecutions. Additionally, a more substantive form of accountability is engaged when private prosecutions provide evidence in matters where witnesses were heard prior to bringing forward charges but their credibility has been undermined by prosecutors. By recognizing this as an issue affecting certain *groups*, Lady Hale also raises the potential for private prosecutions as relevant mechanisms to address systemic failures in state prosecutions, rather than merely as individualized errors.

The following section highlights several examples that illustrate forms of substantive accountability and the public accountability role taken on by victims in contexts of systemic failures on behalf of state prosecutors, rooted in biases and inequalities.

There are several cases wherein sexual assault victims have used private prosecutions to challenge state prosecutorial biases rooted in systemic inequalities—most often relating to gender and social status—on perceived credibility.[47] This is particularly important for victims belonging to

[45] ibid 130.
[46] ibid 133.
[47] Some cases in Scotland have also used or contemplated the use of private prosecutions in cases of sexual violence in which victims are traditionally considered to lack credibility, see Thomas Ross, 'Thomas Ross QC on the Private Prosecution of David Goodwillie and David Robertson' (*Scottish*

marginalized groups, as in the case of *Davies*[48] where two women who were sex workers brought separate private prosecutions, for rape and indecent assault, after the CPS dropped their cases on the basis that there was insufficient evidence for there to be a realistic prospect of conviction. Following these private prosecutions, the Court found sufficient evidence to convict Davies and sentenced him to fourteen years of imprisonment.[49] Grassroots organizations, namely, the English Collective of Prostitutes and Women Against Rape, that helped these women assemble a legal team and bring forward these prosecutions also published a dossier that was part of the trial, which included fifteen cases that bore striking similarities to *Davies* and should have been prosecuted by the CPS.[50] This data suggests systemic flaws rooted in inequalities, notably epistemic injustice,[51] in the way victim testimonial evidence was interpreted and assessed by the state prosecutors in their decision-making process. This highlights the potential for victims as private prosecutors to contribute to substantive and systemic forms of accountability for such state failures. Nevertheless, an important challenge and limitation, discussed below, articulated by victims of this type of violence in recent years is the possibility for the CPS to take over the case and terminate it.[52]

Private prosecutions have also recently been used to support marginalized groups in contexts of state prosecutorial failures to prosecute domestic violence.[53] For instance, in *Moher*,[54] a victim of domestic violence pursued a private prosecution for this offence against her ex-husband, who among other

Legal News, 21 February 2022) <https://www.scottishlegal.com/articles/thomas-ross-qc-on-private-prosecution-of-david-goodwillie-and-david-robertson> accessed 14 June 2023. *Sweeney v X* 1982 JC 70.

[48] English Collective of Prostitutes, 'Successful Private Prosecution of Serial Rapist—R v Davies' (*English Collective of Prostitutes*, 1 January 1996) <https://prostitutescollective.net/private-prosecution/> accessed 24 June 2023.

[49] Tamlyn Edmonds and David Jugnarain, 'Private Prosecutions: A Potential Anticorruption Tool in English Law' (Open Society Foundations 2014) <https://www.justiceinitiative.org/uploads/cb5149bf-6ea8-449a-8260-cea5d8590dfb/legal-remedies-4-edmonds-jugnarain-20160505.pdf> accessed 24 June 2023.

[50] English Collective of Prostitutes (n 48).

[51] Nicola Lacey, 'Criminal Justice and Social In(Justice)' (LSE International Inequalities Institute Working Paper No 84, October 2022).

[52] To avoid this possibility, some victims have undertaken judicial review of decisions not to prosecute instead of a private prosecution. See, eg, *Emily Hunt v the Director of Public Prosecutions* [2020] EWHC 1292 (Admin).

[53] This includes the newly created offence of controlling or coercive behaviour in an intimate relationship, which is an offence contrary to section 76 of the Serious Crime Act 2015 that came into force on 1 October 2018. It can include acts designed to make persons subordinate and/or dependent by isolating them from sources of support, exploiting their resources or depriving them of their independence, and regulating their everyday behaviour. The maximum penalty is five years' imprisonment. Subsequently, the Domestic Abuse Act 2021, for the first time, defines withholding a *get* as a potential form of domestic abuse.

[54] *Moher v Moher* [2019] EWCA Civ 1482.

aspects of abuse, refused to offer her a Jewish divorce (*get*). The case highlights the role of private prosecutions as an option for victims of intimate partner violence, including in culturally specific contexts. The public record does not indicate the reasons why Moher pursued a private prosecution as there is no mention of the CPS's initial role in this case. However, when prompted by the defence, there was a subsequent indication by the CPS that it would not be taking over the case nor interfering, and that the private prosecution was to continue.[55] This prompted the accused to enter a guilty plea for coercive control, resulting in an eighteen-month custodial sentence and an £11,000 payment order towards the prosecution's costs. While the CPS has not provided reasons for failing to take over or to undertake the prosecution, there might be reason to believe that the CPS did not have an appropriate appreciation of how the weaponization of the *get* demonstrated a form of harassment, in addition to the threats that Moher had expressed to his ex-wife. Moreover, the subsequent commentary within Jewish rabbinical law speaks to the controversy of involving secular courts, let alone criminal authorities, in managing aspects of a religious divorce, which could also contribute to why the CPS would have been hesitant to pursue prosecution.[56] These possibilities indicate the CPS's inability to navigate culturally specific and gender-based dynamics. They also highlight the role of private prosecution in holding the state accountable in instances of those types of systemic failures rooted in inequalities.

Relatedly, there are at least two more recent cases of divorced women pursuing private prosecutions for refusal to be granted a *get*.[57] However, in both cases, the *gets* were granted directly before the hearings, which also speaks to the potential private prosecutions to direct behaviour even in circumstances where the full procedure is not carried out. These private prosecutions were brought forward by victims in the public interest and once the *get* was received, the private prosecution was dropped since there was no longer any public interest in pursuing the case. This speaks to the potential for private prosecutions to lessen the power differential in instances of abusive

[55] Luke O'Reilly, 'Property Firm Owner Jailed After Failing to Grant Wife Jewish Religious Divorce' (*Independent*, 1 April 2022) <https://www.independent.co.uk/news/uk/crime/jewish-cps-southwark-crown-court-salford-b2048991.html> accessed 24 June 2023.

[56] Simon Rocker, 'Jailed Businessman Was Not a "Get Refuser", Beth Din Said' (*The Jewish Chronicle*, 19 April 2022) <https://www.thejc.com/news/news/jailed-businessman-was-not-a-get-refuser-beth-din-said-6anQOzSjcchNbfKaWfRvhb> accessed 7 June 2023. According to Jewish law, in order to be valid, a *get* needs to be consented by the husband. Criminal proceedings, such as a private prosecution, can be seen as a form of duress that invalidates any get and apparent consent that could be given.

[57] See, eg, *S v D* (2019), in which a private prosecution included allegations of abuse, including a refusal to provide a *get*. Also, in *Abayahouadayan*, the private prosecution included similar allegations.

gender-based inequalities.[58] Moreover, in these cases, the judges ordered that prosecution costs be paid from governmental (central) funds, which facilitates access to this rebalancing mechanism for marginalized groups and speaks to the importance of its potential for safeguarding the public interest.

Other marginalized groups who have used private prosecutions, with varying degrees of success, include victims of hate crimes and online harassment. In 2019, Alison Chabloz, a blogger, posted several YouTube videos of anti-Semitic songs denying the Holocaust. The CPS decided not to press any charges, which gave rise to a private prosecution by the Coalition Against Antisemitism. This private prosecution was an important process that convinced the CPS to take over the prosecution, which resulted in Chabloz being found guilty of several offences relating to sharing indecent and hate speech online.[59] This case illustrates the use of private prosecution as a tool to address systemic inertia in types of offences that are situated within larger patterns of social violence.

While some private prosecutions have been unsuccessful, they have nevertheless served as important catalysts for wider recognition of systemic racism. For instance, in the 1990s, the CPS opted to not pursue charges following the death of Stephen Lawrence in the context of a racially motivated hate crime. The victim's family brought forward a private prosecution, which ultimately resulted in an acquittal based on insufficient evidence. Following this acquittal, the MacPherson Inquiry was instituted to investigate Stephen Lawrence's murder and examine how racism might have informed the decisions made by both the police and the CPS. The report found a culture of institutionalized racism within the Metropolitan Police Services, which suggests that the lack of evidence, which caused the CPS decision not to prosecute, could be attributed to the police's inaction. Importantly, it is worth highlighting that this failure to collect evidence may also have led to the limits of a private prosecution. In light of such failures, the report also recommended that 'the ability to initiate a private prosecution should remain unchanged'.[60] This suggests that although a private prosecution may not always result in a conviction, this process can be an important mechanism to initiate wider investigations and conversations about systemic failures of policing and police services rooted in inequalities.

[58] Goldsmith Chambers, 'Changing the Legal Landscape for Abuse Victims' (*Goldsmith Chambers*, 27 May 2022) <https://www.goldsmithchambers.com/changing-the-legal-landscape-for-abuse-victims/> accessed 7 June 2023. Specifically, in the case of *S v D* (2019), a criminal trial was averted when the accused consented to the religious divorce, avoiding the threat of a substantial prison sentence.

[59] *R v Chabloz* [2019] Westminster Magistrates' Court, 25 May 2018 (unreported).

[60] William MacPherson, *The Stephen Lawrence Inquiry* (Cm 4262-I 1999) para 40.

The increasing limits of private prosecutions as a mechanism of state accountability and the parallel privatization of interests

Despite its historical importance, the state accountability role of private prosecutions has been increasingly limited in parallel with the expansion of state prosecutorial agencies. While the 1985 law that created the CPS maintained private prosecutions,[61] the CPS's subsequent policies to expand their discretionary powers have substantially limited this mechanism's accountability/constitutional safeguarding function.[62]

For instance, a recent 2009 DPP policy changed the criteria relating to the DPP's power to take over a private prosecution and thereupon to discontinue it.[63] Prior to the 2009 policy, the threshold for the first criterion of the test that guides prosecutions, relating to the strength of the evidence in support of the prosecution, was initially much higher and not merely one that the DPP would not himself proceed.[64] Specifically, prior to the 2009 policy change, the evidential standard the DPP had to ask himself for taking over and discontinuing a private prosecution was whether the evidence clearly failed to disclose a case sufficient for the defendant to be called upon to answer it (clearly no case to

[61] The CPS is a centralized service of prosecutions under the overall leadership of the DPP Private prosecutions, created under section 6(1) of the Prosecution of Offences Act 1985. This Act created a more centralized system despite the Report of the Royal Commission of Criminal Procedure (1979) that recommended a decentralized one. These proposals were made in the hope of setting up an independent prosecution service that would avoid having the same officers investigate and prosecute. This reflects the principle that those responsible for the investigation of the offence should not also be responsible for the conduct of the prosecution. HC, 16 April 1985, vol 77, col 150.

[62] This was confirmed by Lord Wilson's remarks in *Gujra* (n 41) [29], who agreed with Lord Mance's views in *Jones v Whalley* [2007] 1 AC 63 [39]. Since the 1985 Act, some have expressed reservations about whether this mechanism still serves a constitutional safeguard. For instance, Lord Bingham of Cornhill described it as being of 'questionable value' in a speech.

[63] The original stated purpose for which the DPP was given the right to take over the conduct of proceedings was to ensure that cases which ought in the public interest to be pursued were not abandoned or inefficiently conducted, whether through lack of means, inertia, or any other reason. In practice though modelling himself on the Attorney General's right to enter a nolle prosequi (rarely exercised in modern times and if so, usually when he considers the defendant unfit to plead), the DPP used also to take over cases with a view of discontinuing their prosecution. This practice was challenged but upheld at first instance in *Turner v DPP* [1978] 68 Cr App R 70 and on appeal in *Raymond v Attorney General* [1982] QB 839. The threshold for discontinuing private prosecutions was initially much higher and not merely one that the DPP would not himself proceed (see *R v Director of Public Prosecutions, Ex p Duckenfield* [2000] 1 WLR 55). More specifically, prior to 2009, the evidential standard for taking over and discontinuing a private prosecution was whether the evidence clearly failed to disclose a case sufficient for the defendant to be called to answer it. Indeed, it was seen as important for the Executive not to interfere with the citizen's right of free access to the courts and that it is best to control the prosecution by judicial process. In 2009, the DPP changed its evidentiary threshold, to allow the CPS to take over a private prosecution and to discontinue it unless the evidence was such as to render the prosecution more likely to result in a conviction than not to do so, which was upheld in *Gujra* (n 41). In the case of *Campaign Against Antisemitism v Director of Public Prosecutions* [2019] EWHC 9 (Admin), it was described as a public law challenge for which the Court can only intervene if the decision to take over the private prosecution and discontinue it made by the decision maker was irrational, ie a decision to which no properly directed and informed CPS decision-maker could have come.

[64] see *R v Director of Public Prosecutions, Ex p Duckenfield* [2000] 1 WLR 55.

answer test). If his conclusion was that it clearly failed to do so, he then would take over the prosecution and discontinue it; otherwise, and subject to the application of further criteria, notably the public interest, he would decline to take it over. Indeed, courts and the DPP considered this as an important standard for the Executive not to interfere with the citizen's right of free access to the courts and that it is best to control the prosecution by judicial process.[65] Nevertheless, in 2009, the DPP performed a volte-face and introduced a policy that, in his own prior documents, he had described as unfairly limiting the rights of private prosecutors.[66] This policy resulted in changes in its evidentiary threshold, to allow the DPP to take over a private prosecution and to discontinue it unless the evidence was such as to render the prosecution more likely to result in a conviction than not to do so (reasonable prospect test).

This policy change may have severe effects for cases wherein private prosecutions have been undertaken in contexts of state failures to adequately assess the evidence and act in the public interest.

This policy was judicially contested but ultimately upheld as lawful by the majority in *Gujra*.[67] The central issue in this case was whether the DPP's change in policy was lawful—specifically the first criterion relating to the evidentiary standard of the DPP's power to take over a private prosecution and to discontinue it, which implemented the 'reasonable prospect test' instead of the 'clearly no case to answer test'. In this case, Gujra instituted two private prosecutions towards two family members who had allegedly assaulted him. The DPP, acting by the CPS, concluded that the evidence in support of them did not satisfy the reasonable prospect test and, applying the policy, took over and discontinued these private prosecutions. Gujra applied for judicial review of this decision, which was dismissed, and subsequently appealed it to the Supreme Court on the basis that the DPP's current policy was unlawful because it improperly restricted the statutory right of a citizen to bring a private prosecution. The majority reaffirmed the importance of private prosecutions but highlighted that this did not entail that Parliament intended to that the DPP should decline to exercise his discretion so as to intervene and discontinue a prosecution even if it lacks a reasonable prospect of success. Lord Wilson writing for the majority highlights that the new test's focus on the likelihood of conviction was a more relevant question than the previous no case to answer test and gives illustrations of private prosecutions that survive the new test.

[65] ibid.
[66] ibid.
[67] *Gujra* (n 41) 123.

In turn, the dissent in *Gujra* noted that these policy changes go against Parliament's wishes in having access to private prosecution and severely limit the constitutional safeguarding role of private prosecution, stating a much more limited role of private prosecutions: 'to allow the Director to reduce the centuries-old right of private prosecution almost to vanishing point: in effect, to a right to pursue those prosecutions which the CPS are content to have pursued but would prefer to have pursued by some-one else'.[68] These important limitations to the potential for reviewing decisions to take over private prosecutions and discontinue them were subsequently confirmed and described as a public law challenge for which the Court can only intervene if the decision to take over the private prosecution and discontinue it made by the decision-maker was irrational, that is, a decision to which no properly directed and informed CPS decision-maker could have come.[69]

As predicted by the dissent in *Gujra*, one of the effects of the 2009 policy has been to limit the important safeguarding/accountability function of private prosecution. This has also been noted by Stephen James Colman, who highlights the 'difficulties in using private prosecutions as a means to challenge the discretion of the public prosecutor'.[70] Rather, private prosecutions have been increasingly engaged in instances where the CPS would have been content to pursue a case but prefers to have someone else take charge. Indeed, data suggests that within the last decade, there has been an increase in private prosecutions and a decrease in state prosecutions in part due to the 'retrenchment of state activities in many areas where the state had previously provided sufficient funds to enable state bodies to conduct such prosecutions'.[71] Mark Button and others refer to the increasing use of private prosecutions to address financial and corporate crimes as the 'rebirth of private prosecution'[72] by which offences—including large-scale corporate crimes, fraud,[73] and shoplifting[74]—have been increasingly left to be prosecuted by

[68] ibid.

[69] *Campaign Against Antisemitism v Director of Public Prosecutions* [2019] EWHC 9 (Admin).

[70] Stephen James Colman, 'Evaluating Challenges to Decisions Not to Prosecute: Do the Victims' Rights to Review, Judicial Review and Private Prosecution Provide a Coherent and Principled Framework?' (DPhil thesis, University of East Anglia 2020) 155.

[71] *R (Virgin Media) v Zinga* [2014] EWCA Crim 52; 'The State of Private Prosecutions' (*Publications Parliament UK*, 2 October 2020) <https://publications.parliament.uk/pa/cm5801/cmselect/cmjust/497/49705.htm#footnote-108-backlink> accessed 24 June 2023.

[72] Mark Button and others, 'Confronting the "Fraud Bottleneck": Private Sanctions for Fraud and Their Implications for Justice' (2015) 1(3) J Crim Res Policy Pract 159.

[73] ibid.

[74] Kadhim Shubber, 'The British Private Investigator Taking Criminals to Court When the State Won't' (*Financial Times*, 19 May 2023) <https://www.ft.com/content/135ab383-5df7-4824-bed5-1199e60a8597> accessed 7 June 2023.

third-party specialist firms and private companies, without interference from the state prosecutor.

In turn, these policy changes have also diminished the use of private prosecutions to advance the public interest. As illustrated below, these developments have led to the problematic use of private prosecutions as tools to advance private interests, while the state monopolizes the public interest. In parallel, the monopolization of the public interest by the state further constrains the potential for victims to challenge state decisions, notably in the contexts highlighted by Justice Hale in *Gujra*, where state prosecutorial decisions may include biases rooted in systemic inequalities.

Indeed, the current use of private prosecutions by certain profit-based organizations, including those publicly owned, has served increasingly to advance private interests. This is particularly the case when private prosecutions are employed for profit or debt recovery, personal political gain, as well as undertaking these prosecutions even in relatively minor cases. It is worth highlighting that legally, bringing a private prosecution solely for these private interest purposes amounts to an abuse of process, since all prosecutions, including private ones, need to meet the public interest test prior to and throughout the prosecution.[75] For these reasons, as discussed in the cases below, there is an important need for safeguards, transparency, and checks and balances to ensure that all prosecutions—including private ones—are brought in the public interest.

The Post Office and the Royal Society for the Prevention of Cruelty to Animals (RSPCA) cases are notable examples of this development. Both organizations developed specialized familiarity with private prosecutions as a significant feature of their operations. Nevertheless, some of these private prosecutions were pursued to advance private interests, notably to facilitate money recovery or damages, and in ways that gave rise to abusive practices.

In the Post Office case, due technological errors,[76] the Post Office undertook several wrongful private prosecutions[77] against its sub-postmasters employees

[75] *R v Knightland Foundation* [2018] EWCA Crim 1860; *Asif v Ditta* [2021] EWCA Crim 1091.

[76] Approximately 550 former sub-postmasters employees sued the Post Office for having been wrongfully dismissed or prosecuted as a result of accounting and financial errors in the Post Office's internal software, Horizon, which resulted in money disappearing from the system.

[77] Justice Committee, *Private Prosecutions: Safeguards* (2019–2021, HC 495); 'The Post Office Prosecutions' (*Publications Parliament UK*, 2 October 2020) <https://publications.parliament.uk/pa/cm5801/cmselect/cmjust/497/49704.htm#footnote-135> accessed 24 June 2023. The Private Prosecutors' Association questioned whether the Post Office was conducting private prosecutions at all and was in fact a 'publicly-owned entity and a public prosecutor' during the relevant period. There is no clear legal definition of what counts as a 'public prosecutor'. For the purposes of this report, the Post Office is taken to have been operating as a private prosecutor.

for crimes that included theft, fraud, and false accounting. This resulted in over 700 wrongful convictions, and at least one suicide connected to these convictions.[78]

Several reports and investigations into this matter revealed that these private prosecutions were undertaken without appropriate safeguards, transparency,[79] or accountability in ways that increased the risk of wrongful and abusive prosecutions. Specifically, written evidence from the Criminal Cases Review Commission to the Justice Committee problematized the organization's combination of all roles relative to the case, including that of victim, investigator, prosecutor, and political campaigner. Without any mechanisms for transparency or accountability to ensure that decisions were made in the public interest, the Commission identified a strong potential for conflicts of interest and conscious or unconscious bias.[80] This potential for conflicts of interest was also manifest in the numerous evidentiary issues that arose from private prosecutions in this case. Notably, the Post Office failed to respect their prosecutorial duty to disclose material that might assist the defence or undermine the prosecution, as well as their duty to ensure all reasonable lines of inquiry were pursued. Indeed, one of the court cases revealed that the Post Office seemed to adopt an extraordinarily narrow approach to relevance, generally determining that any evidence unfavourable to the Post Office was irrelevant.[81]

Moreover, the abusive use of private prosecution, in this case, contributed to problematic power dynamics. Instead of advancing the public interest, these prosecutions were used to facilitate debt recovery against employees who occupied vulnerable positions within the organization. Indeed, reports also suggested that defendants 'were routinely threatened with the charge of theft, which would not be proceeded with, provided they pleaded guilty to false accounting, made good all losses and did not mention any problems with Horizon.'[82]

[78] BBC News, 'Post Office Scandal: Government Rejects Call to Extend Inquiry' (*BBC*, 27 April 2021) <https://www.bbc.com/news/business-56905442> accessed 7 June 2023; Michael Pooler and Jane Croft, 'Bankruptcy, Jail, Ruined Lives: Inside the Post Office Scandal' (*Financial Times*, 11 September 2020) <https://www.ft.com/content/0138cd7d-9673-436b-86a1-33704b29eb60> accessed 7 June 2023.

[79] *Alan Bates and others v Post Office Ltd* [2019] EWHC 606; *Alan Bates and others v Post Office Ltd* [2019] EWHC 3408 (QB). For instance, it was highlighted that there seems to be a culture of secrecy and excessive confidentiality generally within the Post Office, but particularly focused on Horizon.

[80] Justice Committee (n 77).

[81] *Alan Bates* (n 79) 34.

[82] Justice Committee (n 77). In a 2020 letter to this Committee, the former CEO of the Post Office explained that the Post Office eventually decided to cease all private prosecutions of false accounting, inflating figures, or theft.

The RSPCA's practice of private prosecutions raised similar concerns as seen in the Post Office case. Specifically, the Wooler Report[83] in 2014 highlighted several accountability problems with the investigation and prosecution dually concentrated into the hands of one organization with a political mandate, and without any clear mechanisms for transparency and external accountability.[84] The Report also recognized the presence of a conflict of interest where the interests pursued are not related to the public interest as understood in criminal law. Indeed, it was highlighted that any enforcement strategy must take into account the Society's campaigning, commercial, and de facto regulatory roles, which do not always sit comfortably with the role of prosecutor. It was also suggested that there was an inevitable tension between the RSPCA's very specific objectives as an animal welfare charity versus the broader public policy considerations relevant in criminal law enforcement. This is compounded by the 2006 extension of the ambit of the criminal law and the absence of any powers of official status on the part of the RSPCA relating to enforcement.[85]

Finally, the Report identified a need for more background factual information to be available to RSPCA's Prosecutorial Case Managers (PCMs) to assist in their assessment of the public interest component of the decision whether to prosecute. Indeed, a significant proportion of cases investigated by the RSPCA prosecuted individuals experiencing some degree of marginalization—the elderly or individuals experiencing financial difficulty—which impacted their ability to provide care. Such factors can only be properly taken into account if they are fully known to PCMs at the outset.[86] This highlights the importance of understanding the role of RSPCA as private prosecutors within the relevant power dynamics—notably, the resource disparities between the RSCPA relative to those disproportionately affected by their private prosecutions. In a similar vein, a subsequent review in 2021 by the Environment, Food and Rural Affairs Select Committee led to the organization ending its role as private prosecutor in 2021.[87]

[83] Stephen Wooler, *The Independent Review of the Prosecution Activity of the Royal Society for the Prevention of Cruelty to Animals* (2014).
[84] Indeed, contributors to the review expressed concerns that internal mechanisms of accountability were limited and that there was no external effective avenue for addressing concerns or calling the RSPCA prosecutors to account. ibid 20.
[85] ibid 8, 10.
[86] ibid 60.
[87] BBC News, 'RSPCA Prosecution Powers "To be Examined by MPs" ' (*BBC*, 22 September 2015) <https://www.bbc.com/news/uk-34314004> accessed 7 June 2023; RSPCA, 'We're Reviewing Our Prosecutor Role to Focus on Frontline Cruelty' (*RSPCA*, 28 June 2021) <https://www.rspca.org.uk/whatwedo/endcruelty/prosecution/review> accessed 21 November 2025.

Situating the power dynamics between the prosecutor and prosecuted within a social context based on financial and social capital puts into question how we understand victimhood in these circumstances. This nuance highlights the relevance of understanding the public interest within a framework that is attentive to systemic inequalities. Similar dynamics can be seen in cases where corporations have acted as private prosecutors towards shoplifters, most of whom have a drug addiction problem and where these prosecutions might perpetuate the cycle of offending.[88]

These structural/systemic dimensions as relevant components of the public interest will be further discussed in Chapter 8 to highlight the ways that victims as agents of state accountability can contribute to bringing this type of evidence in state prosecutions.

The recent developments relating to private prosecutions outlined in this section, which include changes in the CPS's policies and practices, suggest an increasing move away from the safeguarding/state accountability role undertaken by private prosecutors to a role of complementary prosecutor. In practice, this role is limited to specific instances where the state prosecutor is content to have certain crimes prosecuted by other entities. As seen, this has been particularly the case in matters of fraud, theft, and shoplifting, giving rise to the use of private prosecutions for private financial gains. In turn, this has begun to reformulate the perception of this mechanism as one to advance private interests, while developing a parallel narrative that considers victims as holders of private interests and state prosecutors as the sole representatives of the public interest.

As highlighted by the dissenting opinion in *Gujra*, it is worth remembering the historical relevance of private prosecutions as a public tool that advances the public interest. Specifically, this mechanism has served to check on state powers and respond to state failures in representing the public interest, including in contexts of systemic inequalities. In parallel, some of the leading case law and reports have underlined the importance for private prosecutions to also adhere to the same standards and obligations as state prosecutors since their decisions are meant to respect public interest standards rather than merely private interests.[89] These obligations include guidelines, transparency, review processes, and evidentiary duties—notably the duty of candour to ensure that all relevant material is made available both for the Court and

[88] See comments by Penelope Gibbs, founder of Transform Justice, a criminal justice reform charity in Shubber (n 74).

[89] Wooler (n 83); In *Gujra* (n 41), the Supreme Court aligned private prosecutions with prosecutions brought by the state by requiring that private prosecutions also meet the public interest grounds.

the defence. Additionally, they may include respecting the Full Code Test (evidentiary and public interest) and paying attention to power dynamics when reaching decisions and implementing private prosecutions to ensure they align with the public interest and their underpinning values, free of conscious and unconscious biases, discussed in Chapter 8.

Judicial review

State accountability in the public interest

Common law judicial review in England and Wales has become a prevalent mechanism of state accountability, which 'reaches to most corners of the administrative state'.[90] Indeed, judicial review is meant to be a tool for citizens to hold the state accountable on the exercise of power itself.[91]

This approach applies to criminal justice, including for victims of crime in England and Wales in response to decisions made by the CPS.[92] Although both decisions to prosecute and not to prosecute can be challenged by way of judicial review, decisions not to prosecute are more often challenged by victims since they are final and not subject to a subsequent trial. If a victim's claim is successful, the Court will quash the decision and may also remit it back to the CPS with a direction to reconsider it in accordance with the findings and judgment of the Court.[93] Importantly, the rise of state prosecutions, coupled with the increasing limitations of private prosecutions as a mechanism of accountability, has contributed to the rise of judicial review as an important tool for victims to hold the prosecutorial state accountable.[94]

Specifically, judicial review can be an important mechanism to hold the state accountable as it allows citizens, including victims of crime, to seek permission to make a claim for review before the High Court in contexts of public interest.

[90] Aronson (n 42) 113.

[91] Jason NE Varuhas, 'Against Unification' in Hanna Willberg and Mark Elliott (eds), *The Scope and Intensity of Substantive Review: Traversing Taggart's Rainbow* (Hart Publishing 2015).

[92] Whilst the DPP is answerable to the Attorney General in relation to matters of prosecution policy, it has been suggested that judicial review may be one of the few effective counterbalances to their large discretion in individual cases. See J Fionda, *Public Prosecutors and Discretion* (Clarendon Press 1995) 60–62; Andrew Ashworth, *The Criminal Process* (Oxford University Press 1998) 200–204. Judicial review was also used to challenge decisions not to prosecute since when the police were the primary prosecutors, before the creation of the CPS. See Colman (n 70) 11; *R v Commissioner of Police of the Metropolis ex parte Blackburn* [1968] 2 QB 118.

[93] A claimant may also be awarded damages in appropriate cases.

[94] In England and Wales, victims have mainly been involved in judicial review of decisions not to prosecute and have been successful in a number of cases. See, eg, *R v DPP Ex p Manning* [2001] QB 330; [2000] 3 WLR 463.

This is particularly useful in circumstances where the CPS has misunderstood or misapplied law or policy, notably the Full Code Test in the Code for Crown Prosecutors—which includes the public interest prong.[95] It may also be useful in circumstances where the CPS has failed to carefully consider evidence, or in situations where it can be demonstrated that the CPS reached a decision as a result of fraud, corruption, or bad faith.[96] Judicial review can also promote state accountability in contexts such as those described by Lady Hale in *Gujra*, where state prosecutorial authorities have made an erroneous assessment of evidentiary credibility rooted in biases that marginalize certain groups. Indeed, as highlighted by Findlay Stark, these contexts provide arguments 'in favour of ensuring that the public prosecution service keeps its approach to certain kinds of cases under review. It is also a point in favour of strengthening judicial oversight of prosecutorial discretion—supervision that, although available in England and Wales, is difficult to exercise effectively.'[97] Several examples of case law, discussed below, illustrate this form of state accountability.

This mechanism predominantly conceives of victims as citizens, situating their interests in matters of state accountability closer to the public end of the spectrum. This parallels private prosecutions since judicial review, to some extent, is an extension of the accountability role private prosecutions were meant to serve prior to their increasing limitations. Indeed, as highlighted by Lord Bingham CJ in the case of *Manning*, discussed more thoroughly below, 'judicial review is the only means by which the citizen can seek redress against a decision not to prosecute'.[98] As suggested by Mandy Burton, Lord Bingham's statement is partially accurate since, as seen above, private prosecutions are also in theory available, albeit increasingly more limited, to challenge some of the decisions made by prosecutors.[99] Burton, however, additionally holds that Lord Bingham neglects to mention that civil actions are also available means for the victim to obtain redress. This statement, however, fails to distinguish between conceptions of redress under judicial review and civil actions. Indeed,

[95] The Code for Crown Prosecutors is issued by the DPP under section 10 of the Prosecution of Offences Act 1985. See Code for Crown Prosecutors (*CPS*, October 2018) <https://www.cps.gov.uk/publication/code-crown-prosecutors> accessed 7 June 2021. According to the Full Code Test, prosecutions should meet the evidential sufficiency test and the public interest element to justify and make decisions about prosecutions.

[96] CPS, 'Appeals: Judicial Review of CPS Prosecuting Decisions' (*CPS*, September 2019) <https://www.cps.gov.uk/legal-guidance/appeals-judicial-review-cps-prosecuting-decisions>.

[97] Findlay Stark, 'The Demise of the Private Prosecution?' (2013) 72(1) CLJ 7.

[98] *Manning* (n 94) 23.

[99] Mandy Burton, 'Reviewing Crown Prosecution Service Decisions Not to Prosecute' [2001] Crim LR 374, 377. The increasing limitations of private prosecutions render this statement increasingly relevant. In the meantime, the VRRS was developed to review prosecutorial decisions not to prosecute as discussed below.

a spectrum of public–private interests introduces greater nuance to highlight that accountability and redress are understood and applied to serve different functions and interests. Specifically, while civil actions and their accompanying redress conceive of victims as holding and serving their personal private interests, judicial review processes view victims as citizens who are meant to engage predominantly public interests in holding the state accountable for its exercise of power.

Despite recognizing victims as citizens who can make legitimate claims relating to public prosecutions, courts have increasingly contributed to a narrative that suggests that state prosecutors hold a constitutional monopoly over prosecutions, including over claims in the public interest. Indeed, in several decisions, courts have stated that Parliament has entrusted the Director (and its officers) as independent professionals, answerable to the Attorney General in their role as guardian of the public interest *and to no other authority*.[100] Similarly, courts have claimed that 'no other authority may exercise these powers or make the judgments on which such exercise must depend'.[101] By emphasizing that the public interest is a matter for the state alone to assess and guard in contexts of prosecutions, they suggest that victims have their own specific roles and interests—aligned with predominantly private interests. Moreover, they have highlighted that reviews may succeed only in very rare cases for the 'good and sound constitutional reason that decisions to prosecute were entrusted under our constitution to the prosecuting authorities'.[102] This claim, which refers to state prosecuting authorities, seems at odds with the history and current role of private prosecutions. Rather, these prosecutions, as well as judicial review, have shown to be necessary to pursue in the public interest when the state has failed in this regard. Despite this increasingly present narrative however, the courts have recognized that the discretions conferred on the Director and state prosecutors are not unfettered and that they must direct themselves correctly in law and that their prosecutorial power must be exercised 'in good faith, uninfluenced by any ulterior motive, predilection or prejudice'.[103]

Finally, it is worth highlighting that the application of a human rights framework to contexts of judicial review and victim participation has also

[100] *R (Corner House Research) v SFO* [2009] 1 AC 756; reaffirmed in *Manning* (n 94); *R (oao 'Monica') v DPP* [2018] EWHC 3508 (Admin). Nevertheless, in *Manning* (n 94), the Court includes greater nuance by highlighting that the responsibility is entrusted to the Director and the responsible staff of the CPS, 'although the power to institute a private prosecution is preserved' (para 21).

[101] *Supreme Court of Fiji in Matalulu v Director of Public Prosecutions* [2003] 4 LRC 712.

[102] *R(L) v DPP* [2013] EWHC 1752, 6.

[103] *Monica* (n 100) [32].

contributed to a narrative that considers victim interests as increasingly private. Specifically, the Human Rights Act of 1998 has expanded the traditional grounds for judicial review to allow for an aggrieved individual to bring a claim on the basis that their human rights have been breached. To have standing, the claimant must show that they have been personally affected, or that they run the risk of being directly affected, by the breach. This rests on a different conception of standing and participation than traditional judicial review that is more closely aligned with public interest claims.[104] Under human rights grounds of judicial review, individual victims of crime would typically have standing to challenge prosecutorial decisions, while campaigning organizations that may have standing under traditional judicial reviews may not. This development has also contributed to the conceptualization of victims of crime as bearing predominantly private interests within a public–private spectrum of interests.

As will be seen in the following chapters, victim participation as part of a human rights framework—rooted in possessive individualism—is prevalent in the United States and its reverberations in England and Wales can also be seen under the VRRS, discussed in greater in the next chapter.

The evolution towards substantive accountability, a lower standard of review, and holding the state accountable for decisions based on unfounded stereotypes rooted in inequalities

Common law judicial review enables a form of accountability that has, at times, engaged in substantive assessments. While historically focusing on process by enforcing statutorily prescribed procedures and staying clear of substance, substantive review has 'grown significantly',[105] including in the context of criminal justice and prosecutorial decisions. This mechanism remains constrained, however, as courts have expressed reluctance to intervene in matters of prosecutorial discretion, highlighting that their power to review decisions is to be exercised sparingly.[106] The rationale that underpins this heightened standard of review is the constitutional independence of the prosecutor coupled with their official/professional expertise.

[104] Varuhas (n 91).

[105] Aronson (n 42) 113, which also specifies that '*Wednesbury* unreasonableness was exceptional for being overtly substantive, but its bar was set so high that it posed no real threat to the basic architecture of judicial review'.

[106] *Manning* (n 94). Other decisions have expressed a similar idea by highlighting that it is meant to be a 'highly exceptional remedy'. See *Sharma v Browne-Antoine* [2007] 1 WLR 780, [14(5)] and very rarely exercised *R (Pepushi) v Crown Prosecution Service* [2004] Imm AR 549, [49]; *R (Bermingham) v Director of the Serious Fraud Office* [2007] 2 WLR 635, [63]; *S v Crown Prosecution Service* [2015] EWHC 2868 (Admin) [2016], 1 WLR 804.

Case law[107] illustrates that the reasons for which the courts seldomly interfere in decisions not to prosecute or investigate are grounded in a public interest rhetoric in two major ways. First, these powers are entrusted by Parliament to the DPP (and the officers) as independent professionals, answerable to the Attorney General in their role as guardian of the public interest, and to no other authority. Second, courts have recognized the polycentric character of official decision-making in policy and public interest considerations, which are not part of the constitutional function nor the practical competence of courts to assess on the merits.[108] Interestingly, contrasting this commentary to private prosecutions adds some nuance in that some iterations of this mechanism empower private actors with legal authority to make such decisions within the public interest.

While this rhetoric of deference remains prevalent in judicial discourse, in practice, it has been tempered. Particularly from the start of the twenty-first century, courts have not only increasingly engaged in substantive forms of review but also clarified that the standard of review should not be placed too high. As highlighted by Burton, 'despite the rhetoric about not interfering with prosecutorial discretion, the courts are increasingly recognising the need for some accountability'.[109]

Specifically, considerations of accountability have had an important role in reconfiguring the scope of judicial intervention. Prior to the twenty-first century, judicial review was predominantly used to challenge the lawfulness of the DPP's policies that were seen to improperly encroach upon certain statutory provisions.[110] Over the years, however, judicial review has developed into a more substantive assessment of prosecutorial accountability, wherein decisions not to prosecute may additionally be reviewed if they were based on legal errors, in breach of the CPS's Code for Crown Prosecutors, or when decisions are so perverse[111] that no reasonable prosecutor would have made them.[112] Courts have specified that:

> In most cases the decision will turn not on an analysis of the relevant legal principles but on the exercise of an informed judgment of how a case against

[107] *Corner House Research* (n 100); reaffirmed in *Manning* (n 94); *Monica* (n 100).

[108] *Matalulu* (n 101) also referenced *in R (On the Application of Corner House Research and Others) v Director of The Serious Fraud Office* [2008] UKHL 60.

[109] Burton (n 99) 376.

[110] *R v Metropolitan Police Commissioner, ex p. Blackburn* [1968] 2 QB 118.

[111] Decisions are labelled 'perverse' where prosecutors have disregarded compelling evidence, or ignored the relevant prosecutorial policy, or a combination of both.

[112] See early body of case law on judicial review of prosecutorial discretion examined by C Hilson, 'Discretion to Prosecute and Judicial Review' [1993] Crim LR 739.

> a particular defendant, if brought, would be likely to fare in the context of a criminal trial. This exercise of judgment involves an assessment of the strength, by the end of the trial, of the evidence against the defendant and of the likely defences. It will often be impossible to stigmatise a judgment on such matters as wrong even if one disagrees with it. So the courts will not easily find that a decision not to prosecute is bad in law, on which basis alone the court is entitled to interfere. At the same time, the standard of review should not be set too high, since judicial review is the only means by which the citizen can seek redress against a decision not to prosecute and if the test were too exacting an effective remedy would be denied.[113]

This statement suggests that judicial review can be a relevant mechanism, although with some limitations, for engaging in a substantive analysis that carefully weighs and examines the various elements of evidence while ensuring that the standard of review is not too high.

Substantive assessments are especially prevalent in instances of judicial review where victims claim that the Full Code Test under the Code for Crown Prosecutors[114] has not been properly understood or applied.[115] In particular, courts have looked at prosecutors' consideration of key evidence, including by assessing the correctness of prosecutors' interpretation of evidence. These grounds for review increasingly delve into the manner of the exercise of the discretion itself, including the proper consideration of the legitimate interests at play, and the quality, weight, and substance of prosecutorial analysis. This dimension of what is considered a correct interpretation arguably has lowered the standard of review in these contexts and brings the analysis closer to a substantive form of assessment within the substantive–procedural spectrum.

The following cases illustrate the implementation of substantive assessments and a lower standard of review in instances of judicial review of decisions not to prosecute. In practice, several of the cases discussed in this section also illustrate the potential for judicial review to respond to state failures towards certain marginalized groups where the actions of prosecutorial authorities are informed by unfounded stereotypes. These include cases of death in state custody, deaths of labourers in contexts of employers' negligence, harms experienced by persons with disabilities, and cases of sexual violence.

[113] *Manning* (n 94) 23.
[114] CPS (n 96).
[115] *R (on the application of Peter Dennis) v DPP* [2006] EWHC 3211.

The case of *Manning*[116] illustrates the evolution towards a more substantive assessment of judicial review. This case concerns the death of Alton Manning, a Black man who died in state custody from asphyxiation following a struggle with prison officers. The circumstances surrounding his death were dehumanizing—as he was naked, directed to have his genitals inspected 'probably without justification',[117] and overpowered by at least three prison officers. Witnesses disagreed on the circumstances surrounding his death as officers claimed he had been properly restrained, while prisoners testified that he was held in a forbidden and dangerous neck-lock. Prosecutors initially decided not to prosecute, directing the case to a prosecutor at Central Casework with special responsibility to review death in custody cases. The reviewing prosecutor reassessed the decision following consultations with counsel and the DPP but ultimately rejected laying charges on the basis that there was insufficient evidence to secure a conviction for manslaughter. In turn, Manning's family sought judicial review of this decision to the High Court on the basis that the prosecutor had wrongly applied a higher standard than the realistic prospect of conviction test set out in the Code, as part of the Full Code Test.

Through substantive analysis, the Court in *Manning* examined prosecutors' assessment of evidence of violence perpetrated by prison officers. The Court ultimately quashed the prosecutor's decision as it found that it had failed to consider important aspects of the evidence,[118] and concluded that prosecutor incorrectly applied the evidentiary test. Specifically, the prosecutor relied on the argument that the contact was accidental and non-continuous, and therefore would not meet the evidentiary bar of the Full Code Test. The Court disagreed with this assessment by highlighting that the prosecutor failed to take into account several aspects of the evidence, while underlining that there was no evidence to suggest that contact was accidental, or non-continuous. Moreover, the Court made clear that the prosecutor provided no explanation of the injury to the deceased's throat and asphyxiation. In this instance, the Court concluded that these were all matters that should have been taken into account on an objective appraisal of the realistic prospect of conviction. As such, the failure to do so vitiated the DPP's decision. The Court also stated that when prosecutors ask themselves the correct questions and consider all

[116] *Manning* (n 94).

[117] ibid [3].

[118] The prosecutor relied on the argument that the contact was accidental and non-continuous and therefore would not meet the evidentiary bar of the Full Code Test. The Court disagreed with this by highlighting that the prosecutor had failed to take into account that there was no evidence of this nor any medical evidence that such contact could have caused or significantly contributed to Manning's death.

the evidence and relevant policy, the Court would have no basis to interfere. Through this clarification, they recognized that different Crown Prosecutors might have reached different conclusions. Rather, the issue was that the prosecutor applied a higher test than that laid down in the Code. While there was no direct engagement with systemic biases relating to racism, a preconception exists within the criminal legal system that diminishes the harm experienced by Black individuals, particularly Black men who are often seen as aggressive and threatening. This mechanism can enable to address such situations when erroneous standards are applied to certain marginalized. Finally, this decision illustrates the ways that accountability in this decision is substantive. Indeed, as suggested within the public law literature discussed in the previous chapter, the High Court's engagement with evidentiary questions can be understood as an analysis towards the substantive end of the spectrum.

Similarly, in *Jones*,[119] the Court considered the Crown Prosecutor's review decision and found that there was no adequate explanation underlying the decision not to prosecute. In this case, a labourer was decapitated by a grab bucket that closed unexpectedly at work. The decision not to pursue charges of negligence manslaughter rested on the argument that the grab bucket procedure had not posed an obvious danger and was assessed erroneously with a subjective culpability standard by the Crown rather than objective liability. Moreover, the Crown Prosecutor had not provided any explanations as to why, in reaching this conclusion, he had preferred the evidence of a service engineer employed by the manufacturer of the crane over the opinion of the manufacturer's service manager. Specifically, the prosecutor's decision, relying principally on the credibility of a single witness stating that the danger had not been sufficiently obvious, was deemed irrational. As such, the Court quashed the DPP's decision not to prosecute on the basis of an error of law and also suggests that, when determinative, prosecutors must provide clear rationales for prioritizing one testimony over another. If not, the ultimate decision would be deemed irrational. This seems to be an assessment of the quality and credibility of a decision draped into a procedural formulation, which leans closest to a substantive-based assessment.

R (on the application of Peter Dennis)[120] provides a further example on Court's engagement in substantive assessment in reviewing prosecutorial decision-making. In this case, the claimant, P, applied for judicial review of a decision by the CPS not to prosecute for gross negligence manslaughter arising

119 *R v Director of Public Prosecutions and others ex parte Jones* [2000] IRLR 373 (High Court).
120 *Peter Dennis* (n 115).

out of the death of his son in an industrial accident. P's son was seventeen years old when he died after falling through a rooflight in his second week of work. P argued that the employer had instructed the labourer to go onto the roof even though he had no previous experience working on roofs or heights. At a Coroner's inquest, which is separate and independent from the criminal process but serves to determine the cause and manner of death in instances of suspicious or unnatural deaths, the jury returned a unanimous verdict of unlawful killing. Following this decision, the CPS considered whether various individuals should be prosecuted for gross negligence manslaughter but concluded that although the employer and others were in breach of duty of care, the degree of negligence exhibited was not such as to amount to a criminal negligence. The CPS explicitly stated several factors that informed this decision, but the Court found that these reasons did not address the case that might be brought against the employer. Furthermore, the Court agreed with the argument that by focusing on the particular moment before the accident, the CPS failed to take into account the seriousness of a failure to give proper instruction on workplace safety in the circumstances. In this sense, the Court found force in the substantive criticism that the CPS failed to take this material evidence into account—suggesting a substantive form of assessment of this decision.

Finally, in *R(B) v Director of Public Prosecutions*,[121] the Court employed a substantive assessment with direct reference to prosecutorial biases in engaging with evidence. In this case, the victim sought judicial review of a decision by the CPS to discontinue a prosecution against the accused for wounding with intent to cause grievous bodily harm and witness intimidation. The CPS's decision to discontinue was made based on the argument that the victim's mental illness prevented him from being placed before the jury as a credible witness. Following a request for judicial review by the victim, the Queen's Bench Divisional Court found the CPS's decision to be unlawful for several reasons. In the first place, the decision was irrational for reasons discussed below. Furthermore, the decision violated the victim's rights under Article 3 of the Convention for the Protection of Human Rights and Fundamental Freedoms, which recognizes the state's positive duty to provide legal recourse against those who commit serious acts of violence against others.

The key evidence at issue in this case was a medical report which concluded that the victim had a mental condition which might affect his perception and recollection of events. The CPS relied on this report to decide that the victim

[121] *R(B) v DPP* [2009] EWHC 106.

could not be put forward as a credible witness when describing the assault. The Court concluded that the CPS's decision was irrational for two reasons. First, the Court suggested that the prosecutor may have misread the report, since it did not logically follow from that report that the victim could not be presented as a credible witness when describing the assault. Alternatively, the Court highlighted that this decision may have been based on an unfounded stereotype on the basis of his disability. Indeed, the victim was perceived to be not credible in any respect because of his history of medical problems. Moreover, the Court made important remarks commenting on the standard of review and judicial deference. The Court recognized that the exercise of the Court's power to intervene will always be exceptional because a decision *not* to prosecute is final subject only to judicial review. However, in practice, the Court admitted that the exercise of the Court's powers will be less rare in these cases than in the case of a decision *to* prosecute because the defendant already has a means to challenge the prosecutor's case in the latter circumstances. This case illustrates the substantive assessment of accountability that judicial review enables as well as the potential for providing accountability to marginalized groups in instances of prosecutorial errors rooted in systemic discrimination as part of the epistemic injustices.

Similarly, judicial review has been a useful tool in addressing the CPS's failures to support victims of sexual violence. This was the case for Emily Hunt, who successfully challenged a CPS decision not to prosecute after she was drugged and sexually assaulted. Initially, the CPS claimed it did not have sufficient evidence to demonstrate that the encounter was non-consensual. After Hunt found out that the assault was filmed, the CPS refused again to prosecute for voyeurism on the basis that the prosecution for this offence was unlikely to succeed. Specifically, the CPS argued that since the recording was made in a place where there would be a reasonable expectation of privacy, the assault would not be legally considered voyeurism.

Hunt initially did not think of judicially reviewing the decision due to an assumption that the CPS would know the law. Moreover, she thought of filing a private prosecution for rape, but dropped this after being advised by a barrister that the CPS could take over the case and terminate it, as is one of the important current limits of private prosecutions relating to accountability discussed above. Instead, she decided to launch a judicial review with the help of the Centre for Women's Justice (CWJ). Not long after, and before the judicial review hearing, the CWJ discovered that the CPS, who had argued there was no basis to prosecute her case, would be arguing the opposite position in criminal division of the Court of Appeal in a case raising the same issue. The Court of Appeal gave Hunt permission to intervene in this separate case[122] in which the CPS was prosecuting a man for secretly filming himself having sex with two other women who had agreed to have sex with him but not filmed. In her intervention, she challenged this legal interpretation of the offence, which prompted the Court of Appeal to decide that even if one consents to sexual activity in a private place, there is a reasonable expectation of privacy, as consent does not extend to agreeing to be filmed without one's knowledge. Therefore, the act of filming is unlawful under the Sexual Offences Act and amounts to voyeurism. In light of this judgment, the CPS revised its initial decision and accepted that their decision in Hunt's case had been unlawful. It proceeded to quash the initial outcome not to prosecute and charge Killick with voyeurism.[123]

The decisions in Hunt suggest that judicial review can be an important mechanism for victims, even indirectly, in bringing their interests forward in holding the state accountable in instances where state actors have rendered biased and unfounded decisions based on erroneous and discriminatory stereotypes. Nevertheless, judicial review also has their limits as in the case of Hunt, considering the circumstances of the offence, there was no consent to any sexual activity and therefore the offence of voyeurism falls short of adequately capturing the nature and gravity of the assault.

The judgments relating to judicial review analysed in this section highlight that it has become important for the state to establish that key evidence has been thoroughly evaluated and correctly interpreted in the review process. This is a direct result of victims acting as agents of state accountability in challenging prosecutorial decisions not to prosecute or to abandon prosecutions through judicial review. A failure on behalf of prosecutors to undertake this evidentiary analysis may give the courts grounds to intervene in the decision, which essentially results in assessments that are closer to substantive forms of accountability and analysed by relying on a lower standard of review in assessing decisions not to prosecute.

In *Manning*, Lord Bingham CJ advocated for this lower standard by highlighting that the standard of review must not be set too high. He justified this decision by recognizing that this is the case in decisions where judicial

[122] *R v Richards* [2020] EWCA Crim 95.

[123] Michael Buchanan, 'Voyeur Sentenced After Woman's Five-Year Campaign' (*BBC News*, 4 September 2020) <https://www.bbc.com/news/uk-england-london-54027088> accessed 13 June 2023; *R v Killick* [2011] EWCA Crim 1608; [2012] 1 Cr App R 10.

review is the only means by which citizens can seek redress against a decision not to prosecute 'and if the test were too exacting an effective remedy would be denied'.[124] Accordingly, if other mechanisms of accountability such as private prosecutions become limited in seeking accountability for state failures, this standard of review becomes important for citizens to obtain some form of redress relating to the broader matter of accountability. Importantly, Lord Bingham relied on the underpinning of this remedy from a citizen's perspective, rather than relying on a discourse of individual personal rights, needs, and interests. This suggests that within the process of judicial review, victims are seen as potential holders of predominantly public roles and interests as agents of state accountability to ensure that appropriate public considerations are taken into account.

Finally, in addition to evidentiary errors in assessment rooted in inequalities, judicial review has also been successful in holding the state accountable in instances where the CPS has made errors in law—which can also be rooted in social inequalities. For instance, the case of Emily Hunt and the errors relating to voyeurism as well as issues relating to consent discussed above provides such an example. Moreover, in *R(F)*,[125] a case in which the DPP refused to initiate a prosecution of a man who sexually assaulted his wife illustrates this potential. In this case, the wife consented to sexual intercourse on the condition that her husband would withdraw before ejaculating, an agreement that he violated, stating that he could do so if he wanted as they were married. The DPP refused to initiate a prosecution on the basis that, whilst the claimant's credibility was secure, the evidence would be insufficient to establish a realistic prospect of conviction for any offence. This was considered an error in law by the Court, who judicially reviewed the decision, since the husband performed a sexual act contrary to her wishes that, according to the Court's interpretation, fell into the definition of rape. This case illustrates the potential for victims to use judicial review as a way of bringing the correct interpretation of legislation and ensuring that the law is adequately implemented in a way that is attentive to power dynamics and inequalities endured by marginalized groups. Erroneous legal interpretations can be based on myths and stereotypes about what is considered consensual sexual intercourse, and these elements can be rectified by this mechanism of state accountability.

[124] *Manning* (n 94) 23.
[125] *R(F) v DPP* [2013] EWHC 945 (Admin).

4. Conclusion

So far, the analysis of available mechanisms in England and Wales suggests that mechanisms of state accountability initiated by victims have, in many instances, been understood as bringing forward citizens' public interests rather than individualized ones. These approaches include an important public component and have, to some extent, enabled substantive forms of assessments of prosecutorial state failures. In practice, this exercise of state accountability rooted in a conception of victims as citizens who can hold public interests has empowered several victims to confront and redress state fallibilities founded on discriminatory stereotypes and within power differentials often rooted in inequalities. Nevertheless, the increasing influence of a narrative that supports the state's monopoly of the public interest in private prosecutions coupled with an individualized and liberal understanding of human rights in the context of judicial review have given rise to a discourse that increasingly conceptualizes victim interests as private. In turn, this has given rise to a different and more limited role of victims as agents of state accountability in England and Wales.

The next chapter examines the recent turn towards an increasingly private conception of victim interests and accountability in England and Wales. In particular, it analyses the development of the VRRS and its impact on the ways victim interests and accountability are conceived with regards to decisions not to prosecute. The chapter highlights that this mechanism has conceived of victims as holders of private interests that has had a considerable impact on the victim's engagement with the public interest in matters of state accountability. In this sense, instead of a direct engagement with the public interest, as seen in traditional private prosecutions and judicial review, victims have seen their role evolve as one where they can contribute in an aggregate way to the public interest. As will be seen, this has also had an impact on the subsequent evolution of judicial review in England and Wales.

5

From Citizens to Private Entities

Towards a Private Conception of State Accountability in England and Wales

1. Introduction

Even within mechanisms that predominantly conceive of victims as holders of public interests, several developments have increasingly led to the rise of a discourse that situates victim interests closer to the private end of the spectrum. As seen, several developments relating to the evolution of private prosecutions along with the development of a human rights framework, rooted in possessive individualism, within the area of judicial review have in part contributed to this shift. These developments along with conceptions brought forward by the courts and the Director of Public Prosecutions (DPP) portraying state prosecutors as holding a monopoly over the public interest have increasingly depicted the interests of victims as private, which has also led to an increasingly private conception of state accountability.

This chapter focuses on another development in England and Wales, namely, the enactment of the Victims' Right to Review Scheme (VRRS)[1] in 2013, which has shaped the role of victims as agents of state accountability by contributing to the privatization of interests and accountability. It begins with an overview of the VRRS as an internal review mechanism within the Crown Prosecution Services (CPS), which was initially proposed by the court as a means to form a more accessible process of substantive review—similar to judicial review and its conception of victims as potential holders of public interests. It then discusses the increasing restrictions that the CPS has placed on the implementation of the VRRS, along with judicial interpretation that has confirmed these restrictions and contributed to the privatization of victim interests. Finally, the chapter discusses the impact that the VRRS has had on the evolution of judicial review.

[1] ibid.

Victims as Agents of State Accountability. Marie Manikis, Oxford University Press. © Marie Manikis 2026.
DOI: 10.1093/9780191993947.003.0007

2. Victims' Right to Review Scheme (VRRS)

This section analyses the VRRS as a mechanism for victims to hold the state accountable.[2] The VRRS was launched in June 2013 by the CPS following the seminal case of *Killick*, which instructed the CPS to implement an accessible and clear prosecutorial review process. This review process allows victims to request an internal review to the CPS of certain CPS decisions not to start a prosecution or to stop a prosecution. Essentially, it is a two-stage review process where victims may seek an internal review to assess whether errors were made in assessing the dual-stage test (Full Code Test), namely, the evidential requirement and the public interest. The first stage of the review process is the local resolution stage and gives the CPS Area responsible for the case the opportunity to verify the decision and ensure that the victim has been given a sufficiently clear and detailed explanation of the decision. This review, although conducted locally, will be carried out by a prosecutor who has had no previous dealings with the case. If the victim is not satisfied, an independent review carried out by the Appeals and Reviews Unit or a Chief of Crown Prosecutor can be undertaken, further discussed below. Reviewing prosecutors will approach the case afresh to determine whether the original decision was right or wrong, which is a different standard than a judicial review. Following the conclusion of the VRRS process, if the victim remains dissatisfied and wishes to challenge it further, the victim can apply to the High Court for a judicial review.

As will be seen, the seminal case of *Killick*, which gave rise to the VRRS, located the victim's role and interests, to some extent, closer to the public end of the spectrum. Nevertheless, subsequent decisions relating to the VRRS have increasingly adopted a narrative which portrays victims as holding interests that are closer to the private end of the spectrum.

Killick: Accountability under the VRRS initially conceptualized as safeguarding interests closer towards the public end of the spectrum

The VRRS was introduced in 2013 in England and Wales, essentially as a result of the Court of Appeal's seminal decision in *Killick*,[3] a case that draws on the long-standing tradition of judicial review of decisions not to prosecute

[2] For a previous study that provides initial data, see Marie Manikis and Mary Iliadis, 'Analysing the Victim Review Scheme of Decisions Not to Prosecute in England and Wales and Within Comparative Jurisdictions' in Pamela Cox and Sandra Walklate (eds), *Victims' Access to Justice: Historical and Comparative Perspectives* (Routledge 2022) 138.

[3] *R v Killick* [2011] EWCA Crim 1608, [2012] 1 Cr App R 10.

in English common law, as well as the Draft European Union Directive (EU Directive)[4] on establishing minimum standards on the rights, support, and protection of victims of crime dated in 2011, which provides that 'Member States shall ensure that victims have the right to have any decision not to prosecute reviewed' to which conceptualizes victim interests as public.

The case of *Killick* involves three complainants with severe disabilities from cerebral palsy, who were allegedly sexually assaulted. The CPS declined to pursue charges against Killick on grounds that there was no realistic prospect of conviction. The complainants challenged this decision internally through the CPS's internal complaints process. Under this process, the CPS's reviewing officer found the decision not to prosecute to be correct. An additional review under this process with additional evidence confirmed the decision that the evidential test for prosecution was not met. In turn, the complainants' solicitors advised the CPS of their clients' intentions to commence judicial review proceedings. This action prompted a third-tier review by the DPP's Principal Legal Advisor who did not restrict herself to deciding whether the previous decisions were reasonable, but considered the matter afresh. She concluded that the original decision not to prosecute was wrong (though not unreasonable), that there was a realistic prospect of conviction, and that it was in the public interest that there should be a prosecution. In response, Killick challenged the refusal to stay proceedings on the grounds of abuse of process. He advanced two distinct bases, notably that (1) representations were made to him that the prosecution would be discontinued and (2) several delays had passed from the time the offences had allegedly taken place and what had happened, suggesting that a fair trial would not have been possible. In dismissing his appeal, the Court of Appeal reaffirmed the victims' right to review while laying grounds for a clearer, more accessible, and formalized internal process of review in England and Wales.

First, as part of its analysis, the Court in *Killick* highlighted the importance of an accessible right to review prosecutorial decisions in English law. Specifically, the Court recognized that there is a well-established right by interested persons to seek judicial review of decisions not to prosecute. Therefore, it would be 'disproportionate for a public authority not to have a system of review without recourse to court proceedings'.[5] Arguably, this clarification suggests that the review mechanism proposed in *Killick* is equivalent to judicial

[4] Directive 2012/29/EU of the European Parliament and of the Council of 25 October 2012, establishing minimum standards on the rights, support, and protection of victims of crime.

[5] *R (on the application of Hayes) v CPS* [2018] EWHC 327 (Admin) [48]; *R v DPP ex p C* [1995] 1 Cr App Rep 136.

review in terms of interests and objectives involved. Additionally, it underlines that accountability mechanisms must accommodate victims' practical needs in recognizing that court proceedings can be cumbersome.

Second and relatedly, the Court in *Killick* considered the right to review under the law and procedure of England and Wales as being 'in essence the same as the right expressed in Article 10 [*sic*[6]] of the Draft EU Directive'.[7] This directive provides that Member States must ensure that victims have the right to review any decision not to prosecute. Although the Court suggests that these two separate rights are equivalent, distinctions should be made between the way common law judicial review has understood the role of claimant-victims versus the rationales behind the EU Directive. As highlighted above, judicial review in England and Wales has been historically understood as a public law mechanism that incorporates public interests, including public views brought forward by victims. In contrast, the rights under the EU Directive seem to be drafted for victims to bring forward their predominantly private interests.

Moreover, the Court addressed the existing confusion between a review process versus a service complaints process. The Court specified that the right to review entails a request to review the correctness of CPS's decision not to prosecute, which has nothing to do with the conduct of a level of service provided by the CPS. The Court explained this distinction by highlighting that the review process revisits the prosecution's decision, whereas a complaints process addresses the victim's negative experiences with services received by the CPS under the *Code of Practice for Victims of Crime*. The Court highlighted that a review process is an integral part of the exercise of a prosecutorial discretion and the use of the term complaint to designate a review under the former policy risks creating confusion between a prosecutorial review process and a service complaints process. This analysis suggests that substantive aspects relating to the public components of the prosecutorial decision may be assessed internally by the CPS, separate from the procedural or process-related flaws in the ways victims are treated.

Third, *Killick* underscores the importance of considering the interests of the State, the defendant, and the victim—'the three interests in a criminal proceeding'.[8] Specifically, the Court recognized finality as an important interest held by the victim during the review process, highlighting that 'as a decision

[6] This passage should have referred to Article 11.
[7] *Killick* (n 4) [49].
[8] ibid [48].

not to prosecute is in reality a final decision for a victim, there must be a right to seek a review of such a decision, particularly as the police have such a right under the charging guidance'.[9] While at first glance, this statement appears to indicate some predominantly private dimension of the interests held by victims, the analogy to the police's right to review hints that these interests may be predominantly public. Indeed, as indicated in Chapter 4, police do not represent their own private interests. Rather, they must incorporate a public dimension in matters of prosecutions and therefore have the ability to hold prosecutors accountable to preserve the public interest when these decisions are erroneous.

Finally, the Court in *Killick* recognized the importance of a clearer and more formal internal review mechanism than the one which existed at the time within the CPS guidance on judicial review. Indeed, this informal mechanism that existed under CPS guidance highlighted that where a decision not to prosecute was challenged and likely to be the subject of judicial review, the decision should be re-reviewed. If upon re-review it was decided that the original decision was wrong, immediate action was to be taken (if possible) to rectify the decision. The standard of review articulated in *Killick* seeks to determine whether the decision was wrong rather than unreasonable—the latter being the standard in judicial review—which suggests a relatively lower standard of correctness that is met in cases of error. While the Court recognized that the CPS was bound to re-review in cases of threats of judicial review, it highlighted that this policy gave rise to ambiguities. Notably, the policy was unclear about the nature and format of the request and its time limits. As such, the Court urged the DPP, as the agent in charge of creating policies for the CPS, to formalize a clearer procedure for review, including guidance on time limits in the interest of incurring reasonable delays for a fair trial.

This decision signalled to the DPP that, as a public authority, it would be disproportionate not to have a system of review of discretionary decisions not to prosecute without recourse to court proceedings. While this process is meant to be similar to judicial review in terms of its objectives and interests, the court makes clear that the procedure should be clear and accessible, with stated time limits and without requiring victims to go to court.

9 ibid.

Accountability for interests conceptualized as closer to the private end of the spectrum

Following this guidance in *Killick*, and in light of the EU Directive, the CPS created the VRRS. While several statements in *Killick*, discussed above, seem to have conceived of victims and their interests as predominantly public, its process quickly diverged from the Court of Appeal's guidance.[10] This section analyses how the VRRS's interpretation by the CPS and subsequent court decisions have situated victims' interests closer to the private end of the spectrum. In turn, this has, to some extent, limited role of victims as agents of state accountability in England and Wales.

In its early days, the VRRS seemed to conceptualize victims somewhat closer to judicial review—as individual citizens who may directly bring forward arguments relating to the public interest. An early example of this can be seen in *Janner*,[11] where a victim successfully challenged a problematic decision made by the state prosecutor on the second prong of the Full Code Test relating to the public interest.[12] In this case, the CPS decided not to prosecute Lord Janner, a former Member of Parliament, over child sexual offence allegations because it would not be in the public interest due to his severe dementia. The victim requested a review under the VRRS, challenging the CPS's assessment of the public interest. Upon review, the DPP concluded that a prosecution would be in the public interest, which led to the prosecution of Lord Janner. This decision suggests that victims have direct representative claims in the ways the public interest is interpreted and defined in decisions not to prosecute. Accordingly, this conception of the public interest can be understood under Grear's unitary theories of the public interest, discussed in Chapter 2, which consider citizen-victims as legitimate entities with common values who can represent the public interest.

Subsequent cases demonstrate a tendency towards an increasingly private conception of victim interests under this scheme, particularly when compared

[10] While its remedial dimension, which includes instituting or reinstituting criminal proceedings, seems to align with more public related remedies, various cases illustrate the ways the CPS and courts have increasingly considered victims as holding predominantly private interests within this mechanism of accountability.

[11] BBC News, 'CPS Grants Lord Janner Review' (*BBC*, 16 May 2015) <www.bbc.com/news/uk-32757978> accessed 4 February 2024.

[12] In recent years, in addition to the Full Code Test, an added layer was added, which highlights that in order to overturn a decision not to prosecute, the reviewer must not only be satisfied that the Full Code Test was wrongly assessed but also that for the maintenance of public confidence, the decision must be reversed.

to the judicial review process discussed above. First, the *Bedford-Turner* case[13] illustrates the private conception of victims within the VRRS, and contrasts it to the predominantly public dimension of direct judicial review. In this case, Bedford-Turner made online content and gave public speeches evoking medieval libels against Jewish people, encouraging expelling them from England to free the country from Jewish control. The CPS initially refused to prosecute, concluding that there was no realistic prospect of a jury finding that Bedford-Turner's speech amounted to incitement to racial or religious hatred. The Chairman of Campaign Against Antisemitism, Gideon Falter, who witnessed the speech, sought review of the decision not to prosecute under the VRRS, but was told that he did not qualify as a 'victim'. In response, Falter took the unusual step to seek judicial review of the CPS's decision. The Court accepted to hear this case under judicial review and explained that it '[raised] potentially important issues for society in the growing area of racist and religious hate crime'.[14] On the evening of the hearing, after a year of claiming that their decision was correct, the DPP agreed that it should be quashed and reviewed by a more senior lawyer. The defendant was ultimately convicted and handed a sentence of twelve months' imprisonment.

This decision offers an important window into the conceptual differences between the way victim interests are conceived under the VRRS mechanism and judicial review—the latter conceptualizing victim interests closer to the public end of the spectrum. Falter's exclusion from the VRRS illustrates a private conception of victims under this scheme. Put otherwise, only individualized victims with personal interests can bring forward requests for review rather than citizen-victims who can speak and make representations in the public interest. In this sense, the VRRS holds similarities to the American conception of the victim, as individuals that bring forward their private interests in the process and therefore have limited standing when they are not recognized as victims having suffered individualized harms.

Second, in the case of *Chaudhry*,[15] the Administrative Court's *obiter* offers additional insights into the predominantly private ways in which victim interests are conceptualized under the VRRS and judicial review that relate to the VRRS. In this case, Mrs Chaudhry seeked judicial review of the legality of the CPS's exclusion from the VRRS of cases in which the CPS decided to charge some suspects

[13] Littleton, 'Jamie Susskind Acts in Landmark High Court Case Over Non-Prosecution of Neo-Nazi' (*Littleton Chambers*, nd) <https://littletonchambers.com/jamie-susskind-acts-in-landmark-high-court-case-over-non-prosecution-of-neo-nazi/> accessed 13 June 2023.

[14] ibid.

[15] *R (on the application of Chaudhry) v DPP* [2016] EWHC 2447 (Admin).

and not others. In response, the Court indicated its reservations as to whether the victim claimant was acting in the public interest in relation to vindicating the rule of law. On this point, the victim argued she had legitimate standing as she was acting in the public interest by bringing forth an issue affecting members of the public who were or might be victims of crime. However, the Court remained doubtful of the victim's public interest claims by highlighting that 'she [had] no real interest in a consideration of the lawfulness of the VRR other than so far as it has impacted her claim'.[16] This reasoning signals that any interest the victim may have in assuming her role within or relating to the legality of this mechanism is considered private. In other words, the victim cannot bring forward or have any public interest component in relation to this scheme. In addition, the Court supported this private interest conception by stating:

> [T]he claimant is an individual, not a representative body or an NGO. The basis for the Claimant acting in the public interest is unclear, at least to me. It is, however, unnecessary to reach a final conclusion. I am prepared to proceed on the assumption (without deciding) that the Claimant has the necessary standing for the claim to be determined on its merits.[17]

Ultimately, the Court justified going forward with this hearing on the pragmatic basis that the parties had fully prepared for it. Therefore, in practical terms, it was convenient to deal with the matter in this Court rather – and less wasteful of public funds. The fact that the CPS did not press objections to the claimant's standing with any vigour was also stated as a reason for accepting to proceed. Nonetheless, one could argue that the Court's analysis failed to consider the public nature of judicial review and to conceptualize the role of victims within the historical, predominantly public understanding. The fact that a victim is an individual rather than an NGO has no basis in law in treating their claims as private rather than predominantly public. Finally, as highlighted in *Killick*, the VRRS was viewed as an extension and a more accessible means of judicial review and therefore was meant to be a public law mechanism. Consequently, it should have considered broadly the role of victims as potential representatives of arguments that are brought in the public interest.

Third, despite the historical role of victims within public prosecutions, there is a growing narrative that displaces victims' legitimate ability to bring forward public interest arguments in favour of expanding the role of state actors

[16] ibid [11].
[17] ibid [13].

as holding the monopoly over the public interest. State prosecutors and courts have a tendency to ignore, disregard, or undermine the citizen-victim's historical role within prosecutions in two ways. First, these actors have suggested that the DPP and CPS, as professionalized state entities, remain the sole legitimate voices that bring forward the public interest. Second, they have articulated that decisions to prosecute have been entrusted, under the constitution, to prosecuting authorities.

Chaudhry is one example of decisions that have undermined the citizen-victim's legitimate role in prosecution by explicitly ignoring the long-standing history of private prosecutions. In this decision, the Court states:

> [P]utting private prosecutions to one side, a criminal prosecution in this jurisdiction is brought by the Crown on behalf of the State or public at large; it is emphatically not a matter of individual vengeance for the victim . . . the prosecutor is required to exercise independent operation judgement . . . in order that it should function as an independent prosecuting authority.[18]

This decision proceeds by emphasizing that victims' predominantly private interests are an element of the public interest that state prosecutors must consider. Indeed, by understanding the victim's interests as forming part of an aggregate understanding of the public interest seems to underscore a privatized notion of the victim. The Court highlights:

> [A]n independent focus on the public interest is not, of course, incompatible with paying adequate attention to the interests of complainants, victims . . . and witnesses . . . indeed, the contrary. For whatever the reason, however, it is fair to acknowledge that, for too long, inadequate attention was paid to the interests of complainants, victims and witnesses—all of whom are entitled to be treated with dignity and respect . . . and to have their respective interests taken into account.[19]

This statement espouses a narrative that brings forward a predominantly private dimension of these interests in relation to the public interest. This is an approach that differs significantly from the historical conception within traditional English common law. Accordingly, this narrative is closer to some of the aggregate ways the United States have conceived the interests of victims.

[18] ibid [14].
[19] ibid [15].

Similarly, in *Chaudhry*, the Court interpreted *Killick* in a way that emphasizes the tensions between the victim and defendant's separate private interests in the process. Specifically, the decision contrasts the victim's interest in the review of a decision not to prosecute with the defendant's interest in the certainty of indications that the matter would be discontinued. Interestingly, in *Killick*, the Court did not speak of victim interests as private and arguably suggested that victims' interests in the finality of criminal law proceedings holds a public dimension, similar to the police or the state. Indeed, the Court in *Killick* clearly highlighted that a decision not to prosecute is, in reality, a final decision for a victim. Therefore, there must be a right to seek review of such a decision, 'particularly as the police have such a right under the charging guidance'.[20] This analogy, which likens the police's right to review to that of victims, suggests that the victim, like the police, have long-standing similar historical public roles and interests in criminal proceedings—as was the case since private prosecutions, discussed in Chapter 4.

Courts' tendencies to conceive of victims' interests relative to VRRS as private has had an important impact on the role of victims as agents of state accountability. As seen in the context of private prosecutions, the rise and increasing power of the CPS has coincided with policies limiting the role of victims and contributed to restrictions on mechanisms available for state accountability. Although *Killick* seems to root the importance of an internal procedure institutionalizing the victims' right to review in public terms to provide a check on prosecutorial powers, the CPS's implementation of the VRRS has started to construct the victim's interests as predominantly private, as discussed above. This conception has resulted in important limits on the VRRS's capacity to hold the state accountable. By claiming a monopoly over the public interest in these decisions, the CPS, endorsed by judicial decisions, signals that victims are not legitimate actors for bringing forward claims relating to the public interest within prosecutions. This perspective tends to relegate victims' interests to the private field that can be relevant to the public interest, albeit in an aggregate way, defined in Chapter 2.

The increasing limits of victim's remit of review under the VRRS

Developments within CPS policies, validated by case law, have introduced several limits to the purview of the VRRS and inevitably to the role of victims

[20] *Killick* (n 4) [48].

as agents of state accountability under this mechanism. Colman has suggested that the VRRS is based on a very narrow interpretation of the requirement to provide a right to review for decisions not to prosecute.[21] Arguably, discourses framing victims' interests as closer to the private end of the spectrum have facilitated these policy decisions along with a view that conceives the state as holders of public interests. This can partly be explained by the predominantly private understanding of victim interests under this scheme, which is seen as coming in conflict with public institutional interests held by the state as well as private interests held by the defendant. Victims' private interests within the criminal public process are considered as holding less legitimacy than other more fundamental interests in criminal proceedings. This serves to limit the victim's accountability role within state prosecutorial decisions as their role as reviewers of prosecutorial decisions may be considered less legitimate within a public process and therefore more easily limited.

Since the VRRS was first introduced, the CPS has created several exclusions to its scope by way of internal guidelines. These policy choices have limited the victim's opportunity to challenge erroneous decisions by the CPS, consolidating prosecutorial power to the CPS. Table 5.1 below illustrates the considerable decrease in the number of qualifying decision, in other words those that can be the subject of review under the VRRS, particularly since an even more restrictive change in policy in May 2021.[22] While in previous years qualifying decisions were around 100K and above, recent restrictions have decreased the number of qualifying decisions to less than 30K. Victims may not engage their right to review in the following decisions: out-of-court disposals, cases where only some of the charges relating to the victim are terminated, decisions to amend the charges or to accept an offer of a guilty plea to a lesser charge, decisions to proceed in respect of some allegations and not others, and decisions to charge some suspects and not others.[23]

Victims have tried to judicially review some of these restrictions but courts have typically had a deferential stance towards qualifying decisions in policy. The lawfulness of the exclusion under paragraph 11(iii) (now para 19(iv)), related to decision to charge some suspects and not others, was challenged

[21] Stephen Colman, 'A Comparison of the Implementation of the Victims' Right to Review in England and Wales, Scotland and Northern Ireland' (2018) 5 Crim LR 365.

[22] Crown Prosecution Service, 'Victims' Right to Review Scheme' (*CPS*, 2025) <https://www.cps.gov.uk/legal-guidance/victims-right-review-scheme> s 6 (version of 16 December 2020, updated 27 May 2021) accessed 24 June 2023.

[23] ibid [19].

Table 5.1 Victims' Right to Review Scheme data

Time Period	VRR Qualifying Decisions	Total VRR Received	Appeals Upheld at Local Review (Original Decisions Overturned at Phase One)	Appeals Upheld by Appeals Review Unit (Original Decisions Overturned at Phase Two)	Total Appeals Upheld (Total Original Decisions Overturned)[a]
June 2013–March 2014	113,952	1,186	114	48	162 (0.14% of all *qualifying* decisions and 14% of total appeals *received*)
April 2014–March 2015	126,589	1,674	137	73	210 (this amounts to 0.17% of all *qualifying* decisions and 13% of total appeals *received*)
April 2015–March 2016	115,941	1,809	123	65	188 (0.16% of all *qualifying* decisions and 10% of total appeals *received*)
April 2016–March 2017	103,113	1,988	122	15	137 (0.13% of all *qualifying* decisions and 7% of total appeals *received*)
April 2017–March 2018	91,133	1,956	136	42	178 (0.20% of all *qualifying* decisions and 9% of total appeals *received*)
April 2018–March 2019	94,727	1,930	152	53	205 (0.22% of all *qualifying* decisions and 11% of total appeals *received*)
April 2019–March 2020	91,912	1,996	210	78	288 (0.25% of all *qualifying* decisions and 14% of total appeals *received*)
April 2020–March 2021	N/A	1,961	206	64	270
April 2021–March 2022	N/A	1,698	179	64	243
April 2022–March 2023	29,543	1,655	204	80	284 (1.03% of all *qualifying* decisions and 17% of total appeals received)

[a] Figures have been rounded up.

Notes: VRR = Victims' Right to Review. Qualifying decisions refer to those made by the Crown Prosecution Service, which could be subject to review under the Victims' Right to Review Scheme.

Source: Crown Prosecution Service, 'Victims' Right to Review Data' <https://www.cps.gov.uk/publication/victims-right-review-data> last updated January 2024.

unsuccessfully in the case of *Chaudhry*.[24] The claimant in this case argued that the CPS had treated this provision as an absolute bar on reviewing a decision not to prosecute, which was unlawful. Alternatively, the claimant argued that even if the CPS policy did not impose an absolute bar, prosecutors had acted unlawfully acting as if such a bar existed, or in failing to indicate to the public the circumstances in which a review apparently barred by paragraph 11(iii) would nevertheless be conducted. The Administrative Court held that this provision was not unlawful as the policy had not limited reviews, which fell outside the policy. It also agreed with the CPS's contention that a more general right of review 'would both significantly undermine operational prosecutorial discretion and have potentially serious implications for the CPS'.[25]

Importantly, paragraph 19(x) of the VRRS excludes the possibility of reviewing decisions where the victim has withdrawn their support for the prosecution. This exclusion suggests that there is no internal review for decisions that have evidentiary errors or have been made contrary to the public interest, notably as a result of discriminatory assumptions and stereotypes. Some of these situations are discussed in greater depth in Chapter 8 and include contexts where marginalized groups may be over-prosecuted, disbelieved, or have their level of responsibility impacted due to affected volition on the basis of substantive inequalities. It also reinforces the role of victims as punitive agents, contrary to studies that have highlighted that victims can play an important role in advancing restraint, which can be consistent with the public interest.[26] Interestingly, despite the discussion above, some of the justifications provided for these limits, which were accepted by the Court, were not based on principled reasons relating to victims' capacity to participate in public matters. Rather, as in *Chaudhry*, the CPS has justified these exclusions due to operational costs and a lack of resources to pursue an expansive review scheme.[27]

Another important limit to the VRRS is the remedial limitations in certain instances where an original prosecutorial decision was wrong (or unreasonable). These instances do not automatically give rise to prosecution as a remedy. For instance, in England and Wales, if the original decision resulted in no evidence being offered at court, it is not possible to recommence proceedings relating to prosecutions as the act of offering no evidence amounts

[24] *Chaudhry* (n 16).
[25] ibid [46].
[26] Marie Manikis, 'A New Model of the Criminal Justice Process: Victims' Rights as Advancing Penal Parsimony and Moderation' (2019) 30(2) CrimLF 201.
[27] *Chaudhry* (n 16) [46].

to an acquittal. Several cases have shared this fate. For example, in the case of *McCrossen-Nethercott*,[28] the complainant was sexually assaulted while asleep and requested a VRRS review on the basis that the prosecutor erroneously relied on a 'sexsomnia' argument in their prosecutorial decision-making. Despite the VRRS's prosecutorial finding that there was indeed an error, and the case should have been brought to trial, the remedy was limited since no evidence was offered at the court that put an end to the case on the basis of an acquittal under the double jeopardy rules. As a consequence, the CPS submitted an apology to the complainant and no new prosecution was possible to bring forward. This significant limit was upheld in *Hayes*,[29] in which the Divisional Court took the view that such an outcome still amounted to an effective right of review and did not leave the victim without satisfaction.

Similar to the justifications provided for limiting the VRRS in *Chaudhry*, the legality of these limits have been justified by referring to institutional factors. Specifically, the court in *Hayes* cited operational effectiveness of the VRRS and the implications for the Magistrates' Court and the Crown Court should a victim make representations before the prosecution acted upon a decision to offer no evidence.[30] Moreover, the restriction was also considered 'justified and proportionate in its balancing of competing interests'.[31] Importantly, as is the case with most decisions under this scheme, the victim's interests, which are predominantly conceived as private, appear to be conflicting with both the defendant's private interests in having proceedings terminated as soon as possible after the decision not to prosecute, as well as the prosecutor's public interest in prosecutorial independence and efficiency.

Limiting the independent internal review and heightening the standard of review within the VRRS

Even in contexts that allow for reviews under the policy, additional discretionary powers have been attributed to the CPS as part of this regime, along with an unclear, and potentially heightened, standard of review—creating additional limits to this mechanism of state accountability. As highlighted in the previous section, these limitations are in part rooted in conceptions of victims

[28] Emma Ailes, 'Claims I had Sexsomnia Destroyed my Rape Case' (*BBC News*, 5 October 2022) <https://www.bbc.com/news/uk-63116989> accessed 24 June 2023.
[29] *R (Hayes) v CPS* [2018] EWCA 327.
[30] ibid [53] (Lord Holroyde).
[31] ibid [52].

as holders of private interests, which serve to consolidate public powers to the state and limiting possibilities for accountability.

As a reminder, the VRRS, as a prosecutorial review mechanism, is comprised of two stages: the local resolution process and an independent review by the Appeals and the Review Unit or relevant Chief Crown Prosecutor, as appropriate. In its initial iteration, the VRRS offered victims who were dissatisfied with the local resolution process the possibility to seek an automatic independent review to the Appeals and Review Unit or a relevant Chief Crown Prosecutor. More recently, the CPS reviewed its scheme to limit this option. Specifically, the policy was amended to allow independent review exceptionally in instances that 'may be available' and 'where applicable' suggesting that this independent appeals process is subject to discretionary approval.[32] In turn, requiring victims to obtain the discretionary approval of state actors creates an additional limit to their ability to pursue their role as agents of state accountability in instances of prosecutorial errors relating to the evidentiary assessment and the public interest.

An additional discretionary element was added to the CPS's assessment of whether an initial wrong decision should be overturned. Specifically, section 10 states that the CPS may overturn a decision not to prosecute in instances where a further review of the original decision shows that the initial decision was wrong. However, the fact that a decision is wrong—on either the evidentiary stage or the public interest—is not sufficient for it to be overturned. Rather, the decision to overturn the initial wrongful decision must also 'maintain confidence in the criminal justice system'.[33] This suggests that even in cases of errors, the CPS may not overturn a decision if doing so will not maintain the confidence in the criminal justice system.

Additionally, the CPS has made changes to the VRRS by removing the automatic appellate possibility, which can give rise to a heightened standard of review. In its initial iteration, the CPS stated that the VRRS's standard of review would 'comprise a reconsideration of the evidence and the public interest i.e. the new reviewing prosecutor will approach the case afresh to determine whether the original decision was right or wrong'.[34] Commenting on that initial standard, the former DPP at the time, Keir Starmer, made clear that the right to review does not turn on the heightened standard of unreasonableness in the *Wednesbury* sense, which was often applicable in instances of judicial

[32] Crown Prosecution Service (n 23) s 6.
[33] ibid s 10.
[34] CPS Appeals and Review Unit [31]; *R (FNM) v DPP* [2016] EWHC 870 (Admin) [13].

review ('so unreasonable that no reasonable person acting reasonably could have made it'[35] but on the less demanding test of whether the original decision was wrong). The current version of the policy is not as clear, as it removed the language stating that the case will be looked at afresh and does not provide victims with the potential to seek an automatic internal appeal, which can provide a more independent assessment. Nevertheless, it continues to use the language of wrong as part of the standard—suggesting a standard of correctness.

The standard of correctness, coupled with automatic internal appeals, has enabled victims to make substantive claims of errors and assessments in the public interest while the case was decided by an independent prosecutor internal to the CPS, which can make a difference in outcome. For instance, in *S v Crown Prosecution Service*,[36] a sexual assault complainant started a review process under the VRRS and argued errors in the assessment of evidence of consent. At the local review level, the claim was unsuccessful and was therefore transferred to the Crown Prosecution Service Appeal and Review Unit in London for review by an independent prosecutor who followed the previous scheme. Conducting a detailed review of the case afresh, the appeals prosecutor concluded that the initial prosecutor did indeed make an error and that the evidence was sufficient to provide a realistic prospect of conviction. Furthermore, the appeals prosecutor decided that in order to maintain the confidence in the criminal justice system, a prosecution should be brought despite the earlier decision. The Court upheld the prosecutorial reviewer's decision and decided that whether the complainant consented or had capacity to consent was a matter that ought properly to be decided by a jury and therefore had to be prosecuted.

This case illustrates the importance of offering the possibility for victims to seek an automatic independent appellate review assessment by a separate CPS unit for greater independence, particularly as professional interests—irrelevant to decisions about prosecutions—may have precedence if decisions are confined to the local level.[37] As suggested by Colman, there can also be substantive advantages of a decision that enables some distance from the original decision at a higher level within the CPS hierarchy.[38] One of those relates to the potential for review of decisions rooted in substantive inequalities that

[35] Keir Starmer, 'Finality in Criminal Justice: When Should the CPS Reopen a Case?' (2012) 7 Crim LR 526, 527.

[36] *S v CPS* [2015] EWHC 2868 (Admin), [2016] 1 WLR 804.

[37] Mary Iliadis and Asher Flynn, 'Providing a Check on Prosecutorial Decision-Making: An Analysis of the Victims' Right to Review Reform' (2018) 58(3) Br J Criminol 550.

[38] Colman (n 22).

can affect credibility. Commenting on the context prior to the enactment of the first iteration of the VRRS, Rogers suggested that 'one imagines that there must have been several cases of rape which were also not prosecuted during that period, which would likely have been reversed if only a system for requiring an independent review had been in place, as later happened under the VRR'.[39] Accordingly, having an independent process to the existing review process can serve as an important tool for holding the state accountable in instances of certain forms of state failures. Moreover, commenting on the previous VRRS policy that enabled victims to seek independent appellate CPS review while applying a lower evidentiary standard of correctness, Rogers noted that

> there should be little danger now that a prosecution will not be brought because just the one prosecutor might wrongly so decide, possibly due to applying an unduly high interpretation of the evidential test. With up to four prosecutors, including one senior one, being involved, and only one of them needing to decide that the case should proceed, one might expect that today a case with genuine merit should be selected for prosecution somewhere along the line.[40]

The discussion above highlights the ways in which the CPS has increasingly defined the limits of internal prosecutorial reviews within the VRRS. These limits inevitably affect the victim's ability to seek prosecutions even in instances of errors, and limit the potential for independent review and reconsideration of the evidence and public interest. Moreover, they can give rise to an unduly high evidentiary standard being applied at the local level as well as other errors, including those rooted in epistemic and substantive inequalities. Moreover, as will be seen below, these changes are part of a wider trend in which the CPS seeks to guard its monopoly over public prosecutions and the public interest, thereby limiting the role of victims as agents of state accountability.

3. The Evolution of Judicial Review Post-VRRS

The VRRS has had a considerable impact on the evolution of judicial review as a mechanism for holding the state accountable in decisions not to

[39] J Rogers, 'A Human Rights Perspective on the Evidential Test for Bringing Prosecutions' (2017) 9 Crim LR 678, 692.
[40] ibid 687.

prosecute—increasingly limiting its substantive potential for accountability, discussed in Chapter 4, and heightening its standard of review. In some ways, it changed and limited the centrality of judicial review as the main mechanism for challenging prosecutorial decisions not to prosecute. Indeed, the VRRS will typically need to be exhausted as a preliminary step before seeking judicial review.[41] Moreover, as highlighted in recent case law, the evidentiary standard for judicial review following an unsuccessful VRRS will be more stringent, since a previous assessment by prosecutors (on the merit) was made under the VRRS, which is meant to use a low standard of correctness.[42] Finally, as will be discussed in greater depth below, the VRRS has developed in ways that increasingly locate victims and their interests towards the private end of the spectrum.

As will be discussed below, it is generally accepted that the standard of review and level of deference courts will apply towards a prosecutorial decision will depend upon the issues to be decided. Where decisions relate to questions of primary fact or assessments of the public interest, the court will be reluctant to hold that the decision-maker's assessment is irrational. However, if the issue is essentially one of law, the decision-maker's experience and expertise are of less force and courts will more easily find that decisions were wrong in law.

Towards procedural review and a heightened standard of review based on state monopoly over the public interest

Similar to the review of rights in the United States, discussed at length in Chapter 7, courts in England and Wales have recognized a procedural dimension to the VRRS. Arguably, the language of due process and individual rights contributes to a predominantly private and procedural conception of victim interests and accountability as the focus rests on the importance of being heard rather than substantive content regarding prosecutorial decisions. In *R (FNM)*,[43] the victim sought judicial review on the basis that prosecutorial decisions were made without providing a victim a fair opportunity to make representations. Specifically, the CPS made its decision regarding the VRRS review

[41] *L v DPP* [2013] EWHC 1752 (Admin).

[42] ibid [10]. Indeed, Sir John Thomas in this decision highlighted that 'it is highly likely that where a review has taken place, and the review can be seen to be careful and thorough, proceedings for judicial review to challenge the decision will be the more difficult to advance . . . if there has been a review in accordance with this procedure, then it seems to me, that the prospect of success will, as I have said, be very small'.

[43] *R (FNM) v DPP* [2020] EWHC 870 (Admin) 9.

prior to the submission of the victim's representations, after she explicitly requested a hold on the decision while she sought legal advice. Importantly, the decision came a month before the deadline the CPS had given for making the decision. The High Court contended that, while the DPP is not required to invite victims to provide representations, victims are entitled to a 'fair opportunity'[44] to make representations when they are told they can do so. It found that by violating the deadline communicated to the complainant, the CPS had failed to provide this fair opportunity that amounted to 'a failure of due process'.[45] Judicial review in this instance is closer to the American model of victims' rights—serving a procedural form of accountability by ensuring that individuals are heard rather than a substantive form that considers the substance of prosecutorial decisions.

Moreover, since the creation of the VRRS, judicial review has also been subjected to a heightened standard of review when compared to the standard applied to victim-initiated judicial reviews of prosecutorial decisions prior to the VRRS. Indeed, as discussed in Chapter 4, less deference was afforded to prosecutorial decisions, where substantive forms of reviews took place. The rationale invoked for this stringent standard is two-fold. Essentially, courts propose that lesser oversight is needed by the judiciary once the CPS has already reviewed its initial decision through the VRRS. This is affirmed by a narrative that suggests that the CPS holds a form of constitutional monopoly over prosecutions that must be respected and treated with the utmost deference.

For instance, in *L v DPP*,[46] Sir John Thomas indicated that once there has been a review in accordance with the VRRS, it is highly unlikely that a court will intervene in favour of the complainant at judicial review, particularly in light of the CPS's constitutional monopoly over prosecutorial decisions. Specifically, Sir Thomas emphasized the monopoly of prosecutions under the constitution to prosecuting authorities, in this case the DPP and those who work under him in the CPS. He made clear that it is very important that the constitutional position of the CPS as an independent decision-maker is respected and recognized by adopting this very strict self-denying ordinance. Moreover, he emphasizes that the CPS has moved to a new policy with the VRRS, which has resulted in new processes of review. For these reasons, he highlighted that the prospect of success under judicial review would be 'very very small, given the constitutional position of the CPS . . . I am not saying

[44] ibid [45] (Bean LJ).
[45] ibid [51] (Bean LJ).
[46] *L v Director of Public Prosecutions and Another* [2013] EWHC 1752 (Admin).

that there will not be such a case, but the chances of a claimant succeeding in them . . . are likely to be small'.[47] He also highlighted that as part of the VRRS, the CPS will determine the scope and depth of review. Indeed, depending on the type of decision, some cases will call for very detailed review while others will be dealt with in short order. Accordingly, 'it is highly likely that where a review has taken place, and the review can be seen to be careful and thorough, proceedings for judicial review to challenge the decision will be more difficult to advance'.[48] In this sense, judicial review will be rejected if it is shown that the CPS has independently reconsidered the decision, and if it cannot be shown that the decision is based on one of three unlawful grounds: (1) because there has been some unlawful policy, (2) because the Director has failed to act in accordance with his own set of policy., or (3) because the decision was perverse; that is to say, it is a decision that no reasonable prosecutor would have reached.

Similarly, in the case of *R(Alina Joseph)*,[49] the Court conducted a judicial review following an unsuccessful review as part of the VRRS in which a specialist prosecutor as part of the Appeals and Review Unit decided not to prosecute on the basis that a prosecution would not be in the public interest. In this case, while there was sufficient evidence giving rise to a realistic prospect of conviction, the reviewing prosecutor in the file as part of the VRRS decided that a prosecution would not be in the public interest. The victim brought a judicial review, which was rejected on the basis of the quasi-unfettered powers of the CPS. The Court specifically rejected the potential of a substantive argument on the public interest, wherein the victims claimed that undue weight was placed on a specific factor in the case, notably the impact of a prosecution on the life of the young defendant. Specifically, it highlighted that the reasons why the courts are very slow to interfere are as follows. First, the court emphasized that state prosecutors are considered to be the only authority who can legitimately make decisions about prosecutions. In this sense, it highlighted that the powers in question are entrusted to the officers identified, and no one else. Second, it invoked the separation of powers by highlighting the 'polycentric character of official decision-making in such matters including policy and public interest considerations which are not susceptible of judicial review because it is within neither the constitutional function nor the practical competence of the courts to assess their merits' (ibid para 31 which cites *Matalulu v Director of Public Prosecutions* [2003] 4 LRC 712, 735–736). Third, they highlight that the

[47] ibid [17]–[18].
[48] ibid [9].
[49] *R(Alina Joseph) v DPP* [2022] EWHC 131 (Admin).

powers are conferred in very broad and unprescritive terms. As such, by articulating that there are no other authorities for prosecutions and that victims and courts do not have the ability to discuss the polycentric notion of the public interest, the Court communicated an increasingly private understanding of the victim's role and interests, which aligns more closely with the ways participatory mechanisms for victims have developed in the United States. Under this approach, victims are considered as holding predominantly private interests in an aggregate way with regards to the public interest and therefore are not recognized as legitimate actors for making substantive claims about elements directly relating to the public interest.

Moreover, the Court in *R(D)*[50] added a further layer of deference in judicial review of matters that have proceeded through the VRRS. It did so by highlighting:

> [I]n assessing challenges based upon perversity, irrationality, *Wednesbury* unreasonableness, failure to take relevant considerations into account or taking irrelevant considerations into account, the Court will proceed with caution—having well in mind that there will already have been a VRR scheme review and that the decision not to prosecute is vested in the *prosecutor* not the Court, a matter of constitutional importance.[51]

Furthermore, if the VRRS reveals an error in reasoning (eg by taking irrelevant considerations into account), this is not sufficient to accept a complainant's argument for judicial review. The approach in *R(D)* signals again that prosecutorial decisions are within the monopoly of the state prosecutor—excluding any acknowledgment of citizen-victims as holding certain prosecutorial functions. This limitation is important and expansive as it highlights that prosecutorial errors are not determinative in judicial review. As seen in Chapter 4 and earlier in this chapter, certain cases illustrated that undue weight afforded on certain aspects of the evidence, along with perspectives relating to the public interest, could give rise to successful decisions to judicially review certain decisions. Moreover, as seen in previous chapter, victims as citizens have long held a role of prosecutors. However, the latest decisions following the VRRS seem to suggest that courts may only intervene as part of judicial review post-VRRS in instances of irrationality or unreasonableness rather than errors made by prosecutors.

50 *R(D) v DPP* [2017] EWHC 1768 (Admin).
51 ibid [25].

In practice, this translates to a new approach by courts to avoid close analysis of prosecutorial decision-making. In *R(D)*,[52] the Court explained that it was unwilling to engage in a close textual analysis of each of the numbered points in the prosecutor's review and instead would need to consider the review as a whole. Put otherwise, the Court stated that each point should not be considered in isolation as they form only part of the decision. This was also reaffirmed in *R (oao 'Monica')*, where it was stated that decision letters 'should be read in a broad and common sense way, without being subject to excessive or overly punctilious textual analysis'.[53] This approach is different from the one undertaken in judicial review decisions prior to the enactment of the VRRS (discussed in Chapter 4), where, for instance, the Court in *Manning*[54] undertook a more substantial and substantive analysis by examining each element of the prosecutor's decision to determine whether the prosecutor took irrelevant considerations into account.

Exceptions: A lower standard of judicial review for legally wrongful decisions under the VRRS

This section highlights the ways that issues that involve assessments of evidence and credibility can be understood as errors of law and give rise to successful judicial review by victims. As discussed in the previous chapter, this stems from a view that victims have long been understood as agents that can bring forward errors made as part of public decision-making, which is not the case as will be seen in the next chapter relating to the experience in the United States.

Indeed, in *Torpey*,[55] the Court reaffirmed its support for a very strict self-denying ordinance in instances of judicial review—highlighting that courts will rarely interfere in VRRS decisions, particularly when the review is careful, detailed, and thorough. Nevertheless, it made clear that this approach may not overlook errors of law. Identifying errors of law and maintaining an expansive view of what qualifies as such reveals a path to engage in a substantive assessment of the reviewing prosecutor's analysis. In this case, the claimant applied for judicial review of the CPS's VRRS decision not to prosecute a police officer for causing death by dangerous driving and/or causing death by careless

[52] ibid.
[53] *R (oao 'Monica') v DPP* [2018] EWHC 3508 (Admin) [46].
[54] *R v DPP Ex p Manning* [2001] QB 330, [2000] 3 WLR 463.
[55] *Torpey, R (On the application of) v DPP* [2019] EWHC 1804 (Admin).

driving. The police officer pursued an individual suspected of theft riding a moped and stayed very closely behind him. During the pursuit, the suspect hit the kerb and lost control, colliding with a traffic pole, which caused his death on the scene.

The Court considered the decision made by the reviewing prosecutor and made several findings. It ruled that the reviewing prosecutor did not undertake the necessary care, thoroughness, and detail in his analysis of the officer's driving prior to reaching any conclusions. Importantly, this was demonstrated by a lack of statements made by the prosecution to support its decision in the evidence. This is an important dimension of the review that warranted a substantive analysis of the evidentiary assessment. Moreover, the Court found that the law on the issue of causation had been misunderstood and misapplied. It decided that the prosecutor had discounted the officer's earlier driving and in doing so, interpreted the legal concept of causation too narrowly. To justify this lower standard of review, it ruled that the interpretation of the criminal law lies within the expertise of the Court and does not usurp any constitutional independence of the CPS. Specifically, the Court stated:

> [T]he issue being essentially one of law, the decision-maker's experience carries less force. In our judgment, the broad and unqualified proposition that none of the Officer's earlier driving had a bearing on the collision amounts to a misdirection of law and one that is susceptible to judicial review on conventional error of law grounds.[56]

In this sense, this form of assessment by the Court can be situated closer towards the substantive end of the spectrum, as the decision examines the way the CPS treated factual evidence—discarding the officer's earlier driving led to an error of law.

In *R(L)*,[57] a domestic worker, L, who had emigrated from the Philippines to the United Kingdom on the promise of domestic work with adequate pay and reasonable hours was instead forced to work excessive hours for very little pay, and with little option to do so. The employers deceived the employee by inducements and violated the terms that brought the worker to the United Kingdom by forcing her to work extremely long hours and paying significantly below what was convened. Moreover, she experienced mistreatment including having her passport taken, her movements restricted, and being

[56] ibid [52].
[57] *R(L) v DPP* [2020] EWHC 1815 (Admin).

denied medical care. Eventually, she escaped and sought help and was referred via the National Referral Mechanism for victims of trafficking by the specialist domestic worker charity Kalayaan, and the Home Office then identified her as a victim of trafficking.

While initially, the police refused to investigate, claiming the perpetrators had diplomatic immunity, it referred the case to the CPS for a charging decision. The CPS also refused to charge the employers of criminal exploitation as they considered that the immunity applied and therefore considered that there was no realistic prospect of a conviction. The decision not to prosecute L's former employer was challenged internally under the VRRS with a first rejection at the first local resolution stage, which confirmed the diplomatic immunity that eliminated any prospect of conviction. The claimant requested a second, independent review under the VRRS. Upon this stage of independent review, the prosecutor who reviewed the file accepted that the residual immunity enjoyed by the employer did not shield the employers from prosecution but concluded that there was no misconduct that amounted to slavery, servitude, forced labour, or compulsory labour under the Asylum and Immigration Act 2004, which relate to exploitation. It was therefore concluded that, although the earlier decision-makers had erred in relying in concluding that diplomatic immunity rendered a prosecution impossible in practice, such errors were not material because there was in any event insufficient evidence to provide a realistic prospect of securing a conviction against the employers. A letter with additional explanations on this point followed to ensure that adequate reasons were offered in conformity with the recent decision in *Torpey*. Among other elements, it noted that the fact that exploitation is narrowly defined and that the employers' facilitating the entry of the complaint to the United Kingdom was not done so with a view to her exploitation.

The claimant challenged this reviewing decision as part of a judicial review and argued that while there was no realistic prospect of a conviction of exploitation on the basis that the employer *intended* her exploitation, the prosecutor-reviewer had nevertheless *failed* to consider whether there was such a prospect of conviction on the basis of *deception* to induce her to provide services in the United Kingdom, which was an additional form of criminal exploitation under the law. In their response, the reviewer within the VRRS assumed that this possibility must have been considered by the CPS, who rendered the initial decision not to prosecute and referenced the case of *R(Monica)*, discussed above, to suggest that decision letters need to be read together as a whole, in a broad and common sense way. This argument was rejected by the Court which stated that although the letter referenced authorities on the adequacy of reasons in public law decision-making, it did not address the complainant's contention. Rather, at issue was the absence of evidence to suggest that the decision-maker had assessed the sufficiency of the available evidence to demonstrate the elements of the offence of exploitation that related to deception. In this sense, there was no indication in the decision letter that the decision-maker considered at all the relevant available evidence for this type of offence.

As in *Torpey*, the Court framed its intervention in light of a heightened level of deference to prosecutorial decision-making with exceptions regarding issues relating to errors of law. Specifically, in its concluding remarks, the Court reminded that 'courts should still be cautious about straying, even subconsciously, into the forbidden territory of assessing the merits of a public decision under challenge by way of judicial review'.[58] Nevertheless, it made clear that courts have a fundamental function of maintaining the rule of law. In this sense, 'proper decision making in a charging context requires the prosecutor to assess the available evidence against the elements of the potential offence'.[59] In this case, the decision was considered fundamentally flawed as it failed to consider evidence relating to deception, which was an important element of the offence of exploitation under the law—thus resulting in an error of law. Specifically, the Court was unable to determine whether the decision would have been substantively the same if the decision-maker's approach had been different and lawful. For these reasons, the application for judicial review was successful and the prosecutorial decision was quashed—requiring the DPP (who was representing the CPS in this case) to reconsider and remake the decision as to whether to charge the employer in light of the evidence.

Following this successful judicial review decision, the DPP reconsidered its initial decision and decided not to prosecute the employer. The claimant brought another successful judicial review case in *R(L)*,[60] where the Court concluded that the DPP had erred in law in its analysis of the power dynamics between employer–employee and whether the employer was expected to safeguard, or not to act against, the financial interests of another person and abused that position, dishonestly, intending by that abuse to make a gain or cause a loss. Interestingly, the Court also found that the DPP's assessment of the credibility of the claimant's account was so flawed and riddled with errors and misconceptions that it was incapable of withstanding scrutiny and was therefore unlawful. It concluded that this case was 'one of the very limited

[58] Initially stated in *R (Plan B Earth) v Secretary of State for Transport* [2020] EWCA Civ 214 [273]; *R(L)* (n 58) [39].
[59] *R(L)* (n 58) [40].
[60] *R(L) v DPP* [2022] EWHC 601.

number of cases where there is a clear-cut basis for concluding the defendant erred in law'.[61] Interestingly, the assessment of credibility is closer to the analysis seen in judicial reviews prior to the VRRS, which remains to some extent still relevant in some cases where the Court has found legal errors.

In brief, the case law relating to judicial review following the VRRS suggests that despite a heightened standard of review in instances of decisions not to prosecute, there are still ways to substantially challenge decisions made by state prosecutors, when factual evidence that apply to legal frameworks and dimensions of victim credibility are considered to have been lacking or interpreted erroneously.

4. Conclusion

As seen in this chapter as well as Chapter 4, earlier developments of victims as agents of state accountability were understood within a conception of victims that hold primarily public interests. In turn, victims held greater legitimacy to make substantive claims and assess the evidence and discuss the public interest in prosecutorial decisions. However, the rise of the professionalized state prosecution and an increasing narrative supporting its monopoly over the public interest have displaced and to some extent limited the victim's public role in prosecutions. Ultimately, the VRRS has both relied upon and reproduced an approach that locates victims' interests towards the private end of the spectrum. As discussed, this has had an important impact on its internal review process of prosecutorial decision-making and mitigated opportunities for state accountability.

Fundamentally, this predominantly private narrative of interests held by victims has limited their legitimacy in bringing forward substantive claims about prosecutorial errors and the public interest within public prosecutorial decisions. In this sense, the more victims' interests are seen as closer to the private end of the spectrum, the less legitimate their voices become within a public process. This conceptual shift has also contributed to an approach that limits the historical public role of victims as citizens within a unitary conception of the public interest meant to hold the state accountable in instances of failures.

[61] ibid [62].

It is worth highlighting that victims still retain a form of legitimacy, even when conceived as predominantly private within an aggregate form of participation. However, as private entities, their claims regarding the public interest do not have as much legitimacy as state actors.

Finally, the increasing shift towards a privatized conception of victim interests within the VRRS has also had some repercussions on the ways judicial review of prosecutorial decisions has evolved in England and Wales. Indeed, it reinforced the quasi-monopoly of state prosecutors on decisions not to prosecute and in relation to the public interest by giving rise to a more stringent standard of review. Nevertheless, despite this evolution and contrary to the context in the United States, substantive possibilities for review continue to be available with a lower standard of review for matters that are understood as errors of law.

The next chapter analyses the ways that the role of victims as agents of state accountability have been understood in the United States. As will be seen, victims are conceived of as holding possessive individualized rights. This framework characterizes victims as holding predominantly private interests in the public criminal law process. This is a notably different conception from England and Wales. In practice, this form of accountability has given rise to important limitations in terms of how victims may work to advance state accountability in instances of prosecutorial errors or decisions that impede the public interest.

6
The Abandonment and Evolving Legacies of the English Common Law in the United States

1. Introduction

The evolution of the role of victims as agents of state accountability in the United States has and continues to differ from that in England and Wales. Within the English common law approach, the recognition of victims as citizens and potential holders of public interests evolved early on to develop a substantive role for state accountability in matters of prosecutions. On the contrary, the approach in the United States has parted quite rapidly and nearly completely from many of the English common law public conceptions of victim interests and practices relating to prosecutions. While some vestiges of the common law remain in some states, they have also been permeated by an increasingly privatizing approach, which sees citizen-victims as holders of private interests. Specifically, this American approach recognizes victims as agents of state accountability in ways that mainly consider them as bearers of predominantly private interests—either within an aggregate or completely private relationship with the public interest. This in turn translates in them having much less legitimacy in holding the prosecutorial state substantively accountable in decisions about whether to prosecute.

2. Towards the Abandonment and Replacement of Private Prosecutions as Holders of Public Interests

Contrary to the context in England and Wales, where citizen participation as private prosecutions was thriving well into the nineteenth century, the United States was sooner to progressively abandon the English common law tradition of private prosecutions. While private prosecutions were widespread in

Victims as Agents of State Accountability. Marie Manikis, Oxford University Press. © Marie Manikis 2026.
DOI: 10.1093/9780191993947.003.0008

the United States in the seventeenth and part of the eighteenth centuries, the United States began replacing the system of private prosecutions with professionalized state agencies before its English counterpart.

In 1704, Connecticut was the first jurisdiction to completely abandon private prosecutions and adopt a professionalized state prosecution process, shortly followed by other colonies.[1] Indeed, some historians have stated that as early as the eighteenth century, prompted by the American Revolution, the state prosecutor had exclusive control over prosecutions instead of any shared responsibility with the victim.[2] Meanwhile, others suggest that even after the American Revolution, citizen-victims typically continued to prosecute cases themselves.[3] As highlighted by Steinberg, within the context of Philadelphia, the public (state) prosecutor adopted a stance of passive neutrality in most cases—one that simply let the private prosecutor and his witnesses take the stand and state their case.[4] Some states went so far as to outlaw the practice of private prosecutions in the nineteenth century.[5] In these jurisdictions, state prosecutors were entrusted with a monopoly over prosecutions that relegated the victim's former participatory role of 'control' over to public prosecutors.

This distinction between states that have kept private prosecutorial remnants and those that have completely abandoned them remains present in modern times. The remnants, discussed below, differ from English common law private prosecutions and include the potential for complaining witnesses, who are the victims of a crime, to enforce the criminal law in minor offences in instances where the state lacks the resources to do so, as well as by enabling forms of citizen access to grand juries. Others, however, have abandoned these vestiges of private prosecutions.

[1] England never tried to make the judicial system in the colonies uniform, and given the isolation of the colonies, colonial courts were left to evolve without much thought and consideration. This gave rise to several experiments with prosecution that flourished through the 1600s, many of which retained some element of private prosecution.

[2] John L Worrall, 'Prosecution in America: A Historical and Comparative Account' in John L Worrall and M Elaine Nugent-Borakove (eds), *The Changing Role of the American Prosecutor* (State University of New York Press 2008) 5–6.

[3] Barth's scholarship suggests that while some historians believed that private prosecution had disappeared at the time of the Constitution's ratification, his works suggests that early America in some respects used a hybrid system of criminal through at least in the middle of the nineteenth century. See Jonathan Barth, 'Criminal Prosecution in American History: Private or Public' (2002) 67 S D L Rev 119, 119.

[4] Allen Steinberg, *The Transformation of Criminal Justice: Philadelphia 1800–1890* (University of North Carolina Press 1989) 56–78.

[5] John Bessler, 'The Public Interest and the Unconstitutionality of Private Prosecutors' (1994) 47 Ark L Rev 511, 518–519, in which the Massachusetts Supreme Court in 1849 suggested that a privately retained prosecutor would void a criminal conviction. Michigan prohibited private prosecutions in 1875.

This parting with the English private prosecutorial tradition involved a reconceptualization of private and state actors' potential in holding public interests. In England and Wales, private prosecutions enjoyed a prevalent perception that they can directly advance the public interest and hold an accountability role as constitutional safeguards against the tyranny and rise of the executive. In contrast, the American approach reflects in part a rejection of a decentralized approach in the hands of locals,[6] who are seen as pursuing criminal charges for personal gain or private interests. In turn, the belief followed that public state prosecutors would act in the public interest and thus curb abuses, such as malicious proceedings. Moreover, the abandonment of private prosecutions was seen as a democratic innovation against the class inequalities of accessing private prosecution.[7] Indeed, some critics in the United States affirmed 'the elimination of the last vestiges of the pernicious practice of private prosecutions by persons who owe no allegiance to society as a whole'.[8] Similarly, scholarly commentary in the United States has expressed an alternative constitutional approach than in England, suggesting that

> because of the common community interest in ensuring that prosecutors treat members of the public fairly, the 'public interest' demands that the use of private prosecutors, who by definition consider private interests, be prohibited under the due process guarantee.[9]

This view conceives of citizens who would be acting as prosecutors as antithetic to the public interest and the public (state) prosecutor as having the monopoly over the public interest.

The perceived incompatibility between private prosecutor and public interest is reinforced by the more recent and predominant American jurisprudence on standing, as a private citizen lacks a judicially cognizable interest in the prosecution or non-prosecution of another. Barriers of standing are rooted in part on the assumption that citizens hold private interests in the United States and that there is no direct nexus between the vindication of their personal interests and the enforcement of the State's criminal laws by the prosecution.[10]

[6] Worrall (n 2) 5–6.
[7] Douglas Hay and Francis Snyder (eds), *Policing and Prosecution in Britain 1750–1850* (Clarendon Press 1989).
[8] *State v Unnamed Defendant*, 441 NW 2d 696 (Wis 1989).
[9] Bessler (n 5) 561–62.
[10] *Linda RS v Richard D*, 410 US 614 (1973).

Part of this reasoning is rooted in the notion that since *crime* is considered a public wrong, a state prosecutor must control its action, rather than the victim, who is considered a private entity with personal interests. This distinction contributed to the evolution of the victim's participative role from 'control' to 'informant', as was described in a 1921 Connecticut court decision:

> The victim of the offense is not a party to the prosecution, nor does he occupy any relation to it other than that of a witness, an interested witness mayhaps, but none the less, only a witness . . . It is not necessary for the injured party to make complaint nor is he required to give bond to prosecute. He is in no sense a relator. He cannot in any way control the prosecution and whether reluctant or not, he can be compelled like any other witness to appear and testify.[11]

In this sense, victims became viewed as entities with predominantly private interests that can, at most, be of use to the state prosecutor who is the sole direct representative and interpreter of public crime and the public interest in prosecutorial matters. The victim's main role was perceived as being a source of information and evidentiary fodder when and if needed by the state prosecutor.[12]

This view is substantially different to the historical role of citizen-victims in common law England described in earlier chapters, and in America at the time of the Founding. As Kaufman highlights in the context of private prosecutions in the United States, criminal law adopted a more

> capacious and in some ways much more radical notion of standing than one that simply allows victims to prosecute crimes. In the heyday of private prosecution, anyone could lay claim to criminal law, on the theory that 'all are interested in the preservation of public order'.[13]

Indeed, historically private prosecutions were brought in the name of the sovereign, not in the name of the individual citizen, which is still the case in England. As highlighted by a dissenting court in New Jersey, 'prosecutions, though brought by a private party, were commonly understood as an exercise of sovereign power—the private party acting on behalf on the sovereign,

[11] *Mallery v Lane*, 97 Conn 133 (1921) 138.
[12] Worrall (n 2) 5–6; *Mallery v Lane* (n 11) 138.
[13] *Stewart v Sonneborn*, 98 US 187, 198 (1878); Emma Kaufman, 'The Past and Persistence of Private Prosecution' (2024) 173(1) U Pa L Rev 89, 93.

seeking to vindicate a public wrong'.[14] In this sense, it was understood that 'the privately retained attorney becomes, in effect, a temporary public prosecutor'.[15] This highlights the historical potential of citizen-victims to bring forward public interest dimensions and challenges the state's monopoly on the public interest.

As will be seen, some of these remnants—including those that allow for citizens' direct access to the grand jury—retain some public interest dimensions of private prosecutions, notably the potential for citizen standing to launch them, rather than being confined to direct victims of crime. Nevertheless, these remnants conceive victim interests closer to the private end of Grear's spectrum than common law private prosecutions but more to the private end of most remnants and the more recent mechanisms of accountability recognized in the United States (discussed in the next chapter). Specifically, it will be seen that these remnants conceive of victims as holders of predominantly private interests but within an aggregate conception that can allow them to contribute indirectly to the public interest.

This increasingly private conception of interests in most states and within the federal context was recently affirmed in *Kinder*,[16] where a district court highlighted that the US Constitution's due process limitations, coupled with federal laws, would preclude the possibility for citizens to have a *private attorney* in matters of prosecutions, putting important limits to the question of possible direct private prosecutions. In this sense, in the United States, without recognizing citizen-victims as prosecutors with the potential to bring forward public interests, they are unable to realize an accountability role as a constitutional safeguard against state fallibilities. Specifically, in the United States, private prosecutors—including when represented by attorneys—are seen in conflict of interest as they are considered to have private duties towards their client thus conflicting with public prosecutors, who are seen as appointed to pursue the public interest, which includes elements of due process for the accused. The Court in *Vuitton* noted this conflicting ethical tension when a private litigator, who had 'an interest in obtaining the benefits of the court's order',

[14] *Robertson v United States ex rel Watson*, 560 US 272 (2010). See also Patrick Devlin, *The Criminal Prosecution in England* (Yale UP 1958) 21.

[15] Andrew Sidman, 'The Outmoded Concept of Private Prosecution' (1976) 25 Am U L Rev 754, 774.

[16] See comment by the court in *State of New Jersey v Kinder* 701 F Supp 486 (DNJ 1988); *Cronan v Cronan*, 744 A 2d 866 (RI 2001). This rests on the US Constitution as well as limits by the federal courts' supervisory power and federal statutes and rules. Moreover, *Young v United States ex rel Vuitton et Fils SA*, 481 US 787, 802 (1987) holds that prosecution is reserved in federal cases for government prosecutors, though federal prosecutors may appoint private attorneys to prosecute cases.

acted as the criminal prosecutor, who is supposed to be 'appointed solely to pursue the public interest in vindication of the court's authority'.[17]

This duty held by the public prosecutor to be detached from a sense of advancing its private interests is captured by a decision in the District of Columbia, which states that

> a public prosecutor, as the representative of the sovereign, must seek justice to protect the innocent as well as to convict the guilty... Our system of justice accords the prosecutor wide discretion in choosing which cases should be prosecuted and which should not. If the prosecutor's personal interest as the defendant in a civil case will be furthered by successful criminal prosecution, the criminal defendant may be denied the impartial objective exercise of that discretion to which he is entitled.[18]

Even in states that have preserved some dimensions of private prosecutions by enabling citizen-victims to hire lawyers in the pursuit of prosecutions, these channels are procedurally constrained based on state prosecutorial monopoly over the public interest. Indeed, in many of these jurisdictions, these processes are only available in particular circumstances. For instance, the state prosecutor must consent to stand aside.[19] Alternatively, private prosecutions may be approved where the prosecutorial state does not have resources to bring an action forward, or for minor offences, such as disorderly person charges, that are not felonies nor misdemeanours and do not result in a criminal record.[20] Isolated to these particular circumstances, the possibility for citizen-victims to hold the prosecutorial state accountable in instances of state failures to represent the public interest is severely limited.

For instance, in New Jersey, a court rule allows any attorney to appear on behalf of any complaining witness to prosecute disorderly persons offences for and on behalf of the state or the municipality. This rule exceptionally recognizes a limited public interest potential pursued by citizen-victims in contexts where the state does not have resources to prosecute, highlighting that

[17] *Young* (n 16).

[18] *United States v Heldt*, 668 F 2d 1238 (DC Cir 1981) 1277.

[19] For instance, Virginia recognizes a common law right of a crime victim to assist in the prosecution by retaining private counsel but the 'public prosecutor must remain in continuous control of the case'. See *Cantrell v Com*, 329 SE 2d 22 (Va 1985) at 28; *State of New Jersey v Kinder* (n 16).

[20] *State of New Jersey v Kinder* (n 16); *People v Wyner*, 207 Misc 673, 142 NYS 2d 393 (County Court, Westchester County, 1955) in which one lower New York court noted that 'the right of the complainant to prosecute the case by himself or hire an attorney to assist him has never been doubted'.

> absent its use, disorderly persons offenses would go unprosecuted, harming not only the state's interest in enforcing its laws, but also the victim's (if not society's) interest in obtaining satisfaction for wrongs committed.[21]

Despite identifying the potential for citizen-victims to represent public interests, the New Jersey Superior Court has limited this possibility to petty offences (quasi-civil offences). This is justified on the basis that the decision to allow for private parties to be represented is discretionary 'and should be based on the seriousness of the case and whether the municipal prosecutor consents to stand aside'.[22] This highlights the hesitation of having citizen-victims recognized as holders of public interests.

In turn, private prosecutions cannot be pursued in instances where the state prosecutor has declined to seek charges nor in cases that involve felonies or misdemeanours that can result in criminal records, a lengthy jail term, and a loss of certain privileges of citizenship.[23] This view holds certain contradictions. On the one hand, it recognizes that, in instances of petty offences, where prosecutors do not have resources to prosecute, citizen-victims can make decisions in the public interest to fill the prosecutorial void. However, citizen-victims cannot act on this void in situations of more serious offences—including state failures—since they are assumed to inherently represent private interests, which are seen as necessarily in conflict with the public interest. As will be seen in Chapter 8, this view can be challenged on a normative basis, particularly in instances where citizen-victims are filling a failure left by the prosecutorial state.

3. Citizen Access to a Grand Jury: The Potential and Limits for State Accountability Based on a Conception of Predominantly Aggregate Private Interests

Despite a tendency to move away from the English common law tradition of private prosecutions in the United States, this section examines some remnants of private prosecutions by way of citizen access to a grand jury as a means for state accountability. This mechanism is referred by the American literature in various ways including as a 'vestige private prosecution',[24] a 'semi-private

[21] *State of New Jersey v Kinder* (n 16) at 488.
[22] *State v Harris*, 620 A 2d 1083 NJ S Ct (1992) at 1088.
[23] *State of New Jersey v Kinder* (n 16).
[24] Caroline Ferguson, 'Actualizing Justice: Private Prosecution Regimes for Modern Social Movements' (2023) 54(4) Colum J L & Soc Probs 578.

prosecution system', and an 'anemic form of "private prosecution"'.[25] Indeed, it holds associations to the common law context of private prosecutions in which 'in an early day in England private parties prosecuted criminal wrongs which they suffered. They obtained an indictment from a grand jury, and it became the duty and the privilege of the person injured to provide a prosecutor at his own expense to prosecute the indicted person.'[26] This quote needs to be complemented by the notion that in English common law not only those who directly suffered from the offence could prosecute but also any citizen, since the wrong was considered public and thus everyone in the public was considered to have suffered.

As will be seen in this section, access to the grand jury is understood as serving a dual role: to initiate actions within the criminal legal process in instances of state prosecutorial failure, while screening out incompetent or malicious prosecutions that seek to advance private interests. Nevertheless, direct citizen access to the grand jury is rare and seldomly seen as facilitating state accountability. In parallel with discourses around private prosecution, many American jurisdictions limit the role of the grand jury on the basis that citizen-victims are generally considered holders of private interests, associated with malicious prosecutions.

The grand jury's evolution can be traced back to the Middle Ages and has taken various shapes in its modern days in the United States. In an earlier iteration, during the reign of Henry II, the accusing jury served both a protective and an investigative function within the judicial mechanism. In this sense it was understood that

> laymen ought not to be put to answer in those courts upon a mere unsworn suggestion of ill fame. Either someone should stand forth and commit himself to a definite accusation, or else the ill fame should be sworn to by twelve lawful men of the neighborhood summoned for that purpose by the sheriff: in other words, the ecclesiastical judge ought not proceed ex officio upon private suggestions.[27]

By the time of the Assize of Clarendon in 1166, the accusing jury had become a prominent institution in England. In every county, twelve men out of every hundred were called to appear before the itinerant judge appointed

[25] ibid.

[26] *State v Peterson*, 218 NW 367 (Wis 1928).

[27] Frederick Pollock and Frederic W Maitland, *History of English Law* (2nd edn, CUP 1968) 151.

by the king, who presented a list of crimes and offences and asked the jurors whether they knew of anyone who in the hundred who had committed to offences enumerated. The jurors relied on their personal knowledge and based on their replies, the judge decided whether the accusations were well-founded.

The fifteenth century saw the grand jury well-established in the English judicial system and, subsequently, in the American colonies of the United States. During the American Revolution, the grand jury was seen as an important institution that enabled independence and resistance to the imperial government. It served to balance state prosecutorial power by determining whether there was probable cause to believe a crime had been committed and protecting citizens against unfounded criminal accusation by either private or public prosecutors. The American founding fathers affirmed this view by referring to the grand jury as both the 'true tribunal of the people' and the 'sacred palladium of liberty'.[28] At a time of colonial resistance to the British monarchy, the widely publicized English case of *Earl of Shaftsbury* 'enhanced immensely the prestige of the grand jury in America' (*State ex rel Miller v Smith* 285 SE 500 (W Va 1981) 503). This case involved Lord Ashley, Earl of Shaftsbury, charged with high treason by the royal prosecutor for taking part in a plot to assassinate the king and '[bring] this kingdom of England to a commonwealth without a king'.[29] The royal prosecutor presented the case to a grand jury in London, who refused to indict and set Lord Ashley free, sending a strong message against absolute monarchical power. The case was subsequently cited for years in the United States, as illustrative of the grand jury's protective power against both the despotism of the Crown and prosecution based on 'partisan passion or private enmity'.[30] Despite this protective role, over the years in England, the grand jury was instrumentalized for monarchical power, which, in part, contributed to its abolition in England.

In modern days, the grand jury in the United States comprises between sixteen and twenty-three citizens, and is a process protected by the Bill of Rights.[31] As in earlier iterations, the American grand jury examines whether there is sufficient evidence of a crime and determines whether an indictment should be returned, as a formal accusation of a crime. At the federal level, felonies, rather that misdemeanours, must have a grand jury indictment. In contrast, only

[28] Saul Padover, *The Complete Jefferson* (Tudor Publishing Company 1943) 128; Richard D Younger, *The People's Panel: The Grand Jury in the United States (1631–1941)* (Brown UP 1963) 41.

[29] *Earl of Shaftsbsury's Case*, 8 st Tr 759, 778 (1681).

[30] *In re Russo*, 53 FRD 564, 568 (CD Calif 1971).

[31] US Constitution amend V reads: 'No person shall be held to answer for a capital, or otherwise infamous crime, unless on a presentment or indictment of a Grand Jury.'

around half of the states employ grand juries, with other states preferring to rely on preliminary hearings to determine whether to indict a defendant on non-federal charges. Additionally, the role of the grand jury varies across states relative to the differing standards of review of the evidence,[32] and degrees of citizen access.[33]

Depending on the state, the grand jury's role is figuratively referred to as a shield or a sword. As a shield, the institution serves 'to protect persons against unfounded or malicious prosecutions by ensuring that no criminal proceeding will be undertaken without a disinterested determination of probable guilt'.[34] Indeed, the grand jury remains a safeguard to the 'innocent against hasty, malicious and oppressive prosecution . . . standing between the accuser and the accused . . . to determine whether a charge is founded upon reason or was dictated by an intimidating power or by malice and personal ill will'.[35] According to this position, fallible prosecutions can come from both the state and from private citizens.

As a sword, its function is seen as a tool for prosecutors, and in some instances, citizens 'to bring to trial persons accused of crime upon just grounds'.[36] Several models of access to the grand jury exist across the United States—ranging from direct citizen access to access with prior court or state-prosecutorial approval. As will be seen, some of these models operate on wider standing that is not solely individualized and enables any citizen to start this process.

Commentators have criticized models that restrict direct citizen access to the grand jury, particularly those that allow this access only through state prosecutors. Critics note that if the grand jury is only available to the prosecuting attorney and the law requires citizens to pass through him, the grand jury can be seen as a 'prosecutorial tool'[37] and more specifically a tool controlled by the state. Insofar as it remains inaccessible to citizen-victims, the grand jury's role is limited from its potential as a tool for safeguarding and accountability in instances of state failures to prosecute, including those resulting from errors and biases in decision-making.

[32] For instance, in Colorado, the prosecution's decision will only be reviewed if it is arbitrary and capricious. Given the stringency of this standard and the broad discretion of prosecutor's, chances of review are very minimal. See *Sandoval v Farish*, 675 F 2d (Sup Ct Colo 1984).

[33] While some states allow citizen access without limitations, others require exhaustion of other remedies available to challenge the charging decision before the citizen may approach the grand jury. See National Crime Victim Institute, *Fifty States and D.C. Survey of Laws that Authorize or Recognize Private-Citizen Initiated Investigation and/or Prosecution of Criminal Offenses* (2015).

[34] *In re New Haven Grand Jury*, 604 F Supp 453 (D Conn 1985).

[35] ibid.

[36] Lester B Orfield, *The Federal Grand Jury*, 22 FRD 343, 394 (1958).

[37] *State ex rel Miller v Smith* 285 SE 500 (W Va 1981).

Loehmann, a relatively recent example from Ohio and one of the catalysts for the Black Lives Matter movement, illustrates this concern. This case shows the potential for citizen-victims to take the role as agents of state accountability, while also illustrating the limits of a process gatekept by a state prosecutor. In *Loehmann*, Tamir Rice, a twelve-year-old Black boy, was shot and killed by a white police officer. Rice's family took part in a process that allows citizens to initiate action by filing an affidavit under state law to an Ohio Municipal Court Judge.[38] This mechanism enables citizens within the community to initiate the criminal process in circumstances where prosecutors fail to do so.

In response to the affidavit, the judge ruled that there was probable cause to charge Loehmann with murder, involuntary manslaughter, reckless homicide, negligent homicide, and dereliction of duty. While the Rice family's affidavit was 'intended to jumpstart the process of prosecution'[39] and 'increase pressure' on the county prosecutor, the murder charge ultimately had to go through a grand jury, which could only be brought by state prosecutors as unique holders of the public interest. The fact that prosecutors decided to present evidence to a grand jury following the judge's findings suggests that the affidavit succeeded in exerting some pressure on the prosecutorial process. Nevertheless, opportunities for state accountability remain limited when state prosecutors who have initially failed to bring forward prosecutions—for potentially biased dimensions—remain the only ones who can bring the case to a grand jury as they are seen as the unique holders of the public interest. As will be seen below, in Nebraska, such failures by state prosecutors in contexts, where there is sufficient evidence to prosecute, can be considered a conflict of interest, which gives rise to the need to replace the state prosecutor by an alternative prosecutorial entity to pursue the case before the grand jury.

Commenting on unprosecuted police brutality, Peter Davis[40] suggests that allowing citizens' access to a grand jury without seeking approval from the state prosecutor would enable marginalized groups to 'ameliorate the problem of

[38] *In re: Affidavits Relating to Timothy Loehmann & Frank Garmback* (Cleveland Mun Ct June 11, 2015). A few other states currently allow private citizens to initiate criminal actions by filing affidavits or formal complaints, namely, Arizona, Idaho, Kentucky, Massachusetts, New Hampshire, Pennsylvania, Rhode Island, West Virginia, and Wisconsin. Some, however, limit this possibility for criminal offences that are on the lower end of the punitive spectrum.

[39] David A Graham, ' "Probable Cause" in the Killing of Tamir Rice" (*ATLANTIC*, 11 June 2015) <https://www.theatlantic.com/politics/archive/2015/06/tamir-rice-case-cleveland/395420/> accessed August 2023.

[40] Peter L Davis, 'Rodney King and the Decriminalization of Police Brutality in America: Direct and Judicial Access to the Grand Jury as Remedies for Victims of Police Brutality When the Prosecutor Declines to Prosecute' (1994) 53 Md L Rev 263.

the symbiotic relationship between police and public prosecutors',[41] which has shielded police criminality from prosecution. While this is true, the analysis of mechanisms that enable citizen-victim access to the grand jury suggests that this access would need to be accompanied by an understanding that the victim can hold public interests in order to directly engage as agents of state accountability. As will be seen, the failure to consider their potential for holding public interests relegates them in a position where they are seen as holders of private interest, at most in an aggregative way that can advance the public interest. A failure to recognize them as potential holders of public interests can impact their ability of achieving state accountability in matters of prosecutions.

Citizens' direct access to the grand jury as witnesses rather than prosecutors

While few states allow direct citizen access to the grand jury, this may be a potential first step in strengthening the role of citizen-victims as agents of state accountability. Even when citizen-victims are allowed this channel, their role is generally considered that of a witness with private interests that can nevertheless contribute—albeit in an aggregate way—to the public interest rather than in a direct way.

Alabama has institutionalized direct citizen access to the grand jury but makes it clear that this role is not the same as a that of a prosecutor. Case law highlights:

> Public policy demands that the citizen . . . may freely bring before the grand jury the fact that a crime has been committed, request an investigation, and furnish such information that he has in aid of the investigation. In this the citizen is not a prosecutor. It is not essential that he have probable cause to believe any individual to be the guilty party. He is merely performing a duty in aid of the tribunal set up to ascertain whether there is probable cause to believe a crime has been committed.[42]

The court goes on to clarify that throughout the grand jury hearing, the party bringing the matter must in good faith aid in the investigation and always believe that the person is actually guilty—otherwise they may be found guilty or

[41] ibid 356.

[42] *King v Second Nat'l Bank & Tr Co of Saginaw*, Mich 234 Ala 106 (1937) 108.

liable of malicious prosecution. As such, the citizen-victim's role presupposes their inability to directly engage with the public interest and substantively hold the state accountable in the event of prosecutorial failures to meet their duties.

This approach in Alabama contrasts significantly to the English approach, wherein citizen-victims are considered prosecutors, partly to ensure a 'constitutional safeguard against capricious, corrupt or biased failure or refusal of those authorities to prosecute offenders'.[43] For these reasons, in England and Wales, there is a strong sense that private prosecution must respect evidentiary standards that apply to state prosecutors, which is not the case in Alabama. Indeed, since citizen access to the grand jury in Alabama is seen foremost as a means to bring forward private interests, as part of an aggregative contribution to the public interest rather than a form of prosecution that directly is made the public interest, it need not abide with prosecutorial evidentiary standards. This view of citizen-victims as mere witnesses who are not required to follow prosecutorial standards relating to evidence in turn places important limits to this mechanism's potential to bring forward substantive arguments about failures to meet the evidentiary standard or elements of the public interest. Since citizen-victims are perceived as unable to meet the standards that lend prosecutors the legitimacy to prosecute in the public interest, this mitigates their role as agents of state accountability in instances of state prosecutorial failures.

Jurisdictions that have recognized direct citizen-victims' access to the grand jury as witnesses have also generally made clear that their role differs to that of privately funded attorneys, at times referred to as 'private prosecutors' within the American literature.[44] Since a privately retained attorney is 'neither a public prosecutor nor a witness',[45] they are forbidden to appear before the grand jury or direct the proceedings absent the permission of the state prosecutor and the court. This view depicts such 'private prosecutors' as holders of private interests, closer to Grear's end of the private spectrum, which differs from an aggregative contribution to the public interest, as well as their historical conception in England and Wales that for an important period. Rather, in England and Wales, these private attorneys were recognized as legitimate prosecutors and agents capable of bringing forward public interests in the prosecutorial process and hold the prosecutorial state accountable in instances of failures.

[43] *Gouriet v Union of Post Office Workers* [1978] AC 435, 498.

[44] This is recognized in several states, including New Mexico, Oklahoma, and Indiana. See discussion in Douglas E Beloof, Paul G Cassell, and Steven J Twist, *Victims in Criminal Procedure* (5th edn, Carolina Academic Press 2024) 212.

[45] ibid.

Citizen-victims empanelling and accessing grand juries with alternative prosecutors as means of holding the state accountable for failures in prosecution

Although it does not fulfil a private prosecutorial role within the meaning of the English context, as a constitutional safeguard towards state failures, some states have nonetheless recognized the potential for both direct and indirect citizen access to the grand jury as a mechanism to hold the prosecutorial state accountable in cases of state failure. As discussed in this section, while these mechanisms have important limitations in enabling citizen-victims to hold the state accountable, they offer wider citizen standing and have to some extent enabled marginalized groups of citizens to bring forward substantive claims about prosecutorial failures rooted in structural inequalities. Importantly, while these mechanisms do not conceive citizen-victims as holders of the public interest, their interests within this accountability role are nevertheless understood as predominantly private—yet in an aggregate way that can contribute to the public interest.

The role of victims as agents of state accountability in parts of the United States can be traced to a legacy of frontier justice. In this sense, these mechanisms have allowed citizens to access legal recourse when they think prosecutors are neglecting to bring charges for a crime. For instance, in Kansas, a law from 1887, which is still active, empowers citizens to gather a certain number of signatures and summon a grand jury to obtain an indictment when they think prosecutors are wrongfully neglecting to bring criminal charges.[46] This law was originally intended to aid citizens frustrated with prosecutors who refused to enforce temperance laws and was most often used to go after saloonkeepers when authorities ignored violations of statewide prohibition.

While largely dormant in modern days, this vestige of private prosecutions was recently exercised by Madison Smith, whose sexual assault case was not taken seriously or considered credible by state prosecutors. In this case, Smith engaged at first in a consensual sexual encounter with a friend, Stolzenburg, who almost immediately began being violent with her while she made the claim that she actively tried to resist.

[46] Peter Kendall, 'A Prosecutor Says No to a Rape Charge, So a College Student Calls Her Own Grand Jury' (*Washington Post*, 19 May 2021) <https://www.washingtonpost.com/national/a-prosecutor-says-no-to-a-rape-charge-so-a-college-student-calls-her-own-grand-jury/2021/05/18/2ea9a130-b766-11eb-a5fe-bb49dc89a248_story.html?utm_campaign=wp_post_most&utm_medium=email&utm_source=newsletter&wpisrc=nl_most&carta-url=https%3A%2F%2Fs2.washingtonpost.com%2Fcar-ln-tr%2F32720c3%2F60a53af19d2fdae302566fd1%2F5ca3e3379bbc0f613a96dff4%2F32%2F68%2F60a53af19d2fdae302566fd1> accessed August 2023.

The day after the assault, Smith told her parents she was raped, reported the crime to the police, and went to a nearby hospital for a forensic exam. The forensic report noted the bruising and abrasion on her neck, as well as bruising inside her mouth. Despite Smith's active cooperation with a local prosecutor, the District Attorney's office declined to file rape charges. The District Attorney justified this decision by suggesting that, since sex had begun consensually, Stolzenburg may not have known that Smith had withdrawn consent. Specifically, the District Attorney stated that 'there isn't anything that any of us felt adequately communicated to him that withdrawal of consent . . . when we have that failure in that communication, then everything from a legal analysis, everything remains consensual'.[47]

Subsequently, Julie Germann, a former Minnesota prosecutor specialized in sexual assault cases, conducted an informal review of the Kansas District Attorney's office's decision for the Smiths. Germann concluded that the attack qualified for a rape charge, since it seemed clear on the facts of the case that there was no ongoing consent. Indeed, Germann stated:

> I would contend that it is clear that if while strangling someone, they are pulling on your hands and grasping for breath, and they are crying, none of that sounds consensual to me . . . I would not have a hard time taking that case to a jury at all.[48]

After three years of prosecutorial inaction, Smith became the first citizen-victim to convene a grand jury for a sex-crime charge using Kansas' 1887 law. Although the grand jury ultimately did not deliver the charge that Smith sought, she expressed satisfaction that her efforts 'brought a lot of awareness to the fact that a lot of sexual assaults get pushed under the rug and ignored'.[49] In the meantime, the county attorney charged Stolzenburg with aggravated battery, which he pleaded guilty to and received two years' probation.

In Illinois, although the state does not allow citizens to directly access grand juries, citizens are able to petition the court to approve a process to start prosecutions in instances of prosecutorial state failures. Indeed, the Supreme Court of Illinois highlighted that although 'the proper channel for presenting

[47] ibid.
[48] ibid.
[49] Peter Kendall, 'A College Student Who Called Her Own Grand Jury Doesn't Get the Rape Charge She Sought for Her Attacker' (*Washington Post*, 3 November 2021) <https://www.washingtonpost.com/nation/2021/11/03/college-student-who-called-her-owngrand-jury-doesnt-get-rape-charge-she-sought-her-attacker/> accessed 11 February 2025.

information to the grand jury is the State's Attorney', the trial court maintains jurisdiction to direct a witness to appear before the grand jury in instances 'where the prosecutor has failed to take action and that failure "will effect a deprivation of due process or result in a miscarriage of justice"'.[50]

The case of *People v Sears* offers an example of such a situation, while also illustrating the challenges emanating from a failure to recognize direct citizen access to the grand jury. This case relates to the 1969 police raids in Chicago, which resulted in the death of Fred Hampton, a twenty-one-year-old Black man and a prominent Black Panther leader. Following the prosecutorial state's failure to empanel a grand jury, several individuals and organizations filed petitions as citizens requesting that the court assign a special prosecutor to investigate the raids. Substantive arguments were made in this petition, including references to critical and unresolved violations of criminal law by employees of both the State's Attorney's Office and the Chicago Police Department. The lower court accepted this request and assigned Barnabas Sears, a Chicago attorney, to act as a special prosecutor. Sears was to investigate the raids as the court held that 'the matters in the petitions are of sufficient importance to confer jurisdiction upon the Court to order a special venire to be issued for a grand jury and that public justice requires it'.[51]

This successful request by citizens highlights the important role of citizens in making claims that advance the public interest in instances when the state has failed its duties. Despite this success, there is still resistance in recognizing citizen-victims as private prosecutors with direct access to the grand jury. Indeed, in this case, Sears, as Special States Attorney appointed by the court, determined which evidence and arguments would be brought to the grand jury. Sears used his prosecutorial discretion to not call certain witnesses in this hearing and, similarly, to not investigate certain police officers and other individuals involved in the raid. The citizens who directed the initial petition for a grand jury tried to have the court hold Sears in contempt for his refusal to subpoena certain witnesses, but ultimately the Illinois Supreme Court found that the circumstances did not 'furnish a sufficient basis for the action of the court, and the order holding Sears in contempt for refusing to subpoena certain witnesses'.[52]

This case is important in defining the contours of the potential for citizen-victim engagement to bring state accountability in Illinois. On the one hand,

[50] *People v Sears*, 273 NE.2d 380 (1971) 389.
[51] ibid 381.
[52] ibid 386.

in initiating a petition, citizen-victims partially held the prosecutorial state accountable for it failing to empanel a grand jury based on potential discriminatory biases present in investigating police misconduct. Their engagement is seen as holders of predominantly private interests with an aggregative potential to contribute to the public interest. However, the case also illustrates that their role falls short due to the failure of recognizing them as entities who can directly engage, hold, and make claims about the public interest. This can be seen with the requirement of assigning a court-assigned prosecutor in lieu of recognizing citizen-victims as private prosecutors who can hold public interests and bring forward evidence in instances of state failures.

Similarly, the state of Nebraska, considered among 'the most robust state regimes'[53] in terms of citizens' ability to empanel a grand jury, illustrates the potential and limits of citizen-victims for holding the prosecutorial state accountable. This can be seen in *State v Chauncey*,[54] which recognized the limits of state monopoly over the public interest and the potential for citizens to partially hold the prosecutorial state accountable in instances of state prosecutorial failure in bringing forward a prosecution. Nevertheless, as discussed below, within this mechanism, citizen-victims are still considered holders of predominantly private interests in an aggregative way, which can halt direct engagement with the public interest.

In this case, a two-year-old child, Juliette, died from what a pathologist referred to as a death by homicide. After four years of state failures to file prosecutorial charges by empanelling a grand jury, community members exercised their right under state law to petition the district court to convene a grand jury. This gave rise to indictments against Dustin Chauncey, Juliette's mother's boyfriend. Chauncey did not challenge the empanelling of a grand jury by citizens but rather the fact that a special prosecutor was appointed by the court for the grand jury hearing rather than a state attorney. The Supreme Court of Nebraska disagreed with Chauncey's claim and highlighted that the district court 'found that a conflict of interest existed in this case because until the petition was filed in July 2012, the county attorney's office had declined to prosecute anyone for Juliette's death since its occurrence in July 2008'.[55] In the context of this state failure, the Supreme Court affirmed the district court's finding that the appointment of a special prosecutor was appropriate.

[53] Ferguson (n 24) 586.
[54] *State v Chauncey*, 890 NW 2d 453 (Neb 2017).
[55] ibid 459.

As experts have underscored, this decision recognizes prosecutions outside the state prosecuting authority's control.[56] To justify this, the judge interpreted the state failure to prosecute as creating a conflict of interest that renders the state prosecutor unfit to try the case. As such, *Chauncey* is particularly interesting as it recognizes that the state prosecution can be in a conflict of interest by serving its *own* interests, viewed as distinct from the 'public interest'. Citizens in this regard are seen as having the legitimacy to identify such state failures to the court and request for alternative prosecutors, who can represent the public interest. Nevertheless, citizens themselves stop short of having the legitimacy to be seen as direct holders of public interests sufficient to be considered alternative prosecutors in such cases.

The federal jurisdiction's rejection of vestiges of private prosecutions as part of the state's monopoly over the public interest

Contrary to relatively rare contexts in the United States that have recognized vestiges to private prosecutions and citizen access to grand juries, most states and most notably the federal jurisdiction are even more restrictive of citizen access to the grand jury and have recognized the power of state prosecutors to veto decisions made by grand juries. Indeed, federal laws do not allow direct access to a grand jury absent a request to do so from the grand jury, prosecutorial or judicial approval.[57] Furthermore, under federal law, the federal prosecutor can veto a grand jury's indictments, which may substantially remove any form of accountability brought on by citizens in instances of federal prosecutorial failures.[58]

The limits placed on citizen access to the grand jury in the federal context stem from the assumption that citizens can be corrupt and may make decisions guided by their private and personal interests. In contrast, state prosecutors are seen as rational agents that serve the public interest. Indeed, this distinction was articulated in *In re New Haven Grand Jury*,[59] which argues that direct citizen access 'would compromise, if not utterly subvert, both the historic

[56] Sara Sun Beal and others, *Grand Jury Law and Practice § 4:2, 2nd edn., & Annual Supplements 1998–2021* (Thomson Reuters 1997); Ferguson (n 24) 585.

[57] Douglas E Beloof, Paul G Cassell, and Steven J Twist, *Victims in Criminal Procedure* (4th edn, Carolina Academic Press 2018) 213.

[58] *United States v Cox*, 231 F 2d 167 (DC Miss 1965).

[59] *In re New Haven Grand Jury* (n 34).

functions of the grand jury, for it would facilitate the pursuit of vendettas and the "gratification of private malice"'.[60] In the same vein, it highlighted that 'the protection of society at large, as well as the preservation of the grand jury as an instrument of justice, requires that the court place limits on direct and unsupervised communications with the grand jury by disgruntled individuals who may have personal axes to grind'.[61] This view is often referenced to reaffirm the prosecutorial state's monopoly—highlighting that the commencement of a federal criminal case by submission of evidence to a grand jury is 'an executive function within the exclusive prerogative of the Attorney General'.[62] This argument is supported by case law highlighting that private citizens in American jurisprudence lack a judicially cognizable interest in the prosecution or non-prosecution of another.[63] Finally, *New Haven* depicts citizen-victims' disagreement with state prosecutorial decisions as irrational suggesting that 'if a complainant is frustrated by a prosecutor's decision not to prosecute, it does not follow that the complainant should have unsupervised recourse to the grand jury'.[64] This position sees victims as a private actor, motivated by irrational vengeance, as opposed to state prosecutors. This reference to the citizen-victim's emotionality is often used to place important limits to citizen-run accountability mechanisms within the federal context.

Overall, the cases presented in this section illustrate the partial role that citizen-victims in the United States have taken in holding the prosecutorial state accountable in certain decision-making choices relating to prosecutions. While considered a vestige of the English common law system of private prosecutions, the American experience has largely removed possibilities for citizen-victims to be considered alternative prosecutors to the state, even in instances of prosecutorial state failures. This is largely due to a conception that victims, particularly in matters of charging decisions, are considered holders of private rather than public, which limits their legitimacy in going forward with prosecutions.

[60] Charge to Grand Jury, supra 30 F Cas At 994-995.

[61] *In re New Haven Grand Jury* (n 34).

[62] *In re Persico*, 522 F 2d 41, 54–55 (2d Cir 1975) cited in *In re New Haven Grand Jury* (n 34).

[63] *In re New Haven Grand Jury* (n 34); *Leeke v Timmerman*, 454 US 83, 85–86, 102 S Ct 69, 70, 70 L Ed 2d 65 (1981), quoting *Linda RS v Richard D*, 410 US 614, 619, 93 S Ct 1146, 1149, 35 L Ed 2d 536 (1973).

[64] *In re New Haven Grand Jury* (n 34).

4. Judicial Review as an Exceptional Mechanism for State Prosecutorial Accountability and Its Limitations

Another mechanism available in very few states that has, to some extent, enabled citizen-victims to hold the prosecutorial state accountable is the possibility of judicially reviewing prosecutorial decisions. Specifically, some states have enacted statutes that allow citizen-victims to seek judicial review of the prosecutor's decision not to prosecute.

Pennsylvania is a notable example that has gone further than most American jurisdictions in allowing for the review of a prosecutor's decision not to charge. Pennsylvania's substantive approach to state accountability is, to some extent, closer to that of England and Wales as it enables citizen-victims to hold the prosecutorial state accountable for errors in assessing the evidentiary standard in a decision not to prosecute. This approach was decided in *Commonwealth v Benz*,[65] an appeal in which the mother of Paaron Jones, an individual who was killed by police, sought review of the District Attorney's decision not to prosecute. While this decision provided a basis for citizen-victims to seek judicial review in instances of prosecutorial errors relating to assessment of evidence, the decision also shielded from judicial review prosecutorial decisions that relied on policy related reasons.

In this case, both Jones and Officer Benz, who was not in uniform at the time, were at a hospital as visitors. Jones was on crutches with a broken leg in a cast and smelled of alcohol. While in the elevator, the two men got into an argument and an altercation ensued in which Jones struck Benz across the back with a crutch. Benz pulled out his badge and firearm and identified himself as a police officer. Jones attempted to flee through the front exit and Benz pursued him with his firearm drawn, stating that he was under arrest, and he should lie face down on the floor. As the two fought, Benz's exposed gun discharged, and a bullet struck Jones to the head. Jones survived but remained in a vegetative state for four years—eventually dying from the gunshot wound. Following Jones' death, the coroner conducted an open inquest and recommended that Benz be charged with voluntary manslaughter. Despite this recommendation, the District Attorney did not file charges. The District Attorney assessed that the eyewitness testimony was disjointed as to make it inconclusive, and highlighted medical evidence of possible powder burns on the victim's head and scientific evidence concerning the retention of the shell of the bullet in the chamber of the gun. This medical and scientific evidence

[65] *Commonwealth v Benz*, 565 A 2d 764 (Pa 1989).

seemed to indicate that the victim was in close proximity to Benz when the gun discharged, supporting Benz's claims that the two men were wrestling over the weapon and that the shot was fired accidently. A review was brought forward by the Attorney General, who found no abuse of prosecutorial discretion and determined that fair investigation had been concluded.

Following this review, Laverda Hicks, the mother of the victim, sought approval of a private criminal complaint to the District Attorney. The District Attorney rejected the request, reiterating that insufficient evidence existed to establish that a crime had been committed. Hicks then sought to obtain judicial review of the matter. While the Court of Common Pleas accepted the petition, they denied approval after a review of the record, holding that the District Attorney did not abuse his discretion. Hicks appealed to the Superior Court for a review of the final order of the Court of Common Pleas pursuant to the existing rules, specifically Rule 133, which 'gives a victim-complainant the right to seek approval from the Court of Common Pleas of a private criminal complaint which has been disapproved by the district attorney'.[66] At this stage, the Superior Court reversed the lower court's decision and determined that evidence was available to establish a *prima facie* criminal case.

The majority of the Superior Court highlighted that judicial reviews and subsequent appeals are possible in instances, like this one, wherein the prosecutor (and the subsequent trial judge) has made errors in their application of the evidentiary standard relating to decisions about whether to press charges. This portion of the judgment is significant as it enables substantive forms of accountability to weave into the assessment of evidence in instances of potential state failures, which may include issues relating to credibility or systemic biases.

Nevertheless, the majority of the Court's holding isolated judicial review to decisions wherein the prosecutor concluded that no crime had been committed. Had the state prosecutor stated policy reasons to support the decision not to prosecute, the Court would have needed to show deference towards such a discretionary use of the executive powers conferred to the prosecution, as a matter of the separation of powers doctrine. In this sense, the Court reminded that, traditionally, the final determination of sufficiency of evidence was a judicial judgment. However, even in instances of sufficient evidence, prosecutors can exercise their prosecutorial discretion not to prosecute for different reasons.

[66] Pa R Crim P 133(B). The term 'victim-complainant' is used in this section as per the court's description of citizen-victims.

The majority's decision was criticized for creating distinctions between elements of prosecutorial decision-making that are reviewable, namely, decisions that relate to the sufficiency of evidence, and matters of policy that are subject to prosecutorial deference as part of the separation of powers doctrine. Specifically, Brown criticized the court's deference to prosecutorial discretion in matters of policy as an unnecessarily restrictive view of the separation of powers doctrine in light of the tradition of broad judicial discretion, the courts' rule-making authority, and policy concerns regardless of public policy concerns.[67] She also pointed out that policy limits to the potential for judicial review ignores the fact that historically, prosecution was not intended as a core executive function.[68] Moreover, the court's approach was seen to severely limit state accountability as prosecutors can easily evade judicial review by articulating their charging decisions based only on policy.[69] As such, this approach can give rise to an alignment with the dominant approach to judicial review of prosecutorial decisions in the United States, which contends that citizen-victims, as holders of private interests, do not have the legitimacy to bring forward public interests as part of prosecutions.

The dissenting judge emphasized the private interests approach, arguing that once a trial judge has agreed with the state prosecutor's judgment, the private complainant cannot appeal the trial judge's decision. The dissent cited the case of *In re Wood*, which confirmed that victim-complainants under Rule 133 have a right to seek approval from the Court of Common Pleas of a private criminal complaint that has been disapproved by the District Attorney. However, the dissent insists that this rule of court does not make the victim-complainant a party to the action and describes the victim-complainant as a private entity who has no standing in criminal prosecutions, by citing *In re Wood*'s claim that

> criminal prosecutions are not to settle private grievances, but are to rectify the injury done to the Commonwealth. The individual who is the victim of a crime only has recourse to a civil action for damages.[70]

He then proceeds to cite the case of *Linda RS*, which states that

[67] Beth Brown, 'The Constitutional Validity of Pennsylvania Rule of Criminal Procedure 113 (b)(2) and the Traditional Role of the Pennsylvania Courts in the Prosecution Function' (1990) 52 U Pitt L Rev 269.
[68] Stephanie Dangel, 'Is Prosecution a Core Executive Function? Morrison v. Olsen and the Framers' Intent' (1990) 99 Yale LJ 1069.
[69] Brown (n 67).
[70] *In re Wood*, 333 Pa Superior Ct 597, 482 A 2d 1033 (1984).

> a citizen lacks standing to contest the policies of the prosecuting attorney when he himself is neither prosecuted nor threatened with prosecution . . . (I) n American jurisprudence at least, a private citizen lacks a judicially cognizable interest in the prosecution or non-prosecution of another.[71]

Based on these reasons, the dissent concluded that, overall, the victim-complainant lacks legitimate interests in the prosecution or non-prosecution and therefore has no standing to seek review and appeal in instances where they disapprove of the District Attorney's judgment not to prosecute.

This opinion is closer to the predominant approach in the United States, which rejects judicial review as a mechanism for prosecutorial accountability. As seen, this rejection rests in part on the notion that citizen-victims hold primarily private interests, rather than public interest, which serves to limit their legitimacy in bringing forward substantive arguments relating to the evidence and discussion of the public interest. Moreover, as discussed by the majority in *Benz*, the resistance to judicial review also relies on a separation of powers doctrine that shields executive/public policy decisions from the remit of judges. This resistance relies on an argument that judges are particularly ill-suited to evaluate prosecutorial decisions, including assessments on the strength of the case, the prosecution's enforcement policies, and the case's relationship to the government's overall enforcement plan.[72] Moreover, reviews are seen to generate costs in the system and are described as risking to 'delay the criminal proceeding, threatens to chill law enforcement by subjecting the prosecutor's motives and decision-making to outside inquiry, and may undermine prosecutorial effectiveness by revealing the Government's enforcement policy'.[73] These comments illustrate the range of justifications made in the United State to shield prosecutorial errors from judicial review brought forward by citizens.

Finally, within the federal context, judicial reviews are not possible. A victim seeking federal charges based on a sufficient nexus between the harm and the criminal remedy would need to show that the refusal to prosecute was a violation of constitutional proportions—notably decisions that are '*deliberately* based upon an unjustifiable standard such as race, religion, or other arbitrary classification'.[74] Accordingly, prosecutorial charging discretion in a manner that reflects implicit biases against certain classes of victims may not be interpreted as deliberate and therefore 'may not be an abuse of discretion or even

[71] *Linda RS v Richard D & Texas, et al*, 410 US 614, 619, 93 S Ct 1146, 1149, 35 L Ed 2d 536 (1973).
[72] *Wayte v United States*, 470 US 598 (1985) at 607–608.
[73] ibid.
[74] *Bordenskirsher v Hayes*, 434 US 357, 364 (1978); *United States v Batchelder*, 442 US 114, 125 (1979).

irrational'.[75] While the court could theoretically review such decisions, barriers presented by standing requirements impose significant obstacles to have cases heard on their merits even in instances of constitutional violations.[76] Moreover, while Congress has the authority to provide review mechanisms of decisions not to prosecute by passing statutes, it has chosen not to do so.

5. Conclusion

Despite the presence of vestiges of private prosecutions, as well as rare possibilities of statutory judicial review available in certain contexts, the predominant American approach has taken a privatization shift more rapidly than in England and Wales. Moreover, even within common law mechanisms that have traditionally been seen as conceiving victims as holders of public interests, there was an earlier tendency in the United States to conceive of victims as holders of private interests. The next chapter focuses on the formalization of this path, resulting in part by the victim's movement and the development of the Crime Victims' Rights Act within the federal context, which has been used by authorities as a rationale to delegitimate citizen-victims' abilities to make claims that advance the public interest in seeking state accountability in decisions about whether or not to prosecute.[77] As will be discussed in greater depth in the next chapter, this conceptualization of victims as holders of predominantly private interests, rather than entities with the potential to make substantive arguments relating to the public interest, has also contributed to the development of a form of procedural accountability within the criminal process that seeks to advance private interests. While it has hindered this role in the context of decisions relating to charges, it has to some extent enabled state accountability at other stages of criminal legal proceedings that are considered less 'public', particularly in matters of restitution.

[75] Josephine Gittler, 'Expanding the Role of the Victim in a Criminal Action: An Overview of Issues and Problems' (1984) 11 Pepp L Rev 117.

[76] Donald G Gifford, 'Equal Protection and the Prosecutor's Charging Decision: Enforcing an Ideal' (1981) 9 Geo Wash L Rev 659.

[77] The federal approach precludes the filing of an information subject to a probable cause review by a prosecutor and/or magistrate. In a case in which a citizen attempted to file a federal information, the Court refused the filing and stated that 'it is well settled that a private citizen has no right to prosecute a federal crime'. See *New York v Muka*, 440 F Supp 33, 36 (NDNY 1977). Moreover, in *Linda RS* (n 71), it was decided that citizen-victims have no standing to use mandamus action to challenge the state prosecutor's charging decision. This decision is often cited to highlight how despite unequal treatment that violates the Equal Protection Clause of the Fourteenth Amendment of the US Constitution, this case was considered within the prosecutor's discretion.

7

A Private and Novel Conception Under the United States' Federal Crime Victims' Rights Act

1. Introduction

In the United States, the conception of the victim's role, interests, and engagement in the prosecutorial process is closer to Grear's[1] private end of the spectrum. In most contexts, the victim's contribution to the public process is framed in primarily aggregate terms—wherein victims are seen as bringing forward their private interests. This private conception has had important implications on the ways that the role of victims within state accountability mechanisms has developed, including under the federal Crime Victims' Rights Act (CVRA), which is analysed in this chapter.

The previous chapter highlighted the initial developments of the victim's role as an agent of state accountability within the few states that have maintained some remnants of common law private prosecutions. It also underlined the elements that have led to this primarily privatized conception of victims and their interests, including the earlier and rapid abandonment of private prosecutions and the steady shift towards a state monopoly over public prosecutions. As seen, this conception has had an important impact on positioning the victim's role as holding a *private* interest in a *public* process—delegitimizing or weakening any claims made in the public interest.

This chapter focuses on the more recent evolution of the role of victims as agents of state accountability under the CVRA, which has developed differently and separately to mechanisms grounded in the English common law discussed in the previous chapter. The CVRA continues to conceive of victims as holding predominantly private interests in the criminal process, to an even

[1] Anna Grear, 'Theorizing the Rainbow? The Puzzle of the Public-Private Divide' (2003) 9 Res Publica 169, 172.

Victims as Agents of State Accountability. Marie Manikis, Oxford University Press. © Marie Manikis 2026.
DOI: 10.1093/9780191993947.003.0009

greater extent than the remnants of private prosecutions discussed in the previous chapter. This has given rise to a context in which in matters of prosecutorial decisions prior to charges, state prosecutors have remained immune from accountability. Prosecutorial decisions that follow charges—notably those that relate to prosecutorial agreements—have been more amenable to some accountability. This has also been the case with those that share some aspects with private torts, such as restitution.

The chapter begins by looking at the victims' rights movement's contribution to the development and codification of a new role of victims as agents of state accountability under the CVRA. This movement that started in the 1980s and 1990s was key in the development of the federal law that has, since its enactment in 2004, served as a model statute for its novel formulation of the victim's accountability role across different state statutes. Notably, the CVRA establishes victim standing in criminal court proceedings to hold the state accountable and obtain redress for violating these rights.

The chapter continues by analysing the ways that victims are understood under the CVRA as well as the implementation of the CVRA's mechanisms of state accountability in case law relating to prosecutorial decisions. The cases discussed illustrate three approaches to the American development of the victim's role. First, the general approach perceives the victim's role and interests as predominantly private and separate from those of the state, establishing a procedural form of accountability in instances of individual rights violations by victims in contexts of prosecutorial agreements. Second, in some contexts that are seen as complementary to the private tort system, notably within restitution, the victim's accountability role takes a substantive form as the victim's interests are considered closer to the private end of the private–public spectrum. Third, the chapter highlights that, in the context of public prosecutions, this underlying privatizing conception of victim interests has served to delegitimize and remove the potential for victims to hold the state accountable in pre-charging/charging decisions. In certain circumstances, this has the effect of protecting erroneous prosecutorial decision-making from state accountability mechanisms, which generally perpetuates systemic inequalities rooted in social injustices.

2. The Victims' Right Movement and Its Conception of a Novel Form of Accountability

The role of victims as agents of state accountability across state and federal jurisdictions developed in great part with the rise of the victims' rights movement during the 1980s. This movement mobilized to advocate for participatory rights for victims to have their interests heard by state agencies. The American victims' rights movement has not so much questioned the victim's lack of public control over criminal prosecutions, but mainly the lack of consideration of the victim's personal interests and well-being at the various stages of the criminal process. As such, earlier iterations of the movement mainly understood participation as 'expression', associated with a personal interests rights-based discourse.[2]

The victims' rights movement worked hard to develop a legal landscape that recognized victim interests as legitimate and relevant within the public criminal process. Specifically, the movement adopted the language of victims' rights, as a parallel to defendants' rights, as relevant private interests in the process, to secure an active, robust, and legitimate form of participation allowing them to bring forward their personal interests in public decision-making.[3] Victims' rights were framed as equal to, and needing to be balanced with, the rights of defendants in the criminal law. The language of rights supposed that victims, like defendants, were private entities who have personal interests to be heard, recognized, and protected within the various stages of criminal proceedings.

The individual rights discourse also suggested that the victim has personal interests that may be different to those held by state agencies. In this sense, like natural theories of rights that impose a limit on state powers to guarantee defendants' individual rights, this Lockean philosophy of 'possessive individualism'[4] was transposed into the context of criminal proceedings to ensure state accountability when states fail to account for these private interests in the process. It conceived victims as individual private entities who suffered direct victimization by the accused, but also 'secondary victimization'[5] by the state that can be harmful and often unresponsive or dismissive to their interests and needs. This conception made clear that since there is also a private dimension to harm suffered by individual victims, in part caused by the state, that the victim's private interests should be heard and protected independently in the

[2] Douglas Beloof, 'The Third Wave of Crime Victims' Rights: Standing, Remedy, and Review' (2005) 2 BYU L Rev 294, 294–96; Jonathan Doak, *Victims' Rights, Human Rights and Criminal Justice: Reconceiving the Role of Third Parties* (Hart Publishing 2008) 248.

[3] Kent Roach, 'Four Models of the Criminal Process' (1999) 89(2) J Crim L & Criminol 671.

[4] Crawford B Macpherson, *The Political Theory of Possessive Individualism: Hobbes to Locke* (OUP 2010) 238; A John Simmons, *The Lockean Theory of Rights* (Princeton UP 1992) 397.

[5] Dean J Kilpatrick and Randy K Otto, 'Constitutionally Guaranteed Participation in Criminal Proceedings for Victims: Potential Effects on Psychological Functioning' (1987) 34 Wayne L Rev 7, 18–22. Examples of secondary victimization include situations where victims are left in the dark about the development and outcome of the process, as well as situations where they have been excluded and their voices are not heard.

criminal process.[6] Importantly, paralleling defendants' rights, the movement was concerned with the *procedural* objectives of ensuring that victims' voices were heard throughout the process and considered that 'procedures should incorporate victims without regard to any changes in outcomes that may result'.[7]

By the 1990s, the victims' rights movement focused on what Beloof described as the 'third wave of victims' rights'.[8] This wave centred arguments to recognize remedies for victims' rights violations by state agencies, contributing to the development of the victim as an agent of state accountability in the United States. Indeed, victim participation expanded from 'expression' to 'accountability' by working towards the creation of robust redress mechanisms that offered victim standing within criminal court proceedings. These mechanisms sought to respond to violations by state agents, notably prosecutors. In this sense, the remedial focus was more court-centric than accountability forums in England and Wales, which have also relied on the creation of internal administrative review processes, such as Victims' Right to Review Scheme (VRRS), seen previously, to challenge prosecutorial discretionary errors.

3. CVRA: A Novel Reconceptualization of the Role of Victims as Agents of State Accountability Rooted in Predominantly Private Interests

The enactment of the CVRA[9] into federal law in 2004 was an important moment meant to recognize the role of victims as agents of state accountability in the United States by offering them standing in criminal proceeding and remedies in instances of state violations of their individual rights. While this statute only applied to federal criminal cases, it served as a model for states to recognize victims' rights in state-related crimes.[10] Victims' rights under the CVRA included (1) the right to be reasonably protected from the accused; (2) the right to reasonable, accurate, and timely notice of any public court proceeding; (3) the right not to be excluded from any such public court proceeding; (4) the right to be reasonably heard at any public proceeding involving release, plea,

[6] Beloof (n 2); Danielle Levine, 'Public Wrongs and Private Rights: Limiting the Victim's Role in a System of Public Prosecution' (2010) 104(1) Nw UL Rev 335, 361; Paul G Cassell and Steven Joffee, 'The Crime Victim's Expanding Role in a System of Public Prosecution: A Response to the Critics of the Crime Victims' Rights Act' (2011) 105 Nw UL Rev 164.

[7] Paul Cassell, 'The Crime Victims' Rights Movement' (2025) 56 U Pac L Rev 387.

[8] Beloof (n 2).

[9] Crime Victims' Rights Act, 18 USC §3771 (2004).

[10] Cassell (n 7).

sentencing, or any parole proceeding; (5) the reasonable right to confer with the attorney for the government in the case; (6) the right to full and timely restitution; (7) the right to proceedings free from unreasonable delays; and (8) the right to be treated with fairness and respect for the victim's dignity and privacy.

Importantly, the CVRA was also meant to establish clear mechanisms to hold the state accountable in instances of failures and breaches. Possibilities for redress under the CVRA have included mechanisms that grant victims standing in criminal proceedings within trial (district) courts for victims to assert their rights, followed by the possibility for review by filing a mandamus action in appellate courts (Circuit Courts) in order to obtain redress when their rights have been ignored or breached by state decision-makers.

Despite debates within case law and legal scholarship,[11] courts initially applied a deferential standard of review when deciding mandamus cases under the CVRA.[12] This was rooted in the idea that a deferential standard should apply to prosecutors and court decisions given the doctrine of separation of powers in which courts should rarely interfere in prosecutorial decisions. Moreover, the private dimensions of victims' rights and accountability has given rise to greater restraint and deference in reviewing state decisions. Despite this predominant approach by courts, Congress overruled these decisions by amending the CVRA and instead adopted a lower standard of review, namely, the ordinary standard of appellate review.[13] Following this decision, appellate courts are currently tasked to apply a lower standard of review, namely, an ordinary standard of appellate review, which prompts them to review district court's legal conclusions *de novo* to determine whether its factual conclusions included clear errors and its discretionary judgments for abuse of discretion.[14] Although a lower standard of review has since been adopted, reviews under mandamus in the United States are still limited as courts do not

[11] For instance, the Second Circuit in *In re Huff Asset Management Co*, 409 F 3d 555 (2nd Cir June 2005) used a more relaxed standard than the traditional mandamus, namely, the standard of 'abuse of discretion' to review the district court's action. On the contrary, appellate decisions in the DC Circuit *United States v* Monzel, 641 F 3d 528 (DC Cir 2011); 5th Circuit (*In re Amy*, 591 F 3d 792 (5th Cir 2009); *In re* Dean, 527 F 3d 391 (5th Cir 2008)); and Tenth Circuit (*In re Olesen*, No 11-4190 (DC No 2:02-CV-00326-TS) (D Utah 2011)) have interpreted the standard of mandamus rigidly as the traditional and discretionary writ of mandamus in common law tradition. For discussion in favour of a relaxed appellate standard of review, see Paul Cassell, 'Protecting Crime Victims in Federal Appellate Courts: The Need to Broadly Construe the Crime Victims' Rights Mandamus Provision' (2010) 87 Denv U L Rev 599; David E Aaronson, 'New Rights and Remedies: The Federal Crime Victims' Rights Act of 2004' (2008) 28 Pace L Rev 623, 662. For arguments in favour of a traditional mandamus standard, see Levine (n 6).

[12] Most recently in *In re Wellcare Health Plans, Inc*, 754 F 3d 1234, 1237 (11th Cir 2014).

[13] See Crime Victims' Rights Act (n 9) §3771(d)(3).

[14] *In re Doe*, 57 F 4th 667, 672–73 (9th Cir 2023) (citing *In re Wild*, 994 F 3d 1244, 1254 n10 (11th Cir 2021) (en banc)).

readily recognize their authority to look into substantive reasoning by prosecutors,[15] particularly when brought forward by victims, who are seen as holders of private interests—limiting their potential for holding the prosecuting state accountable.

Echoing the victims' rights movement, decisions under the CVRA in the US context predominantly view victims as entities who represent their own personal interests in public proceedings. Indeed, victims are seen as having voices and interests independent from the state's, which ought to be heard at various stages of criminal proceedings. Where the state breaches its obligations relative to this participation, victims can assert their rights to the district court in which the proceeding is taking place. If the district court denies the relief sought by victims, they can petition the court of appeals for a writ of mandamus.[16]

In interpreting this legislation, the discussion below illustrates the ways that courts have given credence to, and reaffirmed, the victims' rights movement's conception of the victim as an entity with private interests in the US context. Indeed, as will be seen, the definitional scope of the victim under the CVRA is much narrower than its conception within the English common law approach, and parallels discourse on private and individualized interests. Three approaches have been developed across cases, facilitating varying types of state accountability. First and generally, courts have recognized the victim as a holder of private interests that can, to some extent, legitimately bring these interests forward in the public process, enabling a procedural form of accountability. Consequently, victims' interests have at times been undermined and provided with a limited form of state accountability that is based on a procedural form of engagement rather than a substantive one. Second, in the context of restitution, victims' private interests in criminal proceedings are typically understood as complementary to civil processes and less so as an interference of the public dimension in criminal proceedings. Consequently, this has justified a more substantive understanding of state accountability where victims can substantially engage and bring arguments when these rights are breached. Finally, in contexts of charging decisions, victims' interests are generally considered illegitimate as they are seen to disrupt the monopoly held by state prosecutors, even in instances of potential abuses and errors. In effect, this may shield erroneous prosecutorial decision-making, including those that are rooted in assumptions relating to systemic inequalities.

[15] *In re Ryan*, 88 F 4th 614 (2023) para 627.
[16] Crime Victims' Rights Act (n 9) §3771(d)(3).

Defining victim standing through direct individualizing harm

The concept of victims under the CVRA can be an insightful starting point in understanding the ways victim interests are conceived across the public–private spectrum. This understanding is conveyed in the CVRA's definition of victim as 'a person directly and proximately harmed as a result of the commission of a Federal offense or an offense in the District of Columbia'.[17] This definition is very different to the conception of victims under the English common law. Indeed, as seen in England and Wales, traditional mechanisms of state accountability, such as private prosecutions, considered the victim as a citizen with the ability to directly bring forward elements of the public interest. This historical view is considerably different to the more recent approach developed under the VRRS that has a narrower conception of the victim as bringing forward private components. This latter conception is more closely aligned with the ways victims have been understood in certain contexts in the United States, including by the victims' rights movement and under the CVRA. In this context, directness requires that the offence be the 'but for' cause of the harm, while proximity requires that the harm experienced by the victim must be a 'reasonably foreseeable consequence of the criminal conduct' and not 'merely tangentially linked' to the offence.[18]

The requirement of direct and proximate harm is suggestive of an individualized understanding both of harm and victims, which significantly limits standing under this legislation. For example, in *United States v Ruzicka*,[19] an individual shareholder in a corporation who was the victim of a monetary fraud was refused the status of victim under the CVRA because he was considered an 'ancillary' victim of the fraud, whereas the corporation was the direct victim. This conception delineates individual victims from various members of the public and communities that can also be impacted by crime and who, under foundational notions of criminal law, are understood as harmed by the offence. Indeed, this is substantially different from the understanding of citizen-victims within private prosecutions in England and Wales, where police, NGOs, and a wide range of associations can be considered victims of crime despite not meeting the proximity/direct threshold that is necessary under the CVRA. Accordingly, it appears that the US conception of victims as holding predominantly private interests and forms of state accountability has also contributed

[17] ibid, §3771(e).

[18] *United States v Thuna*, 382 F Supp 3d 166 (DPR 2019); *In re Fisher*, 649 F 3d 401, 402–03 (5th Cir 2011).

[19] *United States v Ruzicka*, 331 F Supp 3d 888 (D Minn 2018).

to a narrower definition of crime victims. This individualized understanding of the victim is particularly important in the US context where, unlike in England and Wales, victims may claim substantial amounts of restitution in criminal proceedings under the CVRA, in complement of the civil approach, discussed below.

Other decisions have demonstrated a somewhat more flexible interpretation of 'direct and proximate' to affirm the rights of victims who have been 'significantly harmed' by a crime.[20] This has been the approach in cases wherein a corporate defendant has harmed multiple victims. For instance, in *United States v Boeing Co*,[21] the judge took an expansive approach to recognize the family members as crime victims when their relatives had died in Boeing aircrafts. At first glance, this suggests a wider ambit of who is to be considered a crime victim. However, the judge maintained that the application of the CVRA depended on family members' ability to demonstrate that the federal offences in question were directly and proximately connected to *their* personal experiences of harm and victimhood.

Importantly, expanding the definition of 'proximity' has the potential to address crimes that extend to larger populations, for example, in the context of environmental justice. In *United States v CITGO*,[22] a group of residents who had experienced health problems due to the misconduct of a nearby oil refinery were recognized as victims as per the CVRA. Initially, the district judge declined to find that residents in the surrounding community were victims, concluding that the residents had failed to demonstrate medically documented physical injuries directly stemming from CITGO's releases. This decision was appealed at the Fifth Circuit and was reversed. While this decision might seem like a widening of victims status, the district court that had to reassess the case still linked it to individualized harms, highlighting that other health complaints, while not life-threatening, were sufficient to trigger victim status and, thus, allowed the residents to be heard during sentencing proceedings. This suggests that an individualized and proximal notion of harm is required as element of standing. Ozymy and Jarrell[23] cite this case and suggest that members of environmental justice communities should be readily recognized as crime victims. They contend that doing so would help address structural

[20] Cassell (n 7).
[21] *United States v Boeing Company*, 2022 US Dist, wl 13829875.
[22] *United States v CITGO*, Crim No CR-06-563 (SD Tex, 27 June 2007).
[23] Joshua Ozymy and Melissa L Jarrell, 'Of Sex Crimes and Fencelines: How Recognition of Environmental Justice Communities as Crime Victims Under State and Federal Law Can Help Secure Environmental Justice' (2020) 38(1) Pace Environ Law Review 109.

and systemic failures in the regulatory state that have not and cannot protect communities from harm or compensate them for their injuries related to ecological harms. Starr, Flack, and Folley comment that this approach comes with some logistical obstacles in the sense that determining who within the larger collective meets the CVRA test of directness and proximity may create an additional stage of litigation.[24]

Despite this widened definition of victims, the notion of harm and accountability for state failures under the CVRA generally remains personal and individualized, iterating victims' private interests in the process. This conception differs from the mechanisms rooted in common law traditions in England and Wales, wherein the public approach would enable those affected as a collective by injustices to bring forward a private prosecution or seek judicial review of decisions not to prosecute. Arguably, conceiving of the victim as holding a public interest in accountability may help address structural/systemic failures in the regulatory state that have not and cannot protect communities from such harms.

The next section illustrates three approaches to the American development of the victim's role as agents of state accountability under the CVRA. First, the general approach perceives the victim's role and interests as predominantly private and separate from those of the state, establishing a predominantly procedural form of accountability in instances of prosecutorial failures relating to prosecutorial agreements once charges have been laid. Second, within the context of restitution, seen as a complement to the tort system, the victim's accountability role takes a substantive form as the victim's interests are considered closer to the private end of the private–public spectrum. Third, the chapter highlights that, in the context of public prosecutions prior to charges being laid, this underlying privatizing conception of victim interests has served to delegitimize and remove the potential for victims to hold the state accountable.

The general approach: victims as holders of predominantly private and aggregate interests in post-charges prosecutorial agreements

In early decisions relating to the CVRA, courts relied on notions of fairness, respect, and dignity to legitimize hearing the victim's private interests in the

[24] Judson W Starr, Brian L Flack, and Allison D Foley, 'A New Intersection: Environmental Crimes and Victims' Rights' (2009) 23(3) Nat Resources & Env't 41.

public process.[25] In *Heaton*,[26] the court held that fairness required allowing victims' views and personal thoughts on a criminal justice decision to be heard before the court. The rhetoric of views and personal thoughts, in order to ensure fairness, respect, and dignity as values tied to their needs, highlights a predominantly private understanding of interests.

As will be discussed in this section, subsequent decisions—particularly in cases where charges have been filed and are subject to a prosecutorial agreement requiring judicial approval,[27] but where state prosecutors have failed to consult with victims regarding guilty plea agreements and deferred prosecution agreements (DPAs)—have primarily understood victims as holders of private interests. Their ability to contribute to the public interest has been framed as limited and largely aggregate, rather than as a direct and substantive contribution.

The power for prosecutors to negotiate and reach agreements with defence is a common and rapidly growing practice in the United States, with some different and lesser traction in England and Wales.[28] This has contributed to a rise in prosecutorial discretionary powers by prosecutors. In the United States, most agreements are made once charges are laid and typically remain subject to review by courts—with a deferential standard towards the prosecution. This is especially the case when dismissal of charges are part of the deal.

As highlighted in these cases, the separation of powers doctrine between the prosecution (executive) and the judiciary is still considered relevant in these cases, but with less emphasis than during pre-charging. Indeed, once charges are laid, judges are seen as having more legitimacy to ensure that decisions are made in the public interest. As will be seen in this section, these agreements typically include plea deals and DPAs, and the CVRA has provided that victims

[25] *Jordan v Dept of Justice*, 173 F Supp 3d 44 (SDNY 2016).

[26] *US v Heaton*, 458 F Supp 2d 1271 (D Utah 2006).

[27] Procedurally, in American law under Rule 11 of the Federal Rules of Criminal Procedure, the judiciary needs to accept guilty pleas and DPAs as they need to serve the public interest. See Fed R Crim Pro 11(c). In practice, however, the prosecutorial state is presumed to be serving the public interest, and judges have treated these requests for approval with great deference as prosecutors are seen as holding the quasi-monopoly over the public interest.

[28] Mary E Vogel, 'The Social Origins of Plea Bargaining: Conflict and the Law in the Emergence of Plea Bargaining, 1830–1860' (1999) 33 L & Soc'y Rev 161. See Mark Motivans, *Federal Justice Statistics 2012—Statistical* Tables, *DOJ NCJ 248470* (Bureau of Justice Statistics 2015) tbl 4.2. In US federal courts in 2007–2011, guilty plea rates increased from 95.8 to 96.9 per cent of all convictions; the percentage of convictions following trial declined from 4.2 to 3.1 per cent. In England and Wales, it has long been said that this practice does not occur. However, research has suggested that tacit forms of bargaining existed and it is not recognized that these practices take place. Most forms of negotiations involve pre-charging contexts such as NPAs, particularly in corporate crime cases. See comparative perspectives in Mary E Vogel, 'Plea Bargaining Under the Common Law' in Darryl K. Brown, Jenia Iontcheva Turner, and Bettina Weisser (eds), *Oxford Handbook of Criminal Process* (OUP 2018).

have a right to provide their views within these agreements—either during negotiations or prior to judicial approval. Non-prosecution agreements (NPAs), which are typically made before any changes are laid, are generally subject to greater deference and, as will be discussed in the third approach, generally do not enable victims to undertake a role in holding the state accountable.

In the case of *In re Dean*, discussed below which involved a plea agreement, the court made clear that 'when criminal charges are submitted for judicial resolution, the courts vigilantly will enforce the public interest, including Congress' command that crime victims are heard and protected' and 'courts must validate the public interest, above all, including rights that Congress has given to crime victims'.[29]

Tied to this private and aggregate conception of victim interests as an element of the public interest, victims have mainly been granted procedural forms of accountability. As discussed in Chapter 3, procedural forms of accountability allow for remedies that recognize the victim's views to be heard but do not recognize substantive engagement on the merits with the state's arguments, notably on the question of elements of the evidence and the public interest. The following analysis illustrates some of the procedural forms of accountability under the CVRA.

Using the CVRA, victims have sought remedies to bring forward their private interests as agents of procedural accountability in cases where state prosecutors failed to consult them prior to deciding whether to accept a guilty plea. In the case of *In re Dean*,[30] victims' families of a fatal explosion at an oil refinery owned by the defendant objected to the government's request that the court accept the defendant's guilty plea and impose a stipulated sentence. The victims challenged the plea agreement as it was reached in violation of their rights under the CVRA to be treated with fairness and to confer with the prosecution. The district court concluded that the government should have explained why it did not notify victims about this plea agreement, as well as shown that it had considered and rejected other alternatives to notifying victims. Despite these failures, the court decided against the victims' arguments, holding that identifying CVRA violations was not inherently grounds to reject a plea agreement—as there are other considerations that form the public interest—and thus allowed the plea agreement, and declined to order any remedy for this breach.

[29] *In re Ryan* (n 15) para 626.

[30] *In re Dean* (n 11) and see related case *United States v BP Products North America Inc*, Crim No H-07-434, 2008 WL 501321 (SD Tex, 21 February 21 2008).

Following this decision, the victims petitioned the Fifth Circuit Court for a writ of mandamus. They argued that the government's failure to consult with them prior to reaching the agreement or to provide them with notice of the plea violated their rights under the CVRA. The Court found that the victims' statutory rights were violated but declined to order any retroactive remedies for the prosecutorial breaches—inviting the district court to hear the victims prior to accepting the guilty plea. It nevertheless recognized separate and legitimate victim standing, resting on two key points. First, the Circuit Court underlined the notion that victims have separate individualized interests from other parties of the criminal process, which extends to plea negotiations. Second, the Circuit Court engaged a form of prospective remedy that further reiterates the procedural nature of this type of accountability by stating its confidence that 'the conscientious district court will fully consider the victims' objections and concerns in deciding whether the plea agreement should be accepted'.[31] In this sense, the Circuit Court concluded that although imperfect, it would be sufficient that the district court has 'the benefit of the views of the victims who chose to participate at the hearing or by their own filings'.[32] This illustrates the private and procedural nature of accountability in this context, as the district court should be expected to see the prosecutor recount that the victim has been consulted on agreement and that the victim's views were heard on the matter. Since these views are personal and are considered to relate to the victim's private interests, it forms but one part of the wider public interest—understood as aggregate. In contrast, a substantive form of accountability would have recognized victims' participation through asserting arguments that substantively challenge the state's decision on the grounds that victims can make direct claims that invoke the public interest.

Similarly, in the recent case of *In re Ryan*,[33] the court applied the same logic as *In re Dean* to a DPA. In this case, Boeing intentionally withheld information relating to their 737 Max aircrafts' change in design from the Federal Aviation Administration, which impacted the level of training required for pilots. This design, coupled with pilots' lack of training, gave rise to two separate fatal crashes, wherein all passengers died. Following these events, the state charged Boeing with conspiracy to defraud the United States,[34] and simultaneously filed a DPA in federal court. As *In re Dean*, the victims' families qualified as victims under the CVRA and the Fifth Circuit Court found that they should

[31] *In re Dean* (n 11).
[32] ibid.
[33] *In re Ryan* (n 15).
[34] Under Crime Victims' Rights Act (n 9) §371.

have been notified of the ongoing DPA discussions and allowed to communicate meaningfully with the government before a deal was concluded. The Circuit Court highlighted that this is particularly true in the circumstances of an agreement that would result in no one, including the company, executives, or employees, being convicted of any crimes, despite the recognition of criminal wrongdoing that had led to the death of 346 people.

However, as in *In re Dean*, the Circuit Court found the mandamus intercession to be premature, reasoning that the victims would have a subsequent opportunity to present their views to the district court. This, the Circuit Court held, would allow the district court to make a decision in the public interest, by considering several interests, including those of the victims—understood as private and aggregate. In its denial of mandamus, the Circuit Court reminded that courts do not have the authority to exercise substantive review over DPAs and that it is up to prosecutors to make these assessments. Nevertheless, district courts may exceptionally refuse to dismiss charges in contexts of DPAs if dismissal is 'clearly contrary to manifest public interest'.[35] In this context, the Circuit Court concluded that it was confident that the district court would uphold the victims' CVRA rights throughout the criminal proceedings by offering victims a procedural opportunity to be heard, especially as judicial approval would be sought to resolve the case in the event that charges were to be dismissed by a DPA. Victims, however, as private entities under the CVRA cannot make direct claims to the substance of the DPA, and their claims about the public interest may be less poignant as they are seen as holders of private interests that can form part of the wider public interest in an aggregate way. Indeed, the standard employed to discuss the public interest suggests that it is one that needs to be clearly contrary to *manifest* public interest which is embedded in the notion that victims are not typically seen as holders of public interests.

Part of the DPA in this case included that Boeing would not be charged for three years and would put in place appropriate corporate compliance safety measures. In May 2024, the state found out that Boeing breached the DPA by failing to put in place appropriate corporate compliance and safety measures. Following this, charges were laid to which Boeing eventually pleaded guilty and reached a guilty plea agreement deal in July 2024, to which the families objected and in December 2024, a district court judge rejected the plea.[36] While

[35] *In re Ryan* (n 15).
[36] *United States of America v The Boeing Company*, No 4:21-CR-5-0, 2024 (ND Tex, 5 December 2024).

the victims objected primarily on the basis that the company was let off too lightly for its wrongdoing, the federal judge rejected the guilty plea, not because of leniency, but because he disagreed with how the independent monitor would be selected and monitored (by the government instead of the court). He argued that public interest requires the court to step in since the selection and monitoring of the independent monitor as part of the agreement undermines public confidence in Boeing's probation.

More recently, in May 2025, however, after a change of government and head of prosecutions at the Federal Department of Justice, the prosecution and Boeing instead announced a new NPA under which the prosecutorial state would agree to dismiss the criminal charges against Boeing (despite having plead guilty and breached its safety compliance measures), provided Boeing would pay an additional penalty of millions to the state and to the families, and make additional investments in safety.

Prior to this NPA, the state prosecution initially had filed a motion to dismiss the criminal fraud matter against Boeing, which would have enabled victims to be heard by the district court in its dismissal requests. Instead, it did a volte-face and told victims that it reached an NPA, which it filed to the federal district court. Part of the NPA stipulates that prosecutors would not proceed with the charges of criminal fraud against Boeing, regardless of how the court rules on the motion to dismiss the criminal fraud. This strategy is seen as a way to avoid judicial oversight as part of dismissal requests that may provide victims with the potential to bring forward arguments about the public interest. In response, victims filed a motion that describe this situation as an unprecedented effort to avoid the judicial review requirement in matters of dismissal agreements, making it void as it is contrary to public policy and deny the motion to dismiss. Victims also argue that the strategy by the state sets a 'dangerous precedent'[37] because it would entail that in all future federal criminal cases involving dismissals, the state would just sign an agreement with the defendants not to prosecute—making the requirement that judges approve the dismissal motion.

While this case remains pending at the time of writing, it will be relevant to see whether the NPA receives the same broad judicial deference as in the third approach—illustrated by *In re Wild*, where the NPA was entered into prior to charges being laid—or whether the district court will afford victims

[37] Clifford Law Office, 'Victims' Families of MAX8 Crashes Files Motion to Oppose DOJ New Non-Prosecution Agreement with Boeing' (18 June 2025) <https://www.cliffordlaw.com/victims-families-of-max8-crashes-file-motion-to-oppose-doj-new-non-prosecution-agreement-with-boeing/> accessed 24 June 2025.

a limited form of accountability. Such accountability would involve hearing victims' views in an aggregate manner in relation to the public interest, while still maintaining a high degree of deference, similar to that typically granted in cases involving plea agreements and DPAs.

These cases illustrate the predominant approach in the United States, once charges are laid in matters involving plea agreements and DPAs. In this context, victim participation is generally understood as an aggregate form of engagement with the public interest. Victims are seen as advancing their own private interests within the broader framework of public prosecutorial decision-making—a contribution that is only considered relevant when it clearly aligns with a clear view of the public interest.

This contrasts to some of the common law mechanisms seen in England and Wales, where victims may bring arguments related to the substantive elements of prosecutorial decision-making as relevant to the public interest. Rather, in the United States, the victim's private interests are understood as forming but one aggregate part of the public interest, which remains within the authority of the executive branch through the state prosecution.

The case of restitution: victims as holders of predominantly private interests considered complementary to civil proceedings with substantive forms of state accountability

In contexts of restitution, a specific approach has been developed by the courts wherein victims' claims are recognized based on the understanding that criminal proceedings retain a complementary function to civil processes. This argument emphasizes the public nature of criminal proceedings, yet recognizes that some of its elements, such as restitution, are complementary to torts—while maintaining that victims hold predominantly private interests. Accordingly, the victim's interest in holding the state accountable for failures to adequately provide compensation avoids the charges of illegitimacy or interference. Consequently, this has contributed to an approach that allows victims as agents of state accountability to contribute substantively to arguments and decisions relating to restitution.

In the case of *In re Brown*,[38] the victim, Carlos Brown, was harmed in a car accident caused by a driver under the influence of alcohol. Rather

[38] *In re Brown*, 932 F 3d 162 (4th Cir 2019).

than pursuing a civil action, the victim sought restitution for lost wages as a condition of the defendant's probation in the criminal case. The district court initially denied Brown's request, redirecting him to instead file a civil suit. Brown then sought a writ of mandamus under the CVRA, which was granted by the Fourth Circuit Court (Court of Appeal). The Court of Appeal decided that the first instance court had failed to properly balance the victim's need for restitution against the burden on the sentencing process, as required under the CVRA. The decision maintained that courts can decline to order restitution if it will unduly delay sentencing, however that was not applicable in *Brown*. This case underlines that victims' personal needs under the CVRA must be balanced with other objectives of the criminal process. Thus, while the interests of victims in proceedings are predominantly private, they remain within the public process. Moreover, by drawing parallels to victims' recourse under civil action, the case further indicates the conception of victims as pursuing predominantly private interests under the CVRA, which in some cases of restitution have provided victims with some legitimacy to make substantive claims to these forms of compensation.

Similarly, the case of *In re Barber*[39] illustrates the complementary approach applied to the relationship between prior civil settlements and restitution under the CVRA. In this case, a crime victim filed a petition for a writ of mandamus under the CVRA after a district court decided that a prior civil settlement reduced the amount of the victim's loss in the calculation for restitution. The Court of Appeal denied the victim's petition, finding that the evidence supported the district court's decision and was neither an abuse of discretion nor legally erroneous. The impact of the prior civil settlement on the victim's rights under the CVRA directly highlights a form of parallel complementarity between the conceptualization of victim interests in civil cases and those of restitution in criminal proceedings.

Finally, the case of *Monzel*[40] illustrates how claims for restitution have permitted victims to contribute substantively to state accountability. In this case, the defendant pled guilty to possession of child pornography. One of the victims, 'Amy', subsequently sought $3.2 million in restitution from the defendant. The trial court awarded $5,000 yet acknowledged that this amount was not enough to remedy the harm the defendant had caused to the victim. The victim

[39] *In re Barber*, 957 F 3d 1381 (9th Cir 2020).
[40] *United States v Monzel* (n 11).

substantively challenged the award on a petition for mandamus,[41] in which the court found that Amy's right to full and timely restitution[42] had been breached since the district court had a corresponding duty to direct the defendant to pay the full amount of her losses. Accordingly, the court remedied this situation by remanding the case to the district court to 'consider anew the amount of Amy's losses attributable to the defendant's offence and order restitution equal to that amount'.[43] This case highlights the substantive nature of accountability that victims can undertake in contexts relating to restitution.

Since restitution is seen as serving a complementary function to private civil claims, victims may articulate their private interests in a way that is not typically seen as delving into discussions on the public interest. While this may lead to a lower amount in restitution, it also lends legitimacy to the victim's role as agent of accountability in a way that has not only enabled them to make substantive claims on the amount of restitution, but also resulted in successful mandamus actions with a lower standard of review, when courts erroneously failed to grant restitution agreed upon during a plea agreement.[44] As such, the approach provides victims with legitimacy to engage substantively as agents of state accountability, in contrast to the decisions discussed above and those in the next section.

Denying state accountability: pre-charging and charging decisions as public decisions insulated from review

The implementation of the CVRA reveals substantial resistance in recognizing the victim's role in holding the prosecutorial state accountable in matters relating to prosecutorial decisions to charge. The decision to charge in the United States consists of two separate steps (two-prong test): the evidentiary stage that assesses the sufficient possibility of guilt, as well as the decision of whether filing criminal charges is in the public interest.[45] The charging role is reserved for federal state prosecutors perceived as public representatives. As such, other than the exceptions seen in Chapter 6, victims' interests in holding the state accountable for breaches of their rights related to charging decisions

[41] The victim also appealed the decision, but the court rejected her appeal on the basis that a victim has no right to directly appeal a criminal defendant's sentence.
[42] Violence Against Women's Act, 18 USC §2259 (1994).
[43] *United States v Monzel* (n 11).
[44] *In re Doe* (n 14).
[45] ABA Standards for Criminal Justice, ch 3, s 4.3(a) (7th edn, 1997).

are generally considered illegitimate. Specifically, there is the concern that victims might disrupt the monopoly held by state prosecutors, even in instances of potential abuses and errors from these actors. Victims, seen to bring forward their own private interests, might reduce the impartiality and fairness of the charging process. This apprehension arises from an image of the victim 'as an overly vindictive individual and an image of the prosecutor as a disinterested, objective individual'.[46] Additionally, part of this illegitimacy is justified as respecting the separation of powers between the executive and the judiciary.

Historically, prosecutors in the United States have benefited from a longstanding authority to decline prosecution for any reason they deem appropriate. Typically, these decisions were considered final without the possibility of external review.[47] Concerned with the scope of this unfettered power, proponents of victims' rights initially thought that the CVRA might offer a tool to redress charging decisions that failed to hear the victims' views.[48] Indeed, the CVRA was meant to provide victims with a mechanism for holding the state accountable in instances of prosecutorial state failures to confer with victims.[49] Nevertheless, case law engaging the CVRA has reaffirmed the prosecutor's power by excluding charge-related decisions from review despite the legislation's goals. While court decisions under the CVRA have recognized the potential for victims to hold the state accountable for state failures to confer with victims in certain prosecutorial decisions, notably those relating to plea agreements, recent cases have largely confirmed that prosecutorial charging decisions are excluded from review, including in instances of errors and unreasonable decisions. These decisions, discussed in this section, highlight an important limitation to the role of victims as agents of state accountability, which differs substantially from the approach in England and Wales.

While charging decisions in England and Wales follow the same two-step assessment, they have historically engaged a different appreciation of victims' interests. As seen in Chapter 4, victims in England and Wales have had a longstanding historical role in public prosecutions, as private prosecutors or as

[46] Josephine Gittler, 'Expanding the Role of the Victim in a Criminal Action: An Overview of Issues and Problems' (1984) 11 Pepp L Rev 117. In a similar vein, referring to the role of the state prosecutor, it was noted that 'part of the function of the public prosecutor is to serve as a check on the understandable desire of a victim to prosecute'. Douglas E Beloof, Paul G Cassell, and Steven J Twist, *Victims in Criminal Procedure* (5th edn, Carolina Academic Press 2024) 197.

[47] Michal Buchhandler-Raphael, 'Underprosecution Too' (2022) 56 U Rich L Rev 409.

[48] Paul G Cassell, Nathanael J Mitchell, and Bradley J Edwards, 'Crime Victims' Rights During Criminal Investigations? Applying the Crime Victims' Rights Act Before Criminal Charges Are Filed' (2014) 104(1) J Crim L & Criminol 59, 61.

[49] Beloof (n 2) 294–6; Paul G Cassell, Bradley J Edwards, and Jordan Peck, 'Circumventing the Crime Victims' Rights Act: A Critical Analysis of the Eleventh Circuit's Decision Upholding Jeffrey Epstein's Secret Non-Prosecution Agreement' (2021) 211 Mich St L Rev 211.

actors who may review charging decisions. Through these channels, the state arguably conceives of victims as prosecutorial entities that can, to some extent, make substantive arguments that engage with evidence, legal interpretation, and the public interest. This is not the case in most of the United States where there is an absolute state monopoly over prosecutorial decisions relating to charges, without the possibility to seek review of these decisions. As will be seen, this deference to the state's authority as prosecutor impacts both procedural and substantive state accountability.

The case of *In re Rivers*[50] illustrates the important limitations of the American approach on the implementation of the CVRA's accountability potential in the context of the pursuit of criminal charges. In this case, the plaintiff, a federal prisoner, alleged to be defrauded by state agencies and a bank, and spoke about this to state and federal law enforcement personnel over several years, but no criminal charges were laid by the prosecution. The plaintiff sought relief under the CVRA along with a court order appointing a prosecutor or advocate to represent her in this matter. Additionally, she sought an order requiring the government to give her materials related to its purported negotiations and agreements with actors who committed crimes against her. The magistrate judge recommended that the district court dismiss the application because, even though she qualified as a crime victim, the government had met all its obligations under the CVRA—highlighting that the CVRA does not impact prosecutors' wide discretion on whether to press charges. Moreover, the magistrate judge stated that the plaintiff had no right under the CVRA to receive the requested investigative materials. This decision underlined that although the CVRA provides that crime victims have a reasonable right to confer with government attorneys in their cases and gives them a voice in this process, it does not entitle them to dictate the manner, timing, or quantity of conferrals. As such, by meeting with the victims and hearing their concerns, the government agents had satisfied their obligations. Accordingly, the court interpreted the CVRA as protecting rights that are limited to the criminal justice process and, simultaneously, silent and unconcerned with victims' rights to file civil claims against their assailants. The court also rejected the plaintiff's claim to remedies under the CVRA based on the foreclosure of another person's home that was used to launder money obtained from her on the basis that 'society is the primary victim of money laundering undertaken for the purposes of concealment'.[51] This case signals to a largely private conception of victims and

[50] *Rivers v United States*, No 6:18-cv-00061, 2020 WL 1527860 (WD Va, 9 March 2020).
[51] Citing *United States v Chambers*, 14 F Appx 140 (4th Cir 2001).

their interests in matters of prosecutions, by opposing society's interests in this offence to her own personal ones. Concurrently, as the victim is understood as having private interests, the case also reaffirms the state prosecutor's monopoly over its discretionary power to decide whether to press charges, including in instances where there may be failures in the exercise of this discretion. Contrary to jurisdictions where victims can bring forward private prosecutions and substantively review aspects of prosecutorial decisions not to prosecute, this case illustrates the limits of such forms of accountability in the United States.

These limits are further demonstrated by some of the more recent decisions in the seminal case of *In re Wild*,[52] which resulted in a series of decisions spanning across several years. These cases underline the victim's private conception and confirm a quasi-unfettered state prosecutorial discretion and lack of victim potential for holding the state accountable even in cases of errors. In this decision, the petitioner, Wild, was one of the more than thirty women who, according to allegations, were victimized by notorious sex trafficker and child sexual offender Jeffrey Epstein. When this was brought forward to the police, Epstein's legal team arranged a guilty plea to a low-level state crime along with a federal NPA providing immunity from federal prosecution to him and his co-conspirators. Similar to the *Boeing* case discussed above, the federal prosecutors failed to confer with the victims prior to reaching this agreement. After the NPA was made public, Wild asserted before the federal district court that federal prosecutors violated her rights under the CVRA by negotiating and executing an NPA with the defence. In particular, she referenced her rights to confer with and to be treated fairly by the government's lawyers. Following years of litigation, the district court in 2011 highlighted that the CVRA applied pre-charging even though the prosecutors had never formally filed federal criminal charges in that case[53] and found that the prosecutors had misled victims and expressly hid the NPA from them—violating their right to confer.[54]

Shortly after the parties filed briefs on the appropriate remedies for the violation of the victims' right to confer in Florida, the FBI arrested Epstein in New York for additional charges, where he supposedly died of suicide in federal detention. The Florida district court in 2019, then, dismissed the Florida CVRA case as moot.[55]

This gave rise to the case of *In re Wild*, in which the victims sought a petition for writ of mandamus (appellate review) to the Eleventh Circuit Court

[52] *In re Wild*, 955 F 3d at 1269 (11th Cir 2020); *In re Wild* (n 14).
[53] *Does v United States*, 817 F Supp 2d 1337, 1341 (SD Fla 2011).
[54] *Doe 1 v United States*, 359 F Supp 3d 1201, 1222 (SD Fla 2019).
[55] *Doe 1 v United States*, 411 F Supp 3d 1321, 1325–26 (SD Fla 2019).

concerning their CVRA rights against other potential defendants. The government filed a response in which it not only opposed Wild's arguments on the merits, but also raised several arguments concerning the scope of the CVRA and the circumstances in which rights under the CVRA are judicially enforceable. In a divided panel, the Circuit Court, in April 2020, denied Wild's mandamus petition and held that CVRA rights, including a victim's right to confer, do not attach before the commencement of criminal proceedings—and thus the CVRA does not provide Wild any judicially enforceable rights. In this sense, despite prosecutorial misconduct, the court ruled that the CVRA does not provide victim standing where there is no pre-existing criminal charges.[56]

Specifically, it argued that since the government never filed charges against Epstein, due to the NPA, there was no pre-existing proceeding in which Wild could have moved for relief under the CVRA. This judgment reconsidered the CVRA's legal interpretation of 2011 and made the CVRA's rights and remedies inapplicable when there are no specific charges brought by an individual in light of an NPA.

Due to the division within that Court, a majority of the active judges of the Eleventh Circuit Court voted to rehear the case en banc in a subsequent case entitled *In re Wild*,[57] which vacated the previous appellate holding. The Circuit Court directed the parties to address two questions: '(1) Whether the CVRA creates rights that attach and apply before the formal commencement of criminal proceedings; and (2) Whether, even assuming that it does so, the CVRA further creates a private right of action, such that any pre-charge right is judicially enforceable in a freestanding lawsuit'.[58]

While acknowledging the profound sympathy for Wild and Epstein's other victims, the majority en banc decision ruled against the victims on procedural grounds. It held that the CVRA does not authorize enforcement by a victim in a free-standing civil action. Moreover, it concluded that it need not resolve, in abstract, the issue decided by the original panel: whether the CVRA applies before the government brings formal charges in criminal proceedings. The only issue that needed to be decided was whether the CVRA authorized Wild to file a free-standing civil suit seeking judicial enforcement of her rights under the CVRA in the absence of any underlying proceeding. The Court decided that the CVRA does not create a free-standing civil action (private right of action). Specifically, it highlighted that the CVRA provides a basis for victims to

[56] *In re Wild* (n 52). For commentary on this decision, see Elkan Abramowitz and Jonathan S Sack, 'Limiting Victims' Rights: Eleventh Circuit Reads CVRA Narrowly' (2020) 263(102) NYLJ 1.

[57] *In re Wild* (n 14).

[58] ibid 1260.

submit a motion, as an incidental matter arising in the progress of a criminal proceeding, but it does not recognize an independent right or remedy.

As part of its reasoning, the majority of the Circuit Court found that there was no clear evidence that Congress intended to create a private right of action and posited that recognizing such right of action would impede prosecutorial discretion—which the charging decision essentially is at its core. It highlighted that

> Ms Wild's reading of the CVRA would permit a putative victim to challenge the correctness, in either case, of the prosecutor's charge decision in court—effectively appealing the prosecutor's exercise of discretion to a federal district judge. Judicial review of a prosecutor's decision whether to prosecute is the very quintessence of an 'impairment of prosecutorial discretion'.[59]

It also proceeded to suggest that

> the commencement of criminal proceedings marks a clear and sensible boundary on the prosecutorial-discretion spectrum. Before charges are filed—when the government is still in the process of investigating and deciding 'whether to prosecute'—its authority and discretion are understood to be 'exclusive' and 'absolute' . . . By contrast, once the charging decision is made, the prosecutor steps into the court's jurisdiction—its 'house', so to speak—and thus necessarily cedes some of her control of the course and management of the case. From that point forward, the court will assume a more active role in administering adjudication of a defendant's guilt and determining the appropriate sentence.[60]

This decision posited important limits to state accountability, in instances of errors or unreasonable decisions relating to decisions not to charge. Accordingly, it reaffirms prosecutorial monopoly and asserts that victims may not bring claims under the CVRA, even in instances where decisions not to charge contain errors and have been made in ways that do not reflect the public interest.

The dissenting opinions in this decision bring to the fore the serious consequences of this case on the potential for victims to serve as agents of state accountability in instances of state failures. These judges highlight the importance

[59] ibid 1262.
[60] ibid 1263.

that CVRA rights apply before charging decisions and the potential for victims to have standing independently from criminal proceedings. Namely, Branch and Hulls argued that situating pre-charge issues outside of the scope of the CVRA would essentially allow the state to engage freely in secret deals (such as the NPA relevant to this case) with wealthy defendants who can afford to have lawyers who negotiate such agreements. In turn, they highlighted that the majority's decision may reinforce socio-economic disparities between defendants, and eliminate accountability mechanisms available to victims in these circumstances. Judge Hull's dissent clearly disapproves of the approach taken by the majority by stating:

> The Epstein victims have no remedy as to the government's appalling misconduct because the Majority rewrites the CVRA to add a blanket post-indictment limitation and reads out of the statute any ability for crime victims to judicially enforce their conferral rights <u>outside</u> of a preexisting criminal proceeding. The Majority's ruling eviscerates the CVRA and makes the Epstein case a poster child for an entirely different justice system for crime victims of wealthy defendants.[61]

In a separate dissent, Judge Branch relied on the plain text of the CVRA to argue that the victim's 'reasonable' right to confer with state prosecutors extended to pre-charge decisions such as the NPA in question. This echoes Cassell and others' views on this matter,[62] which were reaffirmed in scholarship after this decision,[63] and highlight that confining the CVRA's application to post-charge decisions is an inappropriate mechanism to delimit the boundaries of the CVRA since the word 'reasonable' in this legislation already provides sufficient limitations on the extent of review available for charging decisions.

State accountability and systemic misconceptions rooted in inequalities

Prosecutorial decision-making fallibilities relating to decisions about whether or not to prosecute, including those relating to NPAs, can and have taken place at both stages of the two-prong test. First, there can be errors in the first stage

[61] ibid 1327.
[62] Cassell, Mitchell, and Edwards (n 48).
[63] Cassell, Edwards, and Peck (n 49).

relating to the sufficiency of evidence available, particularly in the ways the evidence is interpreted—which can be rooted in systemic inequalities. For instance, credibility related biases towards certain classes of persons can occur at this stage of the assessment. Second, errors can also relate to the way that the public interest is understood, particularly in contexts of power dynamics where defendants in advantageous positions, such as Epstein and corporations, are able to make better non-prosecutorial deals with prosecutions, which are often erroneously presented as advancing the public interest. As will be seen in the next chapter, the concept of public interest can be nebulous and the next chapter seeks to provide a framework rooted in substantive equality to guide the analysis of the public interest and the role of victims in holding the state accountable for decisions that involve the public interest.

As articulated by the dissenting opinions in *In re Wild*, insulating prosecutorial pre-charging decisions from the victims' accountability role under the CVRA risks affecting marginalized victims who are disproportionately impacted by errors by the prosecutorial state. This is especially prevalent in certain contexts, where state prosecutors are prone to make errors rooted in biases and inequalities. Examples can be seen in the context of sexual violence that include high rates of attrition, where only 0.4–5.4 per cent of rapes will be prosecuted due to credibility biases suffered by certain groups of victims.[64] As highlighted by Tuerkheimer,[65] it is important that prejudiced disbeliefs regarding sexual violence be recognized as a distinct type of epistemic error rooted in inequalities. This includes the multiple ways in which gender, racial, and socioeconomic institutional biases intersect in these cases.[66] Sexual assault cases are not the only types of cases that have given rise to such prosecutorial errors. Indeed, multiple other contexts, as seen in previous chapters, have given rise to forms of systemic under-prosecution in part due to misconceptions rooted in inequalities—most notably in contexts of police violence and hate crimes.[67]

[64] Kimberly A Lonsway and Joanne Archambault, 'The "Justice Gap" for Sexual Assault Cases: Future Directions for Research and Reform' (2012) 18 Violence Against Women 145, 146, 157. Another study that examines six jurisdictions across the United States found that the attrition problem in sexual assault cases in the United States stems in great part from prosecutors' frequent refusal to bring criminal charges. See Melissa S Morabito, Linda M Williams and April Pattavina, *Decision Making in Sexual Assault Cases: Replication Research on Sexual Violence Case Attrition in The United States* (National Criminal Justice Reference Service 2019).

[65] Deborah Tuerkheimer, 'Incredible Women: Sexual Violence and the Credibility Discount' (2017) 160 U Pa L Rev 1, 36, 38–41.

[66] ibid.

[67] Buchhandler-Raphael (n 47). The under-prosecution phenomenon in the United States is also manifested in other types of crime, most notably unjustified police violence and hate crimes.

These realities echo some of the dynamics and realities, discussed in Chapter 4, pointed out by Justice Hale in England and Wales,[68] who has problematized the limited state accountability mechanisms in contexts of historically prejudiced victims who have traditionally not been believed or considered less worthy of state protection.

Due to these individual and systemic failures, it is important to provide victims with possibilities to seek state accountability in circumstances where these forms of wrongdoing are undermined or disregarded. In the federal American context, as the CVRA is the primary mechanism used to ensure state accountability within the criminal justice system, excluding pre-charge decisions, such as the decision in *In re Wild*,[69] effectively eliminates the victim's options to seek accountability, including in blatantly erroneous and unreasonable decisions that are rooted in, and perpetuate, inequalities. The recent killing of Ahmaud Arbery,[70] along with many other cases in similar social contexts discussed in Chapter 6, where race and power dynamics are relevant, illustrates some of these difficulties and highlights the importance for victims to have mechanisms for holding the state accountable, particularly in instances where their credibility is undermined due to their positionality within society and in relation to the accused. In this case, three men were accused of killing a Black youth who was jogging in a rural town in Georgia, when three men began to pursue him in two trucks. When surrounded by these vehicles, a struggle ensued, and McMichael shot him three times, once at point-blank range. Importantly, it took more than two months for the men to be arrested and prosecuted in part due to the failures by two of the initial prosecutors to lay charges and advising police not to arrest. Two months after the shooting, a graphic video of the killing started to spread on social media platforms, which prompted the arrest. A case like this one, along with many other examples discussed in Chapter 6 relating to prosecutorial failures to prosecute, would have benefited from a mechanism in which victims can seek reviews of decisions not to lay charges.

As seen in England and Wales, the various mechanisms of accountability that conceive of the victim as an entity who can bring forward the public interest and can substantively engage with rationales that underpin decisions

[68] *R (on the application of Gujra) (FC) v CPS*, [2012] UKSC 52, 132.
[69] *In re Wild* (n 52).
[70] US Department of Justice, 'Federal Judge Sentences Three Men Convicted of Racially Motivated Hate Crimes in Connection with the Killing of Ahmaud Arbery in Georgia' (8 August 2022) <https://www.justice.gov/archives/opa/pr/federal-judge-sentences-three-men-convicted-racially-motivated-hate-crimes-connection-killing> accessed 24 September 2024.

relating to decisions about whether or not to charge an individual can facilitate the recognition, discovery, and substantive engagement with state failures rooted in inequalities.

4. Conclusion

Analysing the evolving role of victims as agents of state accountability under the CVRA highlights the predominantly private and aggregate conception of victim interests within the public criminal process and a form of limited accountability that is often procedural, and only available once charges are laid in the process. This approach that applies post-charging can be seen with several prosecutorial decisions and accountability underpinnings under the CVRA, particularly those that can be subjected to judicial approval, such as plea agreements and DPAs. This predominantly private and aggregate approach has limited the potential for accountability in those instances, since victims are seen to undertake a mere procedural role without possibilities of substantively discussing prosecutorial decision-making. More recently, however, the CVRA's analysis reveals that in some contexts, notably that of restitution, a second approach to accountability is present and seen as more legitimate, offering a substantive form of accountability. Specifically, in the context of restitution, while victims are understood as holders of predominantly private interests, these interests are considered more justified, since restitution within the criminal legal process is seen as complementary to torts and therefore more welcoming of the private role of victims. Finally, a third approach to accountability has emerged in the context of prosecutorial pre-charging decisions. As victims are seen as holders of predominantly private interests in those contexts, their role as agents of state accountability in state prosecutorial decisions about whether or not to charge an individual has been delegitimized under the CVRA. Indeed, contrary to the approaches in England and Wales, discussed in Chapters 4 and 5, this suggests that state prosecutorial decisions about whether or not to prosecute in the federal American context will be shielded from review. Victims are not even seen as having the potential to make aggregate private contributions to the public interest as there is a view that the public interest is purely a matter of state prosecutors even in instances of errors and unreasonable assessments. In this sense, this approach limits the CVRA's general approach to accountability that applies post-charges—namely, its potential for considering a victim's private interests as part of an aggregate component of the public interest.

These decisions highlight the overall limits that stem from considering the victim as holders of private interests, including when they can make claims to the public interests in a private aggregate way. This accountability role is often reduced to one of procedural importance, which does not recognize the victim's legitimacy in making substantive claims in instances of state fallibilities. This limits the victim's contributions towards the public interest, which, as will be discussed in Chapter 8, limits their legitimacy in holding the state accountable in instances of errors and systemic decision-making failures.

PART III
TOWARDS A NORMATIVE FRAMEWORK

8

Strengthening the Citizen-Victim's Role Within a Public Conception

A Normative Framework of State Accountability

1. Introduction

Previous chapters have illustrated how the role of victims as agents of state accountability can be understood differently relative to the location of victim interests along the public–private spectrum. Within the context of prosecutorial accountability, greater engagement, legitimacy, and potential for substantive assessments arise in contexts where victims are viewed as potential holders of public interests. Moreover, mechanisms that conceive of victims as potential holders of public interests widen the notion of the 'victim', extending standing beyond those directly harmed by the offence, encompassing a broader public. Indeed, as seen, when rooted within a public conception, citizen-victims have been able to make substantive claims about prosecutorial decisions in instances of various forms of state failures, ranging from errors of law to fallibilities rooted within wider social inequalities.

Nevertheless, as highlighted in previous chapters, England and Wales is increasingly moving towards an individualizing and privatized approach, mirroring to some extent the United States, where victims are viewed as holding private interests. As seen, this conception can be problematic for state accountability as it rests upon and reinforces the idea that the state holds a monopoly over the public interest. In practice, this translates to forms of state accountability that are more procedural and aggregate as victims are considered to hold less legitimacy to substantively challenge state decisions relating to the public interest—particularly in matters relating to prosecutorial discretion. Nevertheless, as discussed, the approach in England and Wales still holds important differences with the American approach, as it is still rooted within a long tradition of victims as potential holders of public interests within

Victims as Agents of State Accountability. Marie Manikis, Oxford University Press. © Marie Manikis 2026.
DOI: 10.1093/9780191993947.003.0011

prosecutorial decision-making about whether to prosecute, which has contributed to maintaining possibilities for substantive review in instances of errors.

This chapter builds on the preceding analysis by proposing a normative framework to strengthen the role of victims as agents of state accountability, grounded in deliberative democratic theory and a clearer conception of the public interest. It argues for recognizing victims as citizens who may legitimately hold public interests and a role in articulating and defending the public interest, particularly where state actors fall short in doing so. The proposed framework adopts a unitary conception of the public interest rooted in democratic principles that include substantive equality. Within this model, victims are not merely seen as holders of private interests, but civic participants with the capacity, legitimacy, and civic duty to hold prosecutorial decision-making to account when it presents fallibilities, including deviations from the public interest.

This recognition would not only enable victims, as agents of state accountability, to make substantive arguments regarding individual state failures, but would also enable them to address systemic failures, including those rooted in self-interested decisions and inequalities. Underpinning the role of victims within this framework would advance the enterprise of criminal law, including the potential to assign and communicate responsibility with greater nuances and accuracy by being attentive to the criminogenic dynamics which the state contributes to that are rooted in systemic inequalities. As will be seen, considering certain forms of evidence as relevant in decision-making would not only focus on highlighting individual errors but also on addressing systemic failures that can be rooted in institutional power, epistemic injustices, and social inequalities—especially where victims' participation could help identify and contest those systemic flaws. Currently, the role of 'victim' as agents of state accountability is understood as serving red light functions, discussed in Chapter 3—where state errors are viewed as anomalies capable of corrections whereas the framework proposed in this chapter also advances green light functions—rooted in deliberative democratic practices that encourage a state and polity that are self-conscious and in a constant and dynamic state of improvement to support a public interest rooted in values of substantive equality.

This chapter is divided into three sections. First, it presents the various forms of state failures rooted in different types of social inequalities that can affect the enterprise of criminal law by inaccurately ascribing and assessing criminal responsibility. Second, it argues that victims, as citizens, have duties to hold the state accountable for individual and systemic failures by underpinning this role within a communitarian/citizen deliberative democratic framework.

Third, the chapter concludes by illustrating how this role can be integrated within criminal law to ensure prosecutorial decision-making responds to the state's potential to reproduce systemic inequalities.

2. State Fallibilities Rooted in Inequalities

The state, as part of a structure created by and comprising of individuals, is susceptible to human error.[1] As discussed in previous chapters, in the context of criminal justice, the state and its agencies, notably prosecutors, can fail in meeting their duties in decision-making. While many of the failures discussed in cases throughout this monograph have been characterized as interpretative legal errors, misapplications of laws and policies, or errors in judgment made by state professionals, many are increasingly understood as sharing deeper roots in systemic decision-making fallibilities—namely, decision-making biases driven by self-interest rationales as well as implicit biases grounded in broader social inequalities. For these reasons, it is essential for the theoretical framework that underpins the role of victims as agents of state accountability to also strengthen victims' capacity and legitimacy to bring forward forms of state wrongdoing rooted in prosecutorial private interests and implicit systemic social inequalities.

This section proceeds first by identifying the spectrum of state fallibilities that may arise according to Duff and Lacey's frameworks of social inequalities. Next, it outlines those precise state decision-making failures relating to responsibility within criminal legal proceedings—many of which are rooted in substantive inequalities. This will provide the background for the next section that aims to justify the role of victims as legitimate agents to hold the state accountable in these instances. As will be seen, this proposed victims' role is rooted within a framing that considers victims as citizens that can hold public interests within a normative conception of the public interest rooted in substantive equality.

[1] RA Duff, 'When Should We Plead Guilty' in Julian V Roberts and Jesper Ryberg (eds), *Sentencing the Self-Convicted: The Ethics of Pleading Guilty* (Hart Publishing 2023).

Contextualizing state failures

Duff's framework on relative eutopias/dystopias,[2] outlined in Chapter 3, describes two contexts of state failures. First, there are mainly individualized state errors—in other words, human errors that are not necessarily rooted in inequalities. Second, there are those that are mainly rooted within and reproduce various forms of social and structural injustices. These forms of failures can co-exist and intertwine and may affect both offenders and victims. The following discussion offers an overview of these types of errors and their manifestations within the criminal legal process.

Quasi-eutopias

Duff distinguishes between two scenarios that lie near opposite ends of a spectrum ranging from a quasi-eutopia to a quasi-dystopia. The first scenario, referred to as a quasi-eutopia, describes the context of a decent democratic republic in which liberty, equality, and respect are values to which its citizens and government are genuinely and reciprocally committed.[3] In this context, criminal laws are democratically validated and legitimate in their scope; criminal process complies with the rights associated with due process and treats defendants with equality and respect. Punishments in this context are moderate in their severity and constructive in their intent and impact—and do not entail the loss of dignity. A commitment to the prevention of oppression underlies this process, as charges of wrongdoing are put to the test in a way that protects citizens against state decision-making fallibilities, which include private self-interested reasons and implicit biases.[4] Overall, a quasi-eutopia reflects a decent polity, in which defendants are treated—by their fellow citizens and by the state—with equal concern and respect.

Aligning with Duff's framework, this scenario would include equal concern, respect, and treatment of victims as citizens. Processes that relate to prosecutions and determination of responsibility would therefore treat victims and defendants with respect, namely, with a presumption of honesty, good faith, and free from evidentiary stereotypes rooted in substantive inequalities, while pursuing this wider assessment detached from self-serving interests for determining the truth about the public wrong that would merit accurate censure.

[2] ibid.

[3] Ronald Dworkin, *A Matter of Principle* (Harvard UP 1986) 190.

[4] Bruce A Green and Rebecca Roiphe, 'Rethinking Prosecutors' Confiicts of Interest' (2017) 58 BCL Rev 463.

This scenario does not suggest that there is never any state wrongdoing. Duff highlights that 'even in our eutopia, protections against various kinds of potential state oppression are important: it is a society of fallible human beings, including fallible officials and institutions'.[5] Within the quasi-eutopian scenario, most instances of state fallibility would be within the realm of *individual* failures by state actors, including prosecutors and other representatives, relating to the odd individual human fallibility, as opposed to decision-making flaws rooted in systemic failures. This is explained by the fact that, within this scenario, concerns for the public interest rather than self-serving goals, values of respect, and substantive equality are for the most part respected and protect against structural oppression. As the quasi-eutopia recognizes the democratic commitments and capacities of its citizens, these citizens may act to guard against the state's fallibility. Specifically, this would entail processes by which citizens could bring forward and act to redress instances of state fallibilities in criminal law. Conversely, citizens may also be understood as fallible—highlighting the importance of a system of checks and balances in which power would not be held as a monopoly or quasi-monopoly.

Quasi-dystopias

Duff's second scenario, referred as quasi-dystopia, envisions a polity that is significantly dystopian, although not to the extent that law is nothing more than empty rhetoric. In such a context, values of liberty, equality, and of equal concern and respect for all still have *some* purchase within the social fabric and political design. However, these values function more as ideals that the polity radically fails to achieve—or even to pursue with serious commitment. Significant groups within this society are excluded from its benefits—and thus from the status of citizenship. While the law can claim to have some authority, its application is substantively unequal, used for private gains and interests, and disproportionately used against marginalized groups in ways that result in over- and under-criminalization. This produces damaging consequences, particularly to these groups that further exclude them from too many of the rights and benefits of membership in the polity. Most instances of state fallibilities can be attributed to systemic failures.

Lacey's typology of social injustices, rooted in structural inequalities, is particularly useful in conceptualizing the different forms of systemic state failures present within quasi-dystopias,[6] including the criminal legal process.

[5] Duff (n 1) 19.

[6] Nicola Lacey, 'Criminal Justice and Social (In)Justice' in Virginia Mantouvalou and Jonathan Wolff (eds), *Structural Injustice and the Law* (UCL Press 2024); Duff (n 1).

She distinguishes between material injustices, epistemic injustices, and injustices of standing. *Material injustices* refer to the unjust distribution of access to public goods, opportunities, and material resources that are known to be criminogenic. These conditions can shape opportunities for individuals to conform their behaviour to the norms of criminal law—or create special barriers and difficulties in the path of their efforts to do so. They can also limit potential resources for individuals to find safety in contexts of violence. Relatedly, there are *epistemic* injustices,[7] understood as the way knowledge is shaped, received, and validated, rendering claims made by certain groups/individuals less valid and less audible due to their positionality within society. This can be rooted in material injustices that create disparate access to platforming. Epistemic injustices may also flow more subtly from factors such as implicit biases rooted in inequalities of standing, as in assessments of veracity and credibility. Indeed, in scenarios of social injustices, some individuals belonging to certain marginalized groups are considered less credible and respected as their existence and their voices are perceived as illegitimate due to stereotypes and biases.[8] Finally, injustices of *standing* refer to the basic level of participation, recognition, or status within a political community, meant to be marked by reciprocity and the minimal level of respect warranted to participate in such processes. Indeed, this form of injustice can be seen at a more basic level than epistemic injustices, but can also give rise and contribute to epistemic injustices.

As highlighted in scholarship on state fallibilities,[9] many of the self-serving and/or implicit social injustices can be criminogenic. In this sense, responsibility for crime becomes more complicated by the state's involvement in criminogenic realities, which are often ignored and inaccurately assessed by state decision-makers in criminal legal processes. Material, epistemic, and standing injustices can give rise to problematic state decision-making that is often rooted in self and institutional interests as well as biases rooted in substantive inequalities. Specifically, these realities can affect the accurate attribution of responsibility in evidentiary assessments and determination of what constitutes

[7] Miranda Fricker, *Epistemic Injustice: Power and the Ethics of Knowing* (OUP 2007).

[8] There is long-standing evidence in sociology, critical race theory, history, economics, as well as psychology on the operation of implicit biases, as well as on the long-standing impact of gendered and racialized stereotypes that impede the ability of individuals to have their truth claims affirmed. See Patricia Hills Collins, *Black Feminist Thought: Knowledge, Consciousness and the Politics of Empowerment* (Routledge 2019).

[9] Marie Manikis, 'Recognising State Blame in Sentencing: A Communicative and Relational Framework' (2022) 81(2) CLJ 294. Types of state failures include: (1) the state's systemic criminogenic contribution by the creation and maintenance of societal inequalities; (2) the state's systemic and criminogenic contribution through criminalization policies and practices that target or affect marginalized groups; and (3) state's contribution in the production of 'excess harms' from legitimate punishment.

the public interest in criminal legal proceedings—including in decisions about prosecutions—for which, as will be discussed in Section 3, victims as citizens should be legitimate agents to hold the state accountable for.

Failing to account for systemic inequalities in the assessment of responsibility

This subsection outlines those precise state decision-making failings that relate to the assessment of criminal responsibility within criminal legal proceedings for which victims can be legitimate agents to hold the state accountable.

Whether by state prosecutors or judges, state assessments of responsibility in criminal law rely on an indeterminist[10] narrative of responsibility which assumes that crime and decisions are done by agents wholly in control of their decisions and choices. This approach impacts state decision-makers' assessments of evidence relating to responsibility for wrongdoing. In turn, state actors overlook or consider irrelevant the systemic forces rooted, often in inequalities, that may influence their own assessments relating criminal responsibility.[11]

Farmer claims that criminal law has often been pictured a certain way for strategic reasons, despite this picture being in many ways remote from reality. In this sense, a certain kind of orthodoxy has developed within criminalization theory and practice—about the rational and objective character of the criminal law and the subject's agency.[12] These comments are useful in thinking about the state's assignation of responsibility, particularly in contexts under which the state has contributed to criminogenic conditions by its own failures rooted in substantive inequalities.

Contexts of private interests and social inequalities discussed above, including those articulated by Duff and Lacey, highlight the need to provide greater nuances to the state's assessment and communication of responsibility in order to ensure a more accurate ascription of responsibility. Notably, criminal law ought to consider the ways systemic inequalities affect decision-making processes, including in the context of prosecutorial decision-making.

[10] Benjamin Berger, 'Mental Disorder and the Instability of Blame in the Criminal Law' in Francois Tanguay-Renaud and J Stribopoulos (eds), *Rethinking Criminal Law Theory* (OUP 2012).

[11] Kimberlé Crenshaw, 'Mapping the Margins: Intersectionality, Identity Politics, and Violence Against Women of Color' (1991) 43 Stanford L Rev 1241: foundational work outlining how systems fail to account for intersectional vulnerabilities.

[12] Lindsay Farmer, 'Criminal Law as an Institution: Rethinking Theoretical Approaches to Criminalization' in RA Duff and others (eds), *Criminalization: The Political Morality of the Criminal Law* (OUP 2014).

As discussed below, these include decisions about the potential for conviction as part of decisions whether to prosecute, by examining evidentiary and interpretative assessments of credibility, and decisions about pursuits of the public interest.

Accounting for systemic inequalities in the assignment of individual responsibility for crime

Substantively, to ensure a more accurate ascription of criminal responsibility that enables greater fairness and decisions in the public interest, criminogenic social injustices should be relevant considerations for prosecutors and judges when assessing individual responsibility at various stages of criminal legal decision-making. These inequalities can impact individual volition by either influencing mental states during decision-making or by limiting the ability to make free choices.

Social inequalities that affect mental states and decision-making processes include those that contribute to various traumas which impact the emotional regulatory system. Studies in neuroscience and social psychology have made clear that the state's infliction of trauma on an individual can be criminogenic; it may affect the person's ability to make decisions according to their own volition. Indeed, exposure to extreme adversity or toxic stress, including physical abuse and other chronic exposure to state violence, can induce significant and long-standing, yet reversible,[13] alterations in the brain's structure. This may directly affect the neurotransmission pathways that govern emotional regulation, threat perception, and social cues.[14] These alterations have been associated with a greater risk of maladaptive actions and behaviours.[15] These past traumatic experiences can provide reasons that may fall short of the current legal definitions of exculpatory defences such as necessity and duress, yet still be relevant to the degree of moral blameworthiness.[16] Importantly, considering the brain's adaptability and spasticity, alterations can be reversed through adapted relational environments—suggesting the importance of adequately

[13] Federica Coppola, *The Emotional Brain and the Guilty Mind: Novel Paradigms of Culpability and Punishment* (Hart Publishing 2021). Considering the brain's adaptability and spasticity, alterations can be reversed through an adapted relational environment. This is significant in that it suggests the importance of adequately adapted responsive to violence/harms that consider this social context.

[14] Jennifer Mervyn and Stacy Ashton, 'Trauma-Informed Neurobiology and Criminal Behaviour' in Shereen Hassan, Dan Lett, and Leah Ballantyne (eds) *Introduction to Criminology* (KPU Press 2023).

[15] Sophie Aiyer and others, 'Exposure to Violence Predicting Cortisol Response During Adolescence and Early Adulthood: Understanding Moderate Factors' (2014) 43(7) J Youth Adolesc 1066; J Douglas Bremner, 'Traumatic Stress: Effects on the Brain' (2006) 8(4) Dialogues Clin Neurosci 445.

[16] Richard Lippke, 'Chronic Temptation, Reasonable Firmness, and the Criminal Law' (2014) 34(1) OJLS 75.

adapted responses by state decision-makers to violence/harms that are attentive to this social context.

Moreover, social inequalities and chronic systemic discrimination may impact the material conditions that shape individuals' behaviour relative to crime. Writing in the context of the 'dark ghetto' in the United States, Shelby[17] points out that the environment of the disadvantaged, segregated, and disrespected produces conditions that undermine fair equality of opportunities in areas of housing, marketable skills, healthcare, and other basic needs. In turn, ghetto residents experience barriers to conform their behaviour to the norms of criminal law. This highlights the need for state decision-making relating to responsibility to consider those nuances in the ways one understands volition and choice in offending.

As suggested by Morse, contrary to the 'all-or-nothing doctrines' relating to capacity for rationality, control, and hard choices, this approach requires us to consider agency arrayed on a continuum.[18] This framing is important across decisions relating to responsibility—including those made by state prosecutors when assessing whether there is sufficient evidence against the individual to provide a realistic prospect of conviction.

Evidence of the effects of state failure on one's volition can be assessed in different ways, including with sociological and criminological expert reports, studies on criminogenic conditions, as well as social neuroscience, psychological studies, and background-cultural assessment reports.[19] Experiential evidence can also be useful and would be complemented by social scientific research on the specific criminogenic nature of conduct and its effect on volition. Since we are within such a complex field with interconnected variables that may affect levels of volition, evidence by state decision-makers should be admitted with flexibility to draw a fuller portrait of the situational context.

Accounting for systemic inequalities by recognizing relational responsibility for crime

As the previous subsection demonstrates that crime is rarely entirely the result of individual wrongdoing, it is important that the state recognize its own wrongdoing in crime—referred to as a relational form of responsibility to prevent defective practices of attributing responsibility. An earlier

[17] Tommie Shelby, 'Justice, Deviance, and the Dark Ghetto' (2007) 35 Phil & Pub Aff 126; Tommie Shelby, *Dark Ghettos, Injustice, Dissent, and Reform* (Harvard UP 2016).

[18] Stephen J Morse, 'Diminished Rationality, Diminished Responsibility' (2002) 1 Ohio St J Crim L 289, 296.

[19] *R v Ipeelee* 2012 SCC 13.

article has articulated the various ways, rooted in structural inequalities, by which the state can contribute to the creation of crime and argues that those dimensions should be part of state decision-making in sentencing.[20] As highlighted in the previous subsection, this includes systemic forms of discrimination that affect neuropathways as well as create conditions for criminalized behaviour.

Relational responsibility should be considered at every decision-making level within the criminal process including in the context of prosecutorial discretion about whether to charge an individual with an offence or enter into any form of agreement. For instance, prosecutorial agents may recognize legal responses to criminality as criminogenic—such as prosecutions in some instances can indeed be contrary to a public interest that upholds substantive equality. In their assessments, prosecutors would need to engage with empirical data about how decisions relating to criminalization, alternatives to criminalization, entering agreements, or failures to prosecute an individual in certain contexts may impact criminality. Considering these issues by relying on social science research and experiential aspects rooted in substantive equality should form part of prosecutorial analysis and provide more informed responses relating to prosecutions. Arguably, the role of state—and more specifically the prosecutorial state—in creating or reducing further criminogenic conditions should be part of conversations about reasonable responses for context-specific offences and individuals.

Prejudicial assessments and their impact on responsibility in criminal proceedings

In addition to decision-making that inadequately attribute responsibility to individuals, social injustices may also direct prosecutors away from recognizing responsibility of offenders in other circumstances. In contexts of social injustices, certain individuals are deemed less credible and respected as their existence and voices are perceived as illegitimate due to stereotypes and biases. Conversely, some voices are amplified and attributed greater credibility. These decision-making errors relate to Lacey's epistemic forms of social injustices, which may stem from implicit biases rooted in inequalities of standing. These biases often affect how veracity and credibility are assessed, which can significantly impact the attribution of responsibility in state decision-making processes—affecting victims, offenders, and the overall polity.

[20] Manikis (n 9).

State failures that impact the assessment of responsibility may occur due to systemic biases, power dynamics, and misconceptions stemming from inequalities that marginalize the complainant.[21] As seen in previous chapters, this is often the case in contexts of gender-based violence, police brutality against racialized individuals, and other forms of violence that remain under-prosecuted.[22] As emphasized by Deborah Tuerkheimer,[23] it is important to recognize prejudiced disbelief as a specific form of epistemic error rooted in inequalities. The potential for systemic and individual state decision-making errors during the investigative and prosecutorial phases must not be underestimated, especially given the ways in which gender, race, and socio-economic biases intersect in these cases.[24]

These state failures are highlighted by Lady Hale's dissent in *Gujra*,[25] in which she supports citizen-led mechanisms to hold the state accountable in contexts where it has historically failed certain victims—namely, those 'who have traditionally had such difficulty in getting their voices heard or, if heard, believed'.[26]

Relatedly, prosecutorial decisions that are made consciously or unconsciously, as self-serving private-based interests also affect the relevant attribution of responsibility in the criminal process. Green and Roiphe provide several examples, which include conflict of interests that relate to personal and professional relationships between prosecutors and other parties in the process.[27] Most prominent examples that have taken place in the American context include cases of police brutality, political actors, forfeitable assets, and corporate investigations. For instance, professional and personal ties between

[21] Michal Buchhandler-Raphael, 'Underprosecution Too' (2022) 56 U Rich L Rev 409; Kimberly Lonsway and Joanne Archambault, 'The "Justice Gap" for Sexual Assault Cases: Future Directions for Research and Reform' (2012) 18 Violence Against Women 145, 146, 157; Melissa S Morabito, Linda M Williams, and April Pattavina, *Decision Making in Sexual Assault Cases: Replication Research on Sexual Violence Case Attrition in the United States* (National Criminal Justice Service 2019).

[22] In England and Wales, see English Collective of Prostitutes, 'Successful Private Prosecution of Serial Rapist—R v Davies' (*English Collective of Prostitutes*, 1 January 1996) <https://prostitutescollective.net/private-prosecution/> accessed 24 June 2023; *Moher v Moher* [2019] EWCA Civ 1482; *R v Chabloz* [2019] Westminster Magistrates' Court 25 May 2018 (unreported). In the United States, see *In re Affidavits Relating to Timothy Loehmann & Frank Garmback* (Cleveland Mun Ct, 11 June 11 2015); Peter Kendall, 'A Prosecutor Says No to a Rape Charge, So a College Student Calls Her Own Grand Jury' (*Washington Post*, 19 May 2021) <https://www.washingtonpost.com/national/a-prosecutor-says-no-to-a-rape-charge-so-a-college-student-calls-her-own-grand-jury/2021/05/18/2ea9a130-b766-11eb-a5fe-bb49dc89a248_story.html?utm_campaign=wp_post_most&utm_medium=email&utm_source=newsletter&wpisrc=nl_most&carta-url=https%3A%2F%2Fs2.washingtonpost.com%2Fcar-ln-tr%2F32720c3%2F60a53af19d2fdae302566fd1%2F5ca3e3379bbc0f613a96dff4%2F32%2F68%2F60a53af19d2fdae302566fd1> accessed August 2023; *People v Sears*, 273 NE 2d 380 (1971) 389.

[23] Deborah Tuerkheimer, 'Incredible Women: Sexual Violence and the Credibility Discount' (2017) 160 U Pa L Rev 166(1) 1.

[24] ibid.

[25] *R (on the Application of Gujra) (FC) v CPS*, [2012] UKSC 52, 132.

[26] ibid 124.

[27] Green and Roiphe (n 4).

police and prosecutors, such as the ones discussed by Peter Davis,[28] in addition to biases, can also involve personal/private interests by prosecutors. In those scenarios, police departments impermissibly had favoured their own personal interests and those of their officers who were under investigation and failed to recuse themselves.

As seen in Chapter 3, mechanisms of state accountability in England and Wales that view victims as having the ability and legitimacy of holding public interests have enabled marginalized victims to bring forward these forms of state failures.[29] Nevertheless, as discussed in Chapters 3 and 4, when these mechanisms conceive of victims as holders of private interests, their ability to hold the state accountable, including in contexts of systemic inequalities, seems to be increasingly restricted and subject to state resistance. Similarly, as seen in Chapter 5, in the United States, this privatized view of the victim has the effect of insulating erroneous decisions made by state prosecutors rooted in epistemic injustices and inequalities from substantive accountability.[30]

Cognizant of these limitations, the next section offers a theoretical account, rooted in a deliberative democratic framework that conceives of victims as potential holders of public interests. This approach imagines the role of victims as agents of state accountability in ways that recognize their agency and legitimacy in bringing forward evidence of state failures, including those that are rooted in systemic inequalities.

3. Reclaiming the Public Interest: Citizen-Victims, State Fallibilities, and State Accountability Rooted in a Deliberative Democratic Framework

The polity has a direct interest in ensuring that state decisions about criminal responsibility are made in ways that accurately reflect public values and account for inequalities, such as considering the effect of material injustice and interpretational errors relating to epistemic injustice. In turn, victims, as citizens and members of the polity, share this public role and duty to ensure that decisions take these dimensions into account. In this sense, when state

[28] Peter L Davis, 'Rodney King and the Decriminalization of Police Brutality in America: Direct and Judicial Access to the Grand Jury as Remedies for Victims of Police Brutality When the Prosecutor Declines to Prosecute' (1994) 53 Md L Rev 263.

[29] English Collective of Prostitutes (n 22); *Moher* (n 22); *Chabloz* (n 22).

[30] For instance, the case of *In re Wild*, 994 F 3d 1244, 1254 n10 (11th Cir 2021) (en banc) highlights the limits placed on the role of victims in bringing forward prosecutorial decisions rooted in substantive inequalities.

decisions fail to adequately consider these dimensions, victims as citizens have a duty to hold the state accountable—discussed in this section.

Conceptualizing victims as citizens who can hold public interests,[31] as part of a deliberative democratic framework, provides a legitimizing basis for recognizing their role as agents of state accountability. This approach moves beyond conceiving of victims as mere holders of individual private interests and emphasizes their role in making arguments that contribute to the public interest by seeking accountability in instances of state decision-making failures, including those rooted in inequalities. This section also provides some of the contours of this role—notably by justifying and underpinning this role within the public interest rooted within values of substantive equality, defining the concept of victim and standing, as well as drawing out the duties held by citizens-victims as part of this role.

Conceptualizing the public interest in the enterprise of criminal law as rooted in deliberate democratic values that uphold substantive equality

As part of developing the role of victims as agents of state accountability that can hold public interests, it is important to provide some of the relevant underpinnings of this role. This subsection conceptualizes the public interest in the enterprise of criminal law as rooted in deliberate democratic values that suggest they need to make decisions that advance public reasoning which is attentive to substantive equality. It then discusses the ways that a deliberate democratic framework provides the relevant justifications and contours for developing the role of victims as agents of state accountability.

Rooting the notion of the public interest in certain underlying values is an important endeavour. Feintuck warns that the term can be vacuous and at risk of co-optation by those in positions of societal power.[32] Indeed, while the higher courts in England and Wales have repeatedly referred to the 'polycentric character'[33] of decision-making in the public interest, this phrase does not elucidate what has been described as 'ethereal and nebulous nature of this

[31] These interests may align and therefore it may be that the public interest is also in their own personal interests.

[32] Mike Feintuck, *'The Public Interest' in Regulation* (OUP 2004).

[33] *Matalulu v Director of Public Prosecutions* [2003] 4 LRC 712 also referenced *in R (on the Application of Corner House Research and Others) v Director of the Serious Fraud Office* [2008] UKHL 60.

exercise'.[34] Providing a clearer understanding of this term may minimize the risks of seeing this concept co-opted in ways that are used for personal/private reasoning and/or to the detriment of marginalized groups, and benefit the more powerful in society. As such, it is worth anchoring the notion of public interest in a normative set of democratic values—importantly, substantive equality and respect towards fellow citizens. While the purpose of this framing in this section is to infuse dimensions relating to the substantive equality in the public interest as part of the role of victims, this also partly contributes to articulating the relevance of infusing substantive values in prosecutorial decision-making.[35]

Substantive equality has been recognized in democratic frameworks as an alternative to formal equality. As highlighted by Colleen Sheppard, 'formal equality is based on an abstract equal treatment paradigm without regard to the contextual realities of power, or the diverse needs of individuals and communities'.[36] In contrast, substantive equality requires attention to the full context of a given situation and to the persistent systemic discrimination that have operated to limit opportunities available to a certain marginalized group. This notion of systemic discrimination can also be understood as 'a continuing phenomenon which has its roots deep in history and in societal attitudes. It cannot be isolated to a single action or statement. By its very nature, it extends over time.'[37] Indeed, since state failures within criminal law decision-making, discussed in Section 2, are very often rooted in social inequalities, it is paramount that these decisions take into account these power dynamics, notably in their assessment of the evidence and conceptualization of the public interest.

By constructing the public interest so that it is attentive to the power dynamics and unequal social contexts, it becomes a tool available to victims for

[34] See https://www.2harecourt.com/2021/02/01/private-prosecutions-and-the-public-interest/ accessed 23 June 2023; *Mohit v DPP of Mauritius* [2006] UKPC 20, [17], citing *Matalulu v DPP of Fiji* [2003] 4 LRC 712.

[35] As highlighted by Michelle Madden Dempsey, *Prosecuting Domestic Violence* (OUP 2009) 88, very little attention has been paid to the substance of prosecutorial decision-making process, which include some of its underlying values.

[36] Colleen Sheppard, 'Litigating Structural Inequality: Micro, Meso and Macro Dynamics' in Cheryl Milne and Sophia Moreau (eds), *Litigating Equality* (Lexis Nexis 2024). Moreover, on the link between substantive equality and structural inequalities, see Sheila McIntyre, 'Deference and Dominance: Equality Without Substance' in Sheila McIntyre and Sanda Rodgers (eds), *Diminishing Returns: Inequality and the Canadian Charter of Rights and Freedoms* (LexisNexis 2006) 95; Sheila McIntyre, 'Answering the Siren Call of Abstract Formalism with the Subjects and Verbs of Domination' in Fay Faraday, Margaret Ann Denike, and M Kate Stephenson (eds), *Making Equality Rights Real: Securing Substantive Equality under the Charter* (Irwin Law 2009) 99. See also Catharine MacKinnon, 'Substantive Equality: A Perspective' (2011) 96 Minn L Rev 1. In her work, she presents social hierarchy as the 'identifying principle' of substantive equality: see Catharine MacKinnon, 'Substantive Equality Revisited: A Reply to Sandra Fredman' (2016) 14(3) Int'l J Const L 739, 740.

[37] Colleen Sheppard, 'Contester la discrimination systémique au Canada: Droit et changement organisationnel' (2018) 14 La Revue des droits de l'homme <https://doi.org/10.4000/revdh.4161>.

state accountability. Notably, this construction provides a basis for victims to intervene in instances wherein state failures perpetuate systemic injustices. This citizen-based role for victims aligns with the broader pursuit of the public enterprise of criminal justice within deliberative democratic frameworks, which seeks to assign responsibility in a nuanced and accurate manner upholding substantive equality.

Victims as citizens and potential holders of public interests in criminal prosecutions

Rooted within a democratic framework, the enterprise of criminal law is conceived of as the law of citizens to address crime as a public wrong that concerns the polity.[38] This includes assigning responsibility for wrongdoing and calling responsible wrongdoers to public account, in ways that are accurate—in other words, attentive to values of respect and substantive equality, through the criminal legal process that pursues this communicative endeavour.[39] In the context of prosecutions, this includes assessments of responsibility to determine whether a prosecution will charge or not—engaging in what Madden Dempsey has described as 'pursuit and non-pursuit'[40] as part of pursuing or not a communicative denunciation in the public interest. In this context, victims are conceived of as part of the wider citizenry/public, who have a civic responsibility in assisting criminal justice's legitimate and fair enterprise. Marshall highlights that, as part of this endeavour, citizens are responsible both *to* the state, insofar as they are responsible to one another in their role as citizens, and *for* the state.[41] Seen in this light, the criminal law and its processes are a matter for which citizens, qua citizens, are responsible not merely as subcontractors

[38] According to RA Duff, *Answering for Crime* (Hart Publishing 2007) 141, an act is rightly classified as a crime 'because it properly concerns the public, i.e. the polity as a whole'. See also SE Marshall and RA Duff, 'Criminalization and Sharing Wrongs' (1998) 11 Can J L Juris 7, 19-20. On this account, crimes should be understood as wrongs, which concern us all as members of the community, and thus can be distinguished from private wrongs, which concern only those individuals directly involved (and so would be a matter of private redress). Specifically, for Marshall and Duff certain acts, such as rape or residential burglary, 'properly concern' the public as a whole because the wrong is not only the victim's wrong but also ' "our" wrong insofar as we identify ourselves with her . . . the attack on this individual victim is also an attack on us—on her as a member of the group and on us as fellow members'.

[39] Sandra Marshall, 'It Isn't Just About You: Victims of Crime, Their Associated Duties, and Public Wrongs' in RA Duff and others (eds), *Criminalization: The Political Morality of the Criminal Law* (OUP 2015) 298.

[40] Dempsey (n 35) 53.

[41] Marshall (n 39) 298.

of responsibilities to officials, but as participants sharing responsibility for the enterprise of criminal law with state officials.

Victims, as citizens undertaking this role, would therefore have a duty to ensure that responsibility relating to crime is appropriately assigned and communicated in ways that account for the impact of inequalities. This would include proper assessments of prosecutorial decisions and their evidence to ensure that decisions regarding credibility are not based on stereotypes and biases rooted in inequalities, as discussed above. It also includes analysing responsibility for offences in a way that is attentive to the impact that social context and scientific knowledge may have on responsibility—as discussed below. In addition to treating the victim's duty as civic, it should also be guided by a commitment to substantive equality.

Recognizing the victim as citizen supports the role of victims as agents of state accountability enabled to bring forward various forms of state failures that can impact on the assignation and communication of responsibility. Indeed, any failures that affect the ascription of responsibility—including systemic biases relating to credibility, as well as legal and interpretative errors—would be relevant considerations to bring forward by victims as part of addressing defective practices of responsibility and improving the communicative role of the enterprise of criminal law. This possibility and reflexive process would recognize that the state does not always make decisions that are aligned with the public interest, as a notion rooted within substantive equality. Accordingly, this approach recognizes the importance of listening to citizen-victims who may raise some of these concerns to reify the public interest.

Contrary to frameworks that conceive of victims as mere representatives of their own personal/private interests, deliberative democratic frameworks consider victims citizens and thus as relevant participants who are presumed to have the rational ability[42] and responsibility to bring forward justified and well-substantiated considerations to public decisions. As part of the role of victims developed in this monograph, this framework would apply when state agents fail to do so. These frameworks challenge assumptions that consider victims as irrational on the basis that they make decisions strictly based on their private interests—often associated to revenge and anger—or based on stereotypes rooted in social inequalities. For instance, victims who have experienced intimate partner violence are often seen as bringing forward their own personal views and generally thought to be incapable of making rational

[42] Jeffrey Kennedy, 'The Citizen Victim: Reconciling the Public and Private in Criminal Sentencing' (2018) 13(1) Crim L & Phil 83.

decisions. There is no compelling empirical evidence supporting these assumptions. On the contrary, they serve to diminish the voices of victims who can contribute to the public interest through documented and/or experiential knowledge.

Philosophers committed to substantive equality have contributed to our understanding of the relationship between victimization, anger, and constructive engagement, offering insights that are relevant to the present framework. Feminist philosopher Martha Nussbaum, for instance, introduces the notion of 'transition anger',[43] which she carefully distinguishes from irrational forms of anger that are excessive, obsessive, self-deforming, and backward-looking. Transition anger, by contrast, acknowledges the reality of wrongdoing, but turns to the future for a way forward. Nussbaum highlights that transition anger is important for a struggle against injustice as a form of protest to draw attention to the wrong and energize people to address it. Importantly, she argues that this type of anger does not burden the personality and can be imaginative in thinking about solutions to problems. Within the framework proposed in this chapter, instead of an underlying assumption of anger, citizen-victims' potential anger may be a form of 'transition anger' that can be rational and advance the public interest by pointing out to the more complex dynamics that underlie crime—including the state's relational responsibility. Such engagement has the potential to catalyse more thoughtful, inclusive, creative, and long-lasting responses by state decision-makers in assessments of responsibility and related responses.

Victims of crime can bring relevant experiential knowledge relating to the democratic profile they are part of, which would enrich the deliberative process and reveal important errors in state decision-making.[44] In many jurisdictions, including those under analysis, victimization falls disproportionately on specific groups relative to gender, race, socio-economic status, age, profession, and geography. Victims may therefore hold important experiential knowledge relating to social context and background unavailable to state agents in criminal law.

[43] Martha C Nussbaum, 'The Weakness of the Furies' (*Boston Review*, 19 February 2020) <https://www.bostonreview.net/articles/the-weakness-of-the-furies/> accessed 3 July 2025. A constructive form of anger was also brought forward by Martin Luther King Jr, 'Three Views of Violence' in Clayborne Carson (ed), *The Papers of Martin Luther King, Jr: Volume V, Threshold of a New Decade, January 1959–December 1960* (University of California Press 2005).

[44] As highlighted by Bennett Capers, 'Against Prosecutors' (2020) 105 Cornell L Rev 1561, 1601, within the American context, 'given that sixty-three percent of black and forty-eight percent of Latinx have a family member who has been in jail or in prison, she is likely to know firsthand the harm that prisons can do, not just to the incarcerated but also to their families' as well as their communities'.

Moreover, victims belonging to marginalized groups may also hold important information relating to biases held by state actors. As highlighted by Green and Ruben,

> to the extent that varied public interests are at stake, victims will often have expertise in identifying and assessing some of those interests—and possibly greater expertise than the prosecutors. That is because victims will often be more knowledgeable about how various resolutions will affect them, the offender, and the community, to which prosecutors are often a stranger. Prosecutors often make decisions based on folk wisdom, stereotypes, or generalities.[45]

Often, this might point prosecutors to epistemic knowledge rooted within socio-legal contexts that are seldomly used in decision-making. Victims may also expose reasons grounded in partiality, neglect, or discrimination, as well as bring forward power dynamics and choices that may signal over- or under-prosecutions—notably in cases of sexual violence or police violence. Within a deliberative democratic framework, state prosecutors would be required to engage with those claims publicly by providing explanations rather than hiding between discretion.

Finally, citizen-victims may also be well-placed to generate more accurate evidence-based information themselves. As seen in recent years, citizens have generated what is referred to as 'citizen science',[46] which consists of scientific research carried out, in whole or in part, by members of the general public—often in collaboration with or under the guidance of professional researchers. Such contributions can be beneficial in informing certain realities on the ground and yielding more data within certain geographical areas for which citizen-victims may have greater access to than certain researchers. For instance, citizen-victims can help generate data on prosecutorial harms on victims, communities, and other individuals in certain contexts they may be part of. Indeed, citizens have generated data by attending hearings to record prosecutorial decisions and expose issues with plea deals in the United

[45] Bruce A Green and Brandon P Ruben, 'Should Victims' Views Influence Prosecutors' Decisions?' (2022) 87 Brook L Rev 1127, 1150. See also Olwyn Conway, 'Are There Stories Prosecutors Shouldn't Tell?: The Duty to Avoid Racialized Trial Narratives' (2021) 98 Denv L Rev 457, which discusses the role of racial stereotypes in prosecutors' narratives. Robert J Smith and Justin D Levinson, 'The Impact of Implicit Racial Bias on the Exercise of Prosecutorial Discretion' (2012) 35 Seattle U L Rev 795, which discusses the influence of racial stereotyping on various prosecutorial discretionary decisions.

[46] Mordechai Haklay, 'What Is Citizen Science? The Challenges of Definition' in Silke Vohland and others (eds), *The Science of Citizen Science* (Springer 2021) 13.

States.[47] Citizen-victims have also challenged and complemented official data on under-prosecution by gathering sexual violence testimonies as part of creating large-scale qualitative datasets—referred to as shadow datasets, which have documented systemic under-prosecution and discriminatory credibility assessments.[48]

While a public deliberative democratic framework affirms the epistemic value of victims' knowledge, this does not suggest that every claim made by victims is legitimate and acceptable.[49] Indeed, it is important to distinguish deliberative decision-making from aggregative understandings of democracy and individual political standing. In a deliberative process, arguments made as part of democratic deliberation are considered, analysed, and rationally scrutinized by fellow citizens and their representatives with a mind towards the relevance, quality, justifiability, and merits of those contributions.[50] As part of public reasoning, the weight that individual arguments and proposals carry is contingent upon their persuasiveness—on the basis of the more justified argument. The mere fact that an individual requests a certain result does not in itself carry normative weight. The deliberative analysis does not rest on majoritarian or aggregative perspectives, since these approaches find relevant even misinformed, irrational, or self-interested decisions. Majoritarian and aggregate perspectives of citizen input are premised on the notion that the various competing private preferences or interests of individual citizens are given equal weight and aggregated to produce a decision that reflects the quantitative distinction of those preferences or interests. The camp with a majority will determine the decision, even where its decision is based on misinformation, irrational claims, or self-interested positions. For these reasons, the mere election of state prosecutors would not be rooted in a deliberative democratic account proposed in this chapter.

Rather, within a deliberative democratic framework, the validity of arguments brought forward by victims would be assessed on their alignment with an analysis of evidence and a public interest, rooted in substantive equality, rather than victims' personal, private, or subjective preferences. For an argument to hold weight in such a framework, it must be justified and measured based on principles that an informed public—aware of the core values of

[47] ibid.
[48] Trang Le, 'Data, Anecdotes, Anecdotal Data: Feminist Data Activism Against Gendered Violence Post #Metoo' (2024) 11(4) Big Data & Society 1.
[49] Kennedy (n 42).
[50] Amy Gutmann and Dennis Thompson, *Why Deliberative Democracy?* (Princeton UP 2004).

equality and respect—could accept.[51] Victims, as citizens, would need to contribute publicly with acceptable information, perspectives, and arguments that are consistent with these values when seeking to influence public decisions. Such values would be framed in ways that can mitigate, avoid, or actively work against the social injustices discussed above.

Justified contributions could be informed by empirical, experiential, citizen science, and social science knowledge that can evolve in time.[52] For instance, various cases discussed in previous chapters would bring forward the contextual inequalities present in those cases, including those relating to gender, race, disability, and socio-economic status as part of the assessment of the evidentiary threshold and the public interest. Moreover, in instances of non-prosecution agreements (NPAs), determining the public interest rationale behind those agreements would be relevant and would in cases such as Epstein's arguably expose the logics that are contrary to the public interest.

Further, this framework can be an important check on the nefarious effects of corporate privatization, discussed in previous chapters, which do not serve the public interest. Whether in the context of private prosecutions, or other mechanisms discussed throughout this book, there is a legitimate concern[53] that these mechanisms can turn such public interest processes into tools for personal or corporate private ends that are not in accordance with a public interest rooted in substantive equality.[54] Importantly, only arguments that advance the public dimension within criminal legal decision-making would hold force along with considerations of public interest rooted in substantive equality.

For instance, a citizen-victim may be of the view that an offender has committed a public wrong but decides to challenge the state prosecutor's decision to prosecute in a context where the offender has promised the victim a personal favour. This should be seen as a decision that is not in the public interest unless there are additional rationales that may warrant, in the public interest, not prosecuting the individual, notably where there is evidence that other responses, such as diversion in precarious social conditions, may be more beneficial within the context of this individual and the victim. Indeed, there may be contextual and justified reasons, rooted in substantive equality, that can justify

[51] Joshua Cohen, 'Deliberation and Democratic Legitimacy' in James Bohman and William Rehg (eds), Deliberative Democracy: Essays on reason and Politics (MIT Press 1997).

[52] Kennedy (n 42).

[53] Emma Kaufman, 'The Past and Persistence of Private Prosecution' (2024) 173(1) U Pa L Rev 89, 93; Roger A Fairfax Jr, 'Outsourcing Criminal Prosecution: The Limits of Criminal Justice Privatization' [2010] U Chi Legal F 265, pt III.

[54] Kaufman (n 53).

a decision not to prosecute or, instead, to use different and more adapted responses such as diversion or alternative mechanisms.[55] In this sense, based on social contexts, it may be that alternatives to prosecution may serve the public interest in certain situations and would challenge certain assumptions that are themselves rooted in inequalities.

As part of another example, empirical research shows that prosecuting misdemeanour offences mostly serves to punish conduct of the poor and people of colour, in vast numbers, long before they are convicted and often for conduct that are not relevant public wrongs pursued in the public interest.[56] In this context, Green and Ruben highlight that

> the assumption built into the process is that victims want, and will be best served by, prosecutions and retributive punishment. Many prosecutors proceed from that assumption as well. If anything, prosecutors should check their ordinary impulse to use victims' preferences to bolster their own retributive impulses, because otherwise the risk is that prosecutors will pressure victims to come around to prosecutors' views, misinform them, or misconstrue or ignore their legitimate preferences.[57]

In such instances, the framework proposed in this chapter would enable citizen-victims to undertake their role as agents of prosecutorial state accountability. Most cases that would lend themselves to this role would be situations where citizen-victims may bring forward power dynamics and substantive inequalities that affect the ascription of responsibility discussed above. In this sense, they can challenge implicit assumptions relied upon by state prosecutors when their decisions may be contrary to the public interest as a social democratic value rooted in substantive equality. Such transparency and public deliberations with substantive reasoning would challenge the status quo that often does not engage with public reasons and risks giving rise to state fallibilities without potential for accountability.

[55] Berger (n 10).
[56] For example, empirical evidence has challenged the notion of indeterminist criminal responsibility as well as deterrence in instances where social background and inequalities are at play, particularly in instances of misdemeanours. See Issa Kohler-Hausmann, *Misdemeanorland: Criminal Courts and Social Control in an Age of Broken Windows Policing* (Princeton UP 2018); Alexandra Natapoff, *Punishment Without Crime: How Our Massive Misdemeanor System Traps the Innocent and Makes America More Unequal* (Basic Book 2018).
[57] Green and Ruben (45) 1153.

Applying the same public standards across prosecutions

Importantly, assessing the validity of arguments brought forward by citizen-victims in matters of prosecutions would need to follow the same public standards applicable to state agents. This highlights the importance of having state prosecutors and victims provide public justifications and reasons for their assessments. This is an important dimension that serves to preserve the legitimacy of the role of citizen-victims as agents of state accountability. As seen in Chapter 3, this view is generally recognized in the prosecutorial accountability mechanisms in England and Wales, which highlight the importance that the same prosecutorial standards apply to cases brought forward by citizen-victims or state prosecutors.[58] Indeed, this view was highlighted in several reports in England and Wales that note the importance for private prosecutions to adhere to the same obligations as state prosecutors, notably in terms of guidelines, transparency, review processes, and evidentiary duties, such as the Full Code Test (evidentiary and public interest test) regarding decisions about whether or not to prosecute.[59]

Alternatively, an approach that differentiates between prosecutorial standards that apply to citizen-victims versus state prosecutors would undermine citizen-victim perspectives, as the latter would be considered disparate from the public interest of justice. Indeed, this can be seen to a great extent within the American context. Referring to state prosecutors, Gittler argues that

> it is not necessarily appropriate to apply the same standards and norms to victims' decisions to prosecute and to public prosecutors' decisions to prosecute. Public prosecutors represent the interests of the state and have the responsibility of seeing that justice is done, while victims simply represent their own individual interests. Once the proposition is accepted that victims may have restitutive and retributive interests as arising from the crime deserving of vindication through a criminal prosecution of the offender, differences in the handling of criminal cases deriving from differences in the interests of victims are inevitable. The troublesome aspect of this position is that a victim's

[58] In *Gujra* (n 25) 132, the Supreme Court aligned private prosecutions with prosecutions brought by the state by requiring that private prosecutions also meet the public interest grounds. Moreover, in decisions to the VRRS, citizen-victims can make claims relating to the public interest component. See BBC News, 'CPS Grants Lord Janner Review' (BBC, 16 May 2015) <www.bbc.com/news/uk-32757978> accessed 4 February 2024.

[59] Stephen Wooler, *The Independent Review of the Prosecution Activity of the Royal Society for the Prevention of Cruelty to Animals* (2014).

desire to prosecute may be related not to restitutive and retributive interests arising from the crime but rather to motives extraneous to these interests.[60]

Similarly, in the few American states where citizen-victims can initiate prosecutions by directly accessing a grand jury, the standard differs between state prosecutions and those initiated by citizens. As seen in Chapter 6, in Alabama, the court highlighted that in accessing the grand jury, the citizen is not a prosecutor and therefore 'it is not essential that he have probable cause to believe any individual to be the guilty party'.[61] These distinct standards, prevalent within the American context, are rooted in a conception of victims as mere representatives of their own individual interests. In contrast, the state is seen as having legitimacy in making wider public decisions based on its legal and public interest knowledge.

Implementing similar sets of standards between state prosecutors and citizen-victims would render decisions made by citizen-victims more legitimate as they would need to respect the same evidentiary standards and norms around public decision-making. Such standards can also be seen as important safeguards to ensure that assessments relating to state accountability are made in the public interest—rooted within substantive equality—rather than interests that advance purely private interests, such as corporate enrichment, private vengeance, or other dimensions that would be seen as antithetic to the public interest.

The proposed framework in this chapter, which requires justifications in support of decisions whether or not to prosecute, can also serve to diminish the relevance of maintaining a strict application of the separation of powers doctrine in prosecutorial decisions on the basis that prosecutors hold the monopoly of the public interest. Indeed, a strict version of this doctrine has been used to suggest that prosecutorial decisions need to be made independently and therefore require near-absolute immunity with no transparency and minimal possibilities for review. These claims become less defendable if citizens, as much as the state, were required to respect standards and substantive claims that relate to evidence and the public interest. As articulated by Green and Roiphe, state prosecutors—as much as citizens—can be malicious, abusive, self-serving, hold biases, and thus make claims that are contrary to the public interest.[62] This recognition challenges the sanctity of state monopoly over

[60] Josephine Gittler, 'Expanding the Role of the Victim in a Criminal Action: An Overview of Issues and Problems' (1984) 11 Pepp L Rev 117, 156.
[61] *King v Second Nat'l Bank & Tr Co of Saginaw*, Mich 234 Ala 106 (1937) 108.
[62] Green and Roiphe (n 4).

prosecutions while supporting a system of checks and balances that values the ability of state and citizens to make transparent and justified arguments over legal norms and a notion of public interests rooted in substantive equality. This also highlights the importance of checks and balances, such as citizen-victims and an informed judiciary, as a guardian of legality[63] and substantive equality in also providing further checks that powers and duties—held by citizens and the state—are circumscribed and exercised in a way that respects the framework rooted in deliberative democratic theory articulated in this chapter. In this sense, this framework is a call for broadening the polity's relevance in entering deliberative communicative processes of decision-making that entails the possibility of seeking review and self-reflection on the merit of their substantive decisions as part of processes of public decision-making.

Defining victims and standing

As seen in previous chapters, under a conception of victims as holders of predominantly private interests, the role of victims as agents of state accountability is typically limited to individuals who have suffered direct and personal harm as a result of the offence. While this definition was expanded in some instances to include ancillary victims, such as family of deceased victims or a shareholder of a company, generally a strict test for standing applies.[64] This strict test for standing both relies upon and reinforces a conception of victims as holders of predominantly private interests in criminal proceedings.

Rather, a framework that conceives of victims as potential holders of public interests would legitimize an expanded definition of 'victim' in processes for state accountability that can improve the potential of these mechanisms to work in favour of the public interest. Indeed, within the public democratic framework discussed above, the wider community as a victim has important interests and a role within the enterprise of criminal law and therefore this role is not only reserved to direct victims.

As Kaufman suggests, in the context of private prosecutions, public interest or grassroots groups could be mandated to bring prosecutions in cases where

[63] Emmanuel Isaac Onuche, 'Attorney General's Power of Nolle Prosequi: A Relic of Colonialism or a Burden to Rule of Law?' (2021) 5(2) AJLHR 55, 66–70.

[64] See discussion in Chapter 6, which include cases such as *United States v Ruzicka*, 331 F Supp 3d 888 (D Minn 2018). See also the difference in conception between judicial review and the VRRS discussed in England and Wales in Littleton, 'Jamie Susskind Acts in Landmark High Court Case Over Non-Prosecution of Neo-Nazi' (Littleton Chambers, nd) <https://littletonchambers.com/jamie-susskind-acts-in-landmark-high-court-case-over-non-prosecution-of-neo-nazi/> accessed 13 June 2023.

the Crown declines to act—particularly in cases of state violence or institutional abuse.[65] This statement can also expand within the proposed framework to public involvement in review processes to challenge decisions relating to state prosecutions in instances of state fallibilities. In addition to public interest or grassroots groups, associations of lawyers, such as those that had formed in England as early as the eighteenth century, to represent victims could find wider legitimacy, particularly in instances where they can take on pro bono cases. This broader standing would also go a long way towards addressing the issue of cost. Other solutions include government legal aid, grant funding, or cost-recovery mechanisms that would ensure access to private prosecutions and other public law relating mechanisms remain equitable, not exclusionary.

In the context of decisions about whether to prosecute, Bennett Capers suggests that 'the initial power to decide should reside not within the state but with the victim herself and by extension with the people'.[66] While this statement recognizes that victims can make decisions in the public interest, offering the initial power strictly to victims assumes that state prosecutors are not capable of doing so. This is problematic as the state should also be considered capable of doing so provided that decisions outline the ways that they advance the public interest. Indeed, this monograph does not assume that state prosecutors are unable to represent the public interest, but rather that the public interest should not be solely represented by a single entity but by all members of the polity who have the ability to inform decisions that strengthen substantive equality. As seen throughout this book, citizen-victims just as much as the state can make decisions that advance the public interest, including in instances where prosecutors who are meant to advance that interest fail to do so. For these reasons, recognizing that the wider polity, which is not restricted to the state, should have a say in the public interest when the state fails to do so would offer greater safeguards than an approach that offers the monopoly to one party. As highlighted by Angela J Davis, 'we the people' should not just include only crime victims, but should comprise all the residents of a public prosecutor's jurisdiction, including the defendant.[67] Indeed, if the public interest is understood as rooted within values of substantive equality, it may very well be that victims, defendants, and wider communities may have informed contributions to bring forward, particularly in contexts where these groups may be most affected by crime or social inequalities that permeate the

[65] Kaufman (n 53) 144.
[66] Capers (n 44) 1589.
[67] Angela Davis, 'The Perils of Private Prosecutions' (2022) 13(7) Calif L Rev 7, 14.

criminal process. This wider notion would also enable a broader range of citizens to undertake this role to avoid that the burden and risks from this role rest solely on direct victims.

As part of a predominantly public conception of interests that roots the role of victims as agents of state accountability within a deliberative democratic framework, the notion of victims can be expanded. This expanded understanding conceives of victims as citizens who have suffered from crime (even if not the direct victims) and can hold the state accountable for wider state failures that affect the public interest (rather than merely personal/private interests).[68] Expanding the notion of victims this way would, in turn, allow victims to hold the state accountable for various failures, including systemic failures in the criminal legal process, and enable more nuanced and accurate ascription and communication of responsibility for crime.

For example, in the context of environmental injustices, Ozymy and Jarrell[69] suggest that communities that have suffered from corporate ecological harms should be viewed as crime victims. A broader notion of communities impacted would be important for these forms of harms as environmental harms are often obscured as they are embedded into an environment, have cascading effects, as well as intergenerational impacts. A broader notion would also help bring forward and address systemic failures by the regulatory state in protecting these communities. Accordingly, state responses would include acknowledgement, restitution, and wider measures to address these failures.

Instances where victims may be undermined by state prosecution services based on existing stereotypes and biases rooted in inequalities provide additional contexts that can benefit from a public widening of standing. In such contexts, and particularly in contexts of quasi-dystopias where direct victims may be affected by various social injustices, including epistemic and standing, their potential in holding the state accountable may be affected. For those reasons, indirect victims within the polity, such as community groups that can work on behalf of certain marginalized groups, should be able to hold the fallible state accountable in order to offload the risk and burden of this role that can come with this role as well as strengthen direct victims' voices.

[68] Under mechanisms that predominantly conceive victims as holding predominantly public interests, such as judicial review in England and Wales, the notion of victim has tended to be more encompassing by including citizens who can make wider systemic claims about the public interest in instances of state failures. This includes potential for judicial review in cases that raises 'potentially important issues for society in the growing area of racist and religious hate crime'. See the case of *Bedford-Turner* in Littleton (n 64). See also Kaufman (n 53).

[69] J Ozymy and ML Jarrell, 'Of Sex Crimes and Fencelines: How Recognition of Environmental Justice Communities as Crime Victims Under State and Federal Law Can Help Secure Environmental Justice' (2020) 38(1) Pace Environ L Rev 109.

Certain risks and burdens may indeed occur in situations of power imbalances, where state actors and/or offenders may be reticent of having marginalized groups challenge their status and therefore direct victims can benefit from the role of a broadened definition of victims that would also be tasked to take on such a role. Moreover, indirect victims can strengthen direct victims' voices by helping them bring forward relevant social science knowledge and evidence about credibility assessments and injustices affecting specific communities that are rooted in systemic inequalities, which may be relevant to ascribing of responsibility and crafting the public interest. For instance, community groups' participation in holding the prosecutorial state accountable can be particularly relevant in such circumstances of sexual assault victims, as seen in the *Davies* case, since direct victims may be subject to myths and stereotypes or find participation to be traumatic and hold privacy concerns. Indeed, a broader understanding of victim standing can also enable wider members of the polity to bring forward the public interest in instances where direct victims may have suffered harm from powerful offenders, such as instances seen in monograph, including cases of state brutality, environmental injustices, and sexual assault, wherein offenders may have greater social, political, and financial capital than victims. In such instances, the involvement of community organizations, pro bono lawyers, and other citizen actors can help to narrow existing power imbalances, amplify the victim's experiential knowledge, and introduce complementary forms of sociological or contextual expertise that may otherwise be inaccessible to the victim.

The role of victims: civic or legal duty?

Within this public democratic framework, the citizen-victim's role would be understood as a duty rather than as an individual choice or right. This builds on Marshall's argument that the role-based duties of citizens and officials are interconnected and give the criminal law its institutional form.[70] In this sense, she provides an analogy that characterizes ordinary citizens as 'officials in plain clothes' (in parallel to Gardner's 'citizens in uniform'[71]) with the admonition

[70] Marshall (n 39) 298.

[71] One way of characterizing the role of officials in the criminal law and its processes—the 'citizens in uniform' conception—is usefully captured by John Gardner, which can be expressed as an admonition: 'Don't think that when you step into your official role (your "uniform") you stop being yourself and can abdicate responsibility in your capacity as an ordinary member of the public (a "citizen") for the things that you do. You still answer to the law as yourself, and you can't hide behind your public role when you do it.' John Gardner, 'Criminals in Uniform' in RA Duff and others (eds), *The Constitution of the Criminal Law* (OUP 2013) 97.

that citizens cannot abdicate their responsibilities in the criminal legal process and hide behind the role of 'ordinary citizens', since all the roles in this process are ones we inhabit as citizens.[72] This suggests that these duties towards a fair and just enterprise of criminal law are relevant for victims, including a duty to step up when the state fails to act according to its stated values.

As highlighted above, one's unique knowledge relating to a state failure is an important element of legitimacy within a deliberative democratic process. Ashwini Vasanthakumar[73] argues that victims of injustices have duties to resist injustice as they hold knowledge regarding the wrong. She suggests that victims are epistemically privileged with respect to injustice and are thus uniquely positioned to assist fellow victims. Arguably, within a deliberative framework, certain community members—particularly those with lived experience of specific inequalities—may hold deeper insights into injustices, including errors in credibility and responsibility assessments made by state agents. By adopting mechanisms of state accountability that recognize and accommodate citizen-victims' ability to share their experiential knowledge, they can help expose and provide responses to the structural injustices that may otherwise be overlooked, ensuring a more just and equitable finding and ascription of responsibility.

The duties of victims as agents of state accountability can vary depending on the context under which state failure takes place across the quasi-eutopia–dystopia spectrum. This section begins the analysis by asking what responsibilities victims may have in a quasi-eutopian scenario as agents of state accountability and then considers how these responsibilities shift as we move along the spectrum towards progressively more dystopian scenarios.

As highlighted above, close to a quasi-eutopian scenario, the state is engaged in a legitimate and fair enterprise generally committed to serving values of substantive equality, liberty, and respect within the public criminal justice system. As such, the state would recognize its potential for instances of state fallibility, including as part of various forms of systemic and individual decision-making errors. Considering that criminal law is conceived of as the law of citizens of the polity, the victim would have a civic role in assisting a legitimate and fair enterprise of criminal law, which includes a duty to bring forward instances of state fallibility. Indeed, it would be important for victims to seek accountability should the state contribute to oppression, injustice, and make decisions

[72] Marshall (n 39) 298.

[73] Ashwini Vasanthakumar, 'Epistemic Privilege and Victims' Duties to Resist their Oppression' (2018) 35(3) J Appl Philos 465.

contrary to common values and the public interest. In such a system, the state should recognize its own fallibility and offer victims, as citizens, with accessible accountability mechanisms. It would also be a common public expectation to undertake this duty as part of the public interest. Further, this expectation would be reasonable as accountability requests would be made in a decent society in which the system would more favourably and in good faith recognize its fallibility and promptly contribute to a more accurate communication of responsibility.

In a quasi-eutopia, this duty should be characterized as a civic responsibility rather than a legal one. As highlighted by Duff, civic responsibilities are those owed to our fellow citizens by virtue of membership within the polity but are enforceable only by informal persuasion from our fellow citizens, rather than by law.[74] The lack of legal enforceability against a victim who fails to undertake this duty is particularly important. As this duty arises in contexts that relate to state fallibility, the victim should not be held legally responsible by way of state sanction for a failure to bring forward the state's very own legal failure.

As we move along the spectrum towards progressively more dystopian scenarios, there can be certain differences to consider in the victim's duty to hold the state accountable in instances of state fallibility. Indeed, as discussed in the previous section, the state in more dystopian scenarios would be less likely to recognize its own potential flaws and therefore be more resistant to questioning and challenging its actions. In turn, this resistance would create challenges for victims who seek state accountability.

The dystopian scenario creates greater reason to consider this duty as a civic, rather than a legal, responsibility. As in the quasi-eutopia, the state should not pursue a victim for a failure to act upon a state's own failure. This is especially the case in a context where the victim faces state resistance to pursue accountability. Moreover, an additional reason for considering this duty as civic rather than a legal in the context of increasingly dystopian scenarios is the reality that a legal duty against the victim would offer the state even more power to direct towards persecution and abuse.

Moving further along this spectrum, when nearing the actual dystopia in levels of state fallibility, the victim's duty may become unsurmountable and unrealistic. In such situations, where there is no more hope with regards to the state, it might be illusory and illegitimate to maintain that the victim, after experiencing severe state failures, still has a duty to hold the state accountable through the state's own processes and enterprise. In such instances, victims

[74] Duff (n 1).

may have disparate experiences and relationships to the state based on political marginalization.

Where complete dystopia may not be reached for all citizens, those who are in less of a position of vulnerability vis-à-vis the state may be able to successfully navigate state processes for public accountability in criminal law, even as indirect victims. Considering their public standing, those citizens would have a public duty to undertake this role in support of those who may be in more precarious positions.

One may also claim that situations that are closer to dystopias would be increasingly closer to a scenario where the state could potentially lose its standing to punish,[75] and communitarian self-governing frameworks may become the only legitimate response to crimes. These non-state approaches may be caught in cultural frameworks wherein they risk reproducing the same systemic inequalities and power imbalances. The structural nature of this risk highlights the need for duties of accountability in order to preserve the legitimacy of governing frameworks. These challenges represent important limitations to the proposed framework and the role of victims seen in this context.

Nevertheless, even 'towards the dystopian end of the spectrum',[76] the civic duty of holding the state accountable would still be within the realm of possibility as long as the values of a quasi-eutopia still have some purchase. If the state's institutions and its life attempt to pursue these values with some commitment, there is hope in engaging in this common enterprise. Moreover, despite the fact that several groups may be partially excluded from certain rights and benefits, they—along with other members of the polity—may still have the possibility to bring these dimensions forward and have the state recognize individual and systemic failures.

It may be argued that this duty towards the polity becomes even greater in situations in which the state is increasingly holding a monopoly of power with less checks and balances. In the jurisdictions under analysis, where the trial is no longer the main vehicle to determine responsibility for wrongdoing, and where the state relies on prosecutorial diversion, guilty plea agreements, and other forms of prosecutorial agreements, the state prosecutor wields significant discretionary authority. In such a landscape, where access to trial is no longer the norm and often curtailed or avoided due to systemic inequalities,[77]

[75] RA Duff, 'Law, Language, and Community: Some Preconditions of Criminal Liability' (1988) 18 OJLS 189; RA Duff, 'Blame, Moral Standing, and the Legitimacy of the Criminal Trial' (2010) 23 Ratio 123.

[76] Duff (n 1).

[77] ibid.

there is a public responsibility, within deliberative democratic frameworks that value substantive equality, to offer participatory mechanisms to citizens for holding the prosecutorial state accountable for individual and systemic forms of fallibilities within the context of prosecutorial processes. In this sense, the victim's role as a citizen to hold the state accountable in these contexts becomes even more pressing along with the recognition of mechanisms to challenge the state's potential fallibilities that would render the enterprise of criminal law inaccurate and illegitimate.

4. Illustrating the Victim's Role of State Accountability for Prosecutorial Decision-Making

As seen in this chapter, the state can fail in its decision-making processes in several ways that can affect the assessment of responsibility for wrongdoing. This includes the failure to account for the effects of social injustices rooted in inequalities within decisions that relate to prosecutions. Whilst this monograph has analysed and compared mechanisms available to victims as agents of state accountability in England and Wales and the United States,[78] with a focus on prosecutions, the following section highlights some of the ways that citizen-victims, understood within the framework developed in this chapter, can hold the prosecutorial state accountable for failures rooted in inequalities at both stages of the analysis relating to prosecutions. Whilst the focus in this section is on failures regarding decisions relating to prosecutorial decision-making, there may be rationales and mechanisms for expanding this framework beyond prosecutorial decision-making across the various stages of the criminal legal process.[79]

Some of the mechanisms and ways for bringing forward the role of victims as agents of state accountability relating to prosecutorial decisions involves the application of this framework within the mechanisms discussed in this

[78] For instance, we have seen that in England and Wales, victims can seek review of decisions relating to state prosecutions on the basis of individuals failures by state prosecutors can take many forms. First, at the evidentiary stage, examples include cases where the state prosecutor has made an error in understanding the factual evidence, a legal error in understanding the evidentiary threshold required, or a substantive error of interpretation and weight afforded to an element of evidence. Second, at the public interest stage, victims have also sought review of prosecutorial decisions as contrary to the public interest.

[79] For instance, for a discussion on this role for victims in the context of sentencing, see Marie Manikis, 'Victim-related Assumptions Underlying Plea-based Sentence Reductions: A Communicative and Experiential Framework' in Julian V Roberts and Jesper Ryberg (eds), *Pleading Guilty: Ethical Perspectives on Sentencing the Self-Convicted* (Hart Publishing 2023); Manikis (n 9).

monograph, including private prosecutions, judicial review of prosecutorial decisions, as well as administrative prosecutorial review schemes that include independent assessments within prosecutorial offices. Applying the proposed framework within these processes can increase the chances that prosecutorial discretion is exercised in ways that are publicly justified, account and respond to the power imbalances, private conflicts of interest, and substantive inequalities that are often part of the various state fallibilities.

Accountability for prosecutorial state failures rooted in systemic inequalities

The decision to prosecute involves deciding whether there is sufficient evidence and public interest to communicate censure towards a potential responsible wrongdoer for a public wrong. This includes decisions about whether to prosecute along with decisions to enter various forms of agreements. As such, many common law jurisdictions, including those under analysis, have adopted prosecutorial guidelines that generally apply a two-pronged test to determine whether to prosecute an individual.[80] The first part of the test typically involves an evidentiary threshold that aims to assess whether there is a realistic prospect of conviction. At this stage of the process, elements such as the defendant's responsibility, witness credibility, and any defences available in light of the evidence are considered relevant. The second part of the test is an assessment that aims to determine whether a prosecution in a given matter would serve the public interest. Similar considerations are taken into account when determining whether to enter prosecutorial agreements.[81]

Building on the framework developed in this chapter, victims would have an important role in challenging prosecutorial fallibilities within decision-making, including those rooted in inequalities. Indeed, as highlighted in the previous section, prosecutorial decisions about whether to prosecute are relevant to the polity. Therefore, victims, as citizens, are legitimate entities to address state fallibilities within this process, in order to enable an accurate ascription of responsibility as well as decisions that advance the public interest.

[80] In England and Wales, see section 4.4 of the Crown Prosecution Service, *The Code for Crown Prosecutors* (CPS 2023) and within the federal US context, see US Department of Justice, *Justice Manual* (2018) s 9-27.220.

[81] In England and Wales, see paragraphs 2.2–2.3 of the Serious Fraud Office and Crown Prosecution Service, *Deferred Prosecution Agreements Code of Practice* (2014); *Crime and Courts Act 2013*, sch 17. In the United States, see US Department of Justice (n 80) ss 9-27.400–9-27.620.

First, when state prosecutors fail to consider the relevant evidence and social context at the evidentiary stage, victims would have the important role of bringing forward these failures. This may be especially relevant to assessments of credibility as well as a defendant's responsibility. Under the framework proposed, to determine whether a case meets the evidentiary assessment standard, the analysis would need to incorporate values of substantive equality by relying on facts, experiential realities, and social science evidence. We propose that a 'merit-based' approach infused with substantive equality be used to prosecutions as part of the convictability standard. This approach requires the state decide whether there is a reasonable prospect of conviction solely based on the sufficiency of material evidence, rather than allowing the judge's/jurors' potential biases to influence the decision.

Indeed, as highlighted by Buchhandler-Raphael, this assessment should actively incorporate values of substantive equality, otherwise the standard 'might perpetuate racialized, misogynistic or otherwise prejudiced and biased norms that should be repudiated'.[82] Justice Hale in *Gujra* also warns against incorporating a biased standard of convictability, referred to as the 'bookmaker's approach', which 'contemplates that juries may indeed be unreasonable and prejudiced'[83] as part of the evidentiary stage of a decision of whether to prosecute. Under this propensity approach, a prosecutor considers the likelihood of a conviction based on odds and probabilities, similar to how a bookmaker assesses the chances of an outcome in a sporting event. This approach risks considering the assessor's biases as legitimate considerations that also must be incorporated by prosecutors in assessing the propensity of a conviction, which serves to perpetuate myths and stereotypes in all stages of decision-making. Conversely, a 'merit-based' approach requires a prosecutor to evaluate the evidence as a reasonable fact-finder would, considering both the prosecution and defence cases, and deciding whether the evidence supports a conviction on a balance of probabilities. Under this approach, the decision-maker needs to be aware of existing biases and to the extent possible ensure that they are not taken into account in a way that perpetuates discrimination in their decision-making process. As highlighted throughout the framework proposed, the citizen-victim can be well-situated and legitimate in bringing these dimensions forward in instances where the state has failed to do so. As such, it is important to integrate dimensions relating to substantive equality when addressing issues of convictability, which the citizen-victim can help achieve,

[82] Buchhandler-Raphael (n 21) 457.
[83] *Gujra* (n 25) [129].

particularly in instances where the prosecutorial state seems to have relied on assumptions and biases to render its decisions.

State fallibilities at this stage of the process can relate to the evaluation of evidence, particularly when epistemic injustices are part of a given social context. As previously discussed, when certain voices are considered less reliable, and others are amplified, this impacts the treatment of evidence. This is the case in several examples seen in this book as part of the phenomenon of under-prosecution rooted in inequalities. Notably, in cases of gender-based violence, the state may consider the victim to lack credibility, especially when the victim is marginalized according to intersecting identities or experiences. The *Epstein* case, wherein the state entered an NPA for instances of multiple sex offences, illustrates the severe outcomes where prosecutors have failed to take into account systemic inequalities in their assessments of whether to pursue a prosecution. This was similarly the case in *Davies* where community groups that represented victims found several cases of marginalized victims that matched the perpetrator and where prosecutions failed to bring forward prosecutions. Various mechanisms should be made available for victims to raise such systemic failures to ensure that the state does not have the monopoly over wrongful assessments, and can include private prosecutions, review processes, as well as standing within criminal legal proceedings. Importantly, it will be important for these mechanisms to recognize experiential knowledge and evidence from social sciences in order to highlight these state failures.

Conversely, the phenomenon of over-prosecutions is also a relevant reality that is often overlooked by state prosecutors, and which can be brought to account for by victims. This is particularly the case in contexts where accused individuals from marginalized communities have suffered material injustices that affect volition and choices, or where they may be subject to epistemic injustices and considered less credible. Under the proposed framework, victims would have legitimate duties and interests as citizens to bring forward these considerations of prosecutorial decision-making, and state actor—whether prosecutor or judge—would need to take this into account.

Second, victims can also contribute as agents of state accountability in instances where the state has failed to take into account key elements of the public interest or has erroneously judged what the public interest may be in a given case. The framework proposed in this chapter argues that the public interest should be informed by substantive equality and therefore attentive to systemic state fallibilities that contribute to social injustices. Indeed, considerations highlighted as part of social inequalities, discussed above, would be relevant at this stage as they pertain to ascribing responsibility and communicating censure more accurately. Examples can include victims bringing forward information relating to the over-representation of certain groups in criminal justice and their criminogenic effects, as well as the under-prosecution of certain offences by certain groups and their impact on criminality, such as the various ones seen throughout this book, notably sexual and domestic violence, hate crimes, fraud, state brutality, and others, which the state would need to consider in this stage of decision-making. Prosecutorial responses that suggest diversion or exclusion from criminalization (for lack of standing or loss of standing) may also be relevant within this step of the process.

Moreover, certain elements that feature in public interest considerations—including assessments about whether to prosecute or to enter into agreements—involve the potential for recidivism. In this regard, citizen-victims as agents of state accountability can serve an important role by drawing attention to dimensions that are often overlooked in state decision-making. For instance, they may highlight how actuarial risk assessment tools or implicit biases may be used by prosecutors and promote the over-prosecution of marginalized communities, thereby exacerbating systemic inequalities contrary to the public interest.[84] These tools often encode historical biases and disproportionately penalize those from racialized or socio-economically disadvantaged groups.[85] This dynamic contributes to a broader carceral logic that prioritizes incapacitation over addressing the criminogenic social conditions that underlie many offences[86] that occur in contexts of quasi-dystopias.

Victims may also highlight broader concerns about prosecutorial reliance on notions of efficiency that, while expedient, may neglect responses more attuned to addressing underlying criminogenic social conditions. Their engagement can enrich public interest analyses by anchoring them in transparent, evidence-based rationales—drawing from empirical research, contextual knowledge, and lived experience—rather than expedient but potentially harmful decision-making practices.

Finally, citizen-victims may challenge in some instances practices of plea bargaining, NPAs, or deferred prosecution agreements that favour certain privileged groups in society and potentially stem from conflicts of interests and promote social inequalities. This form of participatory engagement can support a more robust conception of the public interest, grounded in justifications from democratic deliberation and responsive to empirical evidence

[84] Sandra G Mayson, 'Bias In, Bias Out' (2019) 128 Yale LJ 2218.
[85] Michelle Alexander, *The New Jim Crow: Mass Incarceration in the Age of Colorblindness* (The New Press 2010).
[86] Lucia Zedner, 'Pre-crime and Post-criminology?' (2007) 11 Theor Criminol 261.

rather than situations of administrative convenience, political expediency,[87] as well as political and institutional pressure. Such participation aligns with principles of democratic accountability, particularly in contexts where trials are rare and prosecutorial discretion is virtually unchecked. This underscores the importance of deliberative frameworks that incorporate victims not as mere consultees seen as holders of private interests, but as epistemic contributors who can enrich institutional understanding through experiential and situated knowledge.

Towards common interests

Contrary to much of the literature on victim participation, which has framed victims' interests as oppositional to those of the accused,[88] victims often share common interests with those of the accused, particularly in contexts shaped by systemic inequalities. While this alignment is supported by empirical studies that examine the rationales of victim engagement in the process, it is also seen in individual cases where victims may favour the withdrawal of prosecutions or advocate for mitigation and alternative responses based on dimensions relating to evidentiary dimensions along with arguments about the public interest.[89]

To enable such possibilities, most of the state accountability mechanisms examined in this book would need to be expanded—not only to allow for the review of decisions *not* to prosecute, but also of decisions *to* prosecute. While some mechanisms, such as judicial review in England and Wales already allow for this, they remain the exception. As highlighted in the literature, potential reforms could include the expansion of these possibilities within administrative processes such as the Victims' Right to Review Scheme (VRRS) in England and Wales[90] as well enabling direct victim access before a grand jury.[91] Turner has suggested, however, that such mechanisms are less likely to be needed, as

[87] National Research Council, *The Growth of Incarceration in the United States: Exploring Causes and Consequences* (The National Academies Press 2014).

[88] The rhetoric of 'balancing rights' or 'balancing interests' of the accused with those of victims reinforces a zero-sum game where victims' interests are in conflict with those of the accused and necessarily advance punitive aims. Kent Roach, 'Four Models of the Criminal Process' (1999) 89(2) J Crim L & Criminol 671.

[89] Marie Manikis, 'A New Model of the Criminal Justice Process: Victims' Rights as Advancing Penal Parsimony and Moderation' (2019) 30(2) Crimi L Forum 201.

[90] Marie Manikis, 'Expanding Participation: Victims as Agents of Accountability in the Criminal Justice Process' (2017) 1 PL 63.

[91] Jenia I Turner, 'Victims as a Check on Prosecutors: A Comparative Assessment' (2022) 13 Calif L Rev 72, 83.

prosecutors are already constrained in various ways formally—by grand jury or judicial review—and practically by victim non-cooperation and limited resources in deciding whether to charge.[92]

While this may be the case, the framework developed in this chapter helps to legitimize this role and ease the current practical and conceptual constraints placed on state prosecutors, particularly those arising from conflict as part of the inadequacy of prosecutorial decision-making to fully account for systemic dimensions. This framework reimagines the prosecutor–victim relationship not as one of conflict, but as a cooperative pursuit of a shared public interest, grounded in deliberative democratic values that includes substantive equality.

In this sense, expanding the scope of accountability to permit challenges to decisions to prosecute would be particularly valuable in cases where victims possess additional forms of knowledge or experiential insight that can demonstrate why prosecution would be unprincipled as contrary to the public interest. Moreover, this form of accountability would enable victims to bring relevant perspectives in instances where state prosecutors may have based their decisions on faulty assumptions or counter-narratives presented in decisions that misrepresent their views. Finally, victims may offer additional checks in instances where grand juries may be tied to the prosecution, a phenomenon that has been raised by some commentators relating to the tendency of some grand juries to be instrumentalized by state prosecutors.[93]

The framework discussed in this chapter provides a means to reconcile the interests of victims, offenders, and state as shared public interest towards a more adequate ascription of responsibility that recognizes and responds to social inequalities. As seen in this chapter, victims can bring forward the complex realities that accused people may have suffered material injustices and wider instances of systemic inequalities rooted in race, gender, and other aspects of one's social position that may provide context for certain offences. These criminogenic dimensions are often attributable to the state and can be relevant considerations in the assessment of the evidence in a given case along with the public interest. In this sense, victims can also engage in discussions about the state's relational responsibility by highlighting the ways that the state has contributed to the creation of criminogenic conditions. Moreover, victims can also bring forward various assumptions relating to victims that are rooted in social inequalities. These reflections can eventually affect the wide range of responses

[92] ibid 83.
[93] *State ex rel Miller v Smith* 285 SE 500 (W Va 1981).

to criminality and determination of whether prosecution may be the way forward in a given case.

Some may argue that implementing such a framework would demand too much time and resources from an already over-burdened system. While enabling victims to bring forward state fallibilities can indeed require time and resources, it may ultimately prove more efficient and principled as in the long run, as certain matters may be better addressed through processes outside the criminal legal system—within other state systems that are more adapted to respond to situations of criminogenic injustices. Moreover, a framework that incorporates the state's relational responsibility within prosecutorial decision-making may be better positioned to create conditions that mitigate, rather than contribute to, criminogenic environments.

5. Conclusion

In conclusion, this chapter has articulated a framework rooted in deliberative democratic theory to justify and describe the ways that citizen-victims may hold an important role as agents of state accountability in instances of state fallibilities, including those that are rooted in social inequalities. An understanding of victims as citizens who can hold a public role and interests can legitimize and expand the role of victims as agents of state accountability to address various state failures, including in the assignation of responsibility in criminal law, often rooted in inequalities. Indeed, this novel participative role for victims would rely on communicative theories of punishment and recognize the importance for victims as part of the polity to attribute nuanced and accurate responsibility, notably by recognizing the state's relational share.

This framing would create an important civic responsibility on the part of victims in bringing forward a nuanced understanding of responsibility situated within social context. In turn, this might provide a lens to align the victim's interests with those of the accused in criminal justice, particularly by reflecting on state wrongdoing and harms as systemic. While this analysis is focused on prosecutorial decisions as part of the assessment of evidence and public interest dimensions, it may also find relevance at other stages of the criminal legal process.

9
Conclusion

1. The Relevance of State Accountability

Holding the state accountable for its public decisions and actions is a cornerstone of democratic societies.[1] This is especially crucial in the context of criminal justice, where the state wields extensive power and control—particularly in relation to prosecutions for crimes understood as public wrongs.[2] Decisions relating to public prosecutions are increasingly wide-ranging and can have lasting effects on society, on victims, and on individuals facing prosecution. These decisions vary across jurisdictions and may include decisions whether to take over or discontinue private prosecutions, whether to initiate or pursue public prosecutions, and whether to enter into prosecutorial agreements and negotiations. Overall, state prosecutors undertake important communicational decisions and can decide to begin an important denunciatory process.[3] In this sense, early on, they make initial assessments of responsibility, and all their decisions need to be made in the public interest.

Importantly, state prosecutors are seen as entities that hold a monopoly over the public interest, which promotes a narrative that sees victims as not legitimate actors who can make contributions in the public interest. As discussed, part of this dynamic stems from the historical role of the Attorney General in colonial jurisdictions, who was tasked with implementing English criminal law and, in doing so, acquired significant powers and centralized control over prosecutions. This development contributed to a concentration of prosecutorial authority in the hands of the state, which was also seen as a way to limit the abuses of private prosecutions. A similar trajectory increasingly emerged in England and Wales, where the role of the state in prosecution was progressively strengthened. However, private prosecutions have persisted and, for

[1] Marcus Bovens, 'Analysing and Assessing Public Accountability: A Conceptual Model' (European Governance Papers (EUROGOV) C-06-01, 16 January 2006).

[2] RA Duff and SE Marshall, 'Communicative Punishment and the Role of the Victim' (2004) 23(2) Crim Just Ethics 39.

[3] Michelle Madden Dempsey, *Prosecuting Domestic Violence* (OUP 2009).

Victims as Agents of State Accountability. Marie Manikis, Oxford University Press. © Marie Manikis 2026.
DOI: 10.1093/9780191993947.003.0012

some, continue to serve as a vital mechanism for ensuring state accountability, particularly in cases of prosecutorial inaction. Historical and contemporary experience reveals that both private and state-led prosecutions are vulnerable to failure and abuse—failures that may run counter to the democratic values underpinning the public interest. These fallibilities demonstrate how public interests can be appropriated or distorted to serve private aims and highlight the potential for prosecutorial decision-making to be shaped by systemic bias rooted in social inequalities.

While the analysis affirms that the state should retain its legitimacy to prosecute crime as a public wrong, acknowledging the capacity of victims to speak in and for the public interest—particularly when the state fails to do so—may open the door to larger questions about widening the legitimacy of other groups, entities, and individuals—who are not state prosecutors—in making initial decisions about prosecutions.

As the state, including its prosecutors, is comprised of humans, errors in the exercise of discretionary powers are inevitable. This monograph discusses these fallibilities both theoretically and through case studies, illustrating their wide-ranging nature. As seen, these errors may be either conscious or unconscious and can range from technical or interpretational individualized legal mistakes to those rooted in power dynamics, private interest-related conflicts, and systemic biases—often stemming from broader social inequalities.

For these reasons, it is crucial for criminal legal scholarship to engage with questions of state accountability in the context of criminal justice—and specifically prosecutions—through both empirical and normative lenses that can advance the conversation and deliberative practices around prosecutorial decision-making that strengthen accuracy and accountability in prosecutions.

Although accountability can take multiple forms and originate from a range of institutions and actors, this monograph focuses on the role that victims have played, continue to contribute to, and can further develop in this endeavour. Scholarship has often overlooked this role, despite initial forms of this type of victim participation have historically started to take shape within the English common law tradition. In recent years, England and Wales as well as the United States have in different ways and to varying degrees recognized additional legal mechanisms for victims to hold the prosecutorial state to account within the criminal legal process.

A comparative analysis of these mechanisms reveals important insights into how victims and their interests are understood within those mechanisms and how their accountability roles have evolved depending on the ways their interests are understood. In turn, this enables a clearer understanding of the limitations of these mechanisms—helping to identify where resistance to this form of victim participation lies and to critically assess whether such resistance is justified.

2. Comparative Findings and Analysis

A contextual and empirical analysis of the implementation of these mechanisms—through policy developments and case law—reveals that when victims are primarily viewed as holders of private interests, their ability to hold the state accountable for substantive decisions within the public process is constrained. In such cases, their role as agents of state accountability tends to be limited to an aggregate contribution to the public interest and as raising primarily procedural state failures related to their inclusion in certain aspects of the public process.

Even in England and Wales—where victims have historically been recognized as legitimate bearers of public interests in prosecutions—state prosecutors and judges have increasingly reframed victims as holders of private interests under several mechanisms of state accountability. This shift has, to some extent, restricted their role in holding the state accountable for substantive failures relating to the content and rationales of decision-making.

As discussed in this monograph, this privatizing narrative has extended into the realm of private prosecutions, a mechanism that has traditionally conceived of victims as potential holders of public interests. This shift has contributed to the growing delegitimization of what was once a public function carried out by citizens who were seen as capable of carrying out evidentiary assessments and advancing arguments in the public interest—at times advancing substantive equality.[4] This extension has also given rise to cases where private for profit interests were funnelled into this mechanism, with very little checks, resulting in wrongful and abusive prosecutions and mixed calls for reform or its abolition.[5] Nevertheless, as this monograph illustrates,

[4] English Collective of Prostitutes, 'Successful Private Prosecution of Serial Rapist—R v Davies' (*English Collective of Prostitutes*, 1 January 1996) <https://prostitutescollective.net/private-prosecution/> accessed 24 June 2023; Tamlyn Edmonds and David Jugnarain, 'Private Prosecutions: A Potential Anticorruption Tool in English Law' (Open Society Foundations 2014).

[5] For instance, some proposals were made in England and Wales for a binding code of standards and greater oversight. Michael Savage, 'Plans to Reform Private Prosecutions After Post Office Horizon Scandal' (*The Guardian*, 13 January 2024); Ministry of Justice, *Consultation on the Oversight and Regulation of Private Prosecutors in the Criminal Justice System* (CPd 43/2025, March 2025) <https://assets.publishing.service.gov.uk/media/67c57c4f72e83aab48866ce8/oversight-regulation-private-prosecutors-consultation.pdf> accessed 7 June 2025. As seen in this monograph, in the United States, this discourse has contributed to its abolition with some vestiges left in very few states.

when private prosecutions are required to meet the same public interest standards as state-led prosecutions, they can serve as legitimate tools through which citizen-victims can make substantive claims regarding prosecutorial decisions in the public interest when the state fails to act appropriately. Similarly, judicial and prosecutorial review mechanisms have increasingly adopted a privatized conception of victims, viewing them as representatives of private interests. These mechanisms, however, should not be redirected to serve victims' private aims or abolished due to potential private interest abuses, but rather structured to recognize citizen-victims as entities that have abilities to pursue public interests.

Recognizing that victims have the potential to hold public interests does not mean that these interests cannot also align with some of the private interests they may also hold. The analysis relating to state accountability however would not be focused on how these interests may benefit an individual victim but rather on whether this advances the public interest, which as discussed in this book, should be understood as more than an aggregate understanding of interests. In this sense, the victim's involvement in holding the state accountable should rely on substantiated public 'reasons to call the wrongdoer to account' rather than was it commonly perceived as 'reason to stand up for oneself against a wrongdoer'[6] as part of a private interest conception of victims.

In the United States, the legal narrative surrounding the privatization of victim interests has existed for much longer than in England and Wales and remains particularly robust at the federal level. This narrative, coupled with a strong commitment to preserving and reaffirming the state's monopoly over prosecutorial charging and negotiating decisions, has led to significant restrictions on the victim's role as an agent of state accountability in cases of prosecutorial fallibilities.

Indeed, in instances where charges have been laid by state prosecutors but negotiations are ongoing, victims have been able to assert their role—though primarily in relation to procedural failures affecting their inclusion in the process. When plea deals or similar agreements are subject to judicial scrutiny, their role as agents of state accountability is typically framed as an aggregate form in relation to the public interest.

In contrast, where no charges have been laid, victims have been effectively barred from holding the state accountable, even in cases involving serious breaches of the public interest. The case of *Wild*,[7] involving the victims

[6] Dempsey (n 3) 191.

[7] *In re Wild*, 955 F 3d 1269 (11th Cir 2020); *In re Wild*, 994 F 3d 1244 (11th Cir 2021) (en banc).

of sex trafficker Jeffrey Epstein, illustrates these limitations. Despite having been misled by state prosecutors and excluded from discussions surrounding a secret non-prosecution agreement (NPA) with Epstein, the victims were denied the possibility to challenge both procedural and substantive state failures relating to this agreement. The court held that under the Crime Victims' Rights Act, victims lack standing to challenge prosecutorial decisions when no formal criminal proceedings are underway. This interpretation raises serious concerns for future cases—particularly those involving marginalized victims harmed by powerful individuals—by effectively sanctioning covert NPAs that may undermine the public interest, without any mechanism for oversight or accountability.

Only in a few instances has the narrative of privatization enabled victims to hold the state substantively accountable for violations of their interests. In such cases within the United States, public criminal processes have increasingly taken on characteristics of private law mechanisms—most notably in the context of restitution claims. As demonstrated in relevant case law, victims have, in these limited circumstances, succeeded in asserting substantive claims to restitution, which are seen as complementary to tort law. These claims, however, tend to reinforce the conception of victims as holders of individualized private interests rather than as participants advancing broader public interests, which can serve to delegitimize victims their claims at other stages of the process that are seen as more public.

Interestingly, even in states that have retained certain vestiges of common law-based mechanisms, these remnants remain partial and have been shaped by the broader narrative of privatization. Nevertheless, in some of these states, there is recognition that victim-citizens may access grand juries and take part in certain mechanisms that allow courts to appoint special prosecutors—thereby offering a partial means of holding the state accountable.[8] Indeed, these mechanisms also recognize the possibility that state prosecutors may be influenced by private interests[9] when making prosecutorial decisions. As a result, they provide victims with avenues to request the appointment of a special prosecutor. Finally, a very limited number of states have allowed for judicial review of prosecutorial decisions. While this brings these processes closer to the approach found in England and Wales, it remains a partial approach as victims

[8] *People v Sears*, 273 NE 2d 380 (1971) 389; *State v Chauncey*, 890 NW 2d 453 (Neb 2017).
[9] Bruce A Green and Rebecca Roiphe, 'Rethinking Prosecutors' Conflicts of Interest' (2017) 58 BCL Rev 463.

in the United States are not generally recognized as entities who can make arguments in the public interest.

Conversely, when victims are recognized as citizens capable of making claims in the public interest, there tends to be a broader recognition of their role as agents of substantive accountability. This framing enables victims to engage substantively with legal and normative arguments in cases of potential prosecutorial failures. In England and Wales, several cases illustrate how victims have successfully invoked judicial review to substantively challenge errors in prosecutorial decision-making—particularly regarding the interpretation and evaluation of evidence.[10] As seen, such challenges often go beyond procedural failings and require engagement with the reasoning and substance of prosecutorial decisions.

Moreover, marginalized victims—when conceived as holders of predominantly public interests in England and Wales—have also made some headway in holding the state accountable for failures rooted in epistemic injustices. In cases involving private prosecutions and judicial review, victims have contested prosecutorial decisions that relied on unfounded stereotypes about their credibility and social status.[11] These cases demonstrate that marginalized victims, including sex workers, victims of domestic violence, and victims of hate crimes, are perceived as having greater legitimacy in holding the state accountable for prosecutorial failures when they are understood as holders of public interests rather than purely private interests. This recognition supports a more inclusive and equality-driven conception of the public interest, one that acknowledges systemic inequalities and seeks to respond to them through more substantive forms of accountability.

Resistance to the victim's role as an agent of state accountability is largely rooted in long-standing assumptions and narratives that frame victims as holding personal, individualized, and subjective views—perceived as incompatible with the objective and rational processes associated with decision-making in the public interest. This resistance is also at times explained by the state's reluctance to acknowledge its own fallibility, coupled with a desire to control and monopolize the definition and articulation of the public interest. Moreover, it is often assumed that transparent engagement with external actors, including citizens, victims, and judges, poses a threat to prosecutorial

[10] See discussion in chapter that provides illustrations. Mandy Burton, 'Reviewing Crown Prosecution Service Decisions Not to Prosecute' [2001] Crim LR 374, 377; *R v DPP Ex p Manning* [2001] QB 330, [2000] 3 WLR 463.

[11] See, eg, English Collective of Prostitutes (n 4); *Moher v Moher* [2019] EWCA Civ 1482; *R v Chabloz* [2019] Westminster Magistrates' Court, 25 May 2018 (unreported).

independence and undermines the separation of powers. These rationales have frequently been used to shield the state from accountability, reinforcing a system that limits meaningful scrutiny. As a result, victims are precluded from occupying more substantive roles as agents of state accountability in instances of prosecutorial failure, institutional bias, or discretionary errors.

While prosecutorial independence and the separation of powers doctrine are foundational principles in democratic systems—designed, among other aims, to safeguard the public interest from undue private interference—these ideals should not be invoked as pretexts to avoid transparency and withholding decision-making rationales behind prosecutorial assessments. As this monograph argues, victims should be seen as capable, rational contributors to the public interest discourse, and their participation can enhance accountability in prosecutorial decision-making. Moreover, when prosecutors fail to uphold this role, judges too can complement this process and serve to promote public accountability.

Importantly, accountability need not be confined to formal judicial processes. Internal review mechanisms within independent prosecution services, if structured appropriately, can also serve this function. However, the Victims' Right to Review Scheme (VRRS) in England and Wales presents two critical shortcomings. First, it often lacks a genuinely independent review process, which can result in conflicts of interest where decisions are reviewed by the same institution that made them. Second, the VRRS reflects an increasing shift towards a privatized understanding of victim interests—framing victims primarily as holders of personal interests notably in aggregate ways rather than direct contributors to the public interest. This framing, also present in the United States for certain decisions, and to a greater degree excluding victims' contribution in an aggregate way, has served to limit both the legitimacy and substantive impact of their participation.

Furthermore, this privatization has contributed to a narrowing of access to judicial review. In England and Wales, courts have increasingly required that the VRRS process be exhausted before a judicial review claim can be brought and they have signalled a more deferential standard of review once the internal process has been completed. This represents a departure from earlier models of state accountability, in which victims could directly access judicial review without such constraints and deference. In the United States, access to judicial review is limited. In most states and at the federal level, such review is unavailable in cases involving prosecutorial decisions not to lay charges. At the federal level, limited judicial oversight is generally confined to contexts once charges are brought—including those that involve plea agreements or deferred prosecution agreements (DPAs). Even in those instances, victims are perceived as forming an aggregate component of the public interest that limits legitimacy. Failures to recognize victims as agents of state accountability in instances prior to charges being laid creates a significant accountability gap in situations where prosecutors decline to prosecute. As a result, there is often no meaningful mechanism to assess or challenge prosecutorial decisions that may involve serious errors, omissions, or failures to properly assess the public interest in pursuing a case.

A similar resistance is also reflected in academic literature, where victims are frequently portrayed as pursuing private, subjective interests that are considered irrelevant to public decision-making and potentially threatening to the rights of the accused. Ironically, even segments of the victim advocacy literature have reinforced these assumptions by framing victim engagement primarily in terms of personal and individualized harm, needs, and views in the process. This perspective positions victims as lacking the objectivity required to advance arguments in the public interest, thereby limiting their perceived legitimacy in holding the state substantively accountable for prosecutorial failures. Consequently, the victim's role is often reduced to a form of procedural accountability—allowing for challenges to basic procedural shortcomings, such as the failure to be notified or heard within an aggregate understanding, but rarely permitting substantive engagement with prosecutorial reasoning or the public interest of decision-making. This limitation is particularly significant for marginalized communities, who may possess experiential and empirical knowledge relating to inequalities that can meaningfully inform legal and policy prosecutorial deliberative reasoning.[12] Reframing victims as capable and informed citizens across the legal culture—rather than as passive or private-interest seeking groups—would enhance their legitimacy in contesting state failures and contributing to a more transparent, deliberative, and accountable prosecutorial process.

3. Normative Reflections

Building on these findings and drawing from theoretical arguments grounded in deliberative democratic and communitarian frameworks, this monograph

[12] Jeffrey Kennedy, 'Beyond Judicial Solitude: Listening in the Politics of Criminal Sentencing' (2024) 43(3) Crim Just Ethics 225.

proposes a normative framework that justifies victims' ability to hold the state accountable—both procedurally and substantively—for various forms of state failures, including those rooted in systemic inequalities. Within this framework, victims are conceived as citizens capable of advancing public interests in a unitary rather than an aggregate way. These interests should be understood to encompass core democratic values, most notably substantive equality. Such a reconceptualization would facilitate more accurate and transparent discussions about responsibility in criminal law and prosecutions, as well as more rational and inclusive deliberations regarding the definition of the public interest.

This monograph contributes to the broader field of criminal law and justice, which has traditionally framed victims primarily as holders of private interests. It challenges this dominant narrative by introducing a public framework through which victims' roles and interests can be more fully understood. As discussed, adopting a broader conception of victims—one that recognizes them as public citizens—allows for the integration of diverse forms of knowledge and experiences into the legal process. This, in turn, can lead to more accurate communicative representations of responsibility and more substantive evaluations of the public interest, particularly in contexts where the state has failed in its assessments. Furthermore, this work engages with dimensions of the public interest in criminal law and prosecutions, addressing a gap in the current legal literature. Much of that literature remains rooted in assumptions that seldomly address underlying values and elements of legitimacy and standing relating to the public interest.

The framework advanced in this monograph does not propose for a complete shift towards a model of private prosecutions, in which victims or other citizens would assume full control over prosecutorial functions. Rather, its central focus lies in exploring and strengthening the mechanisms through which the state can be held accountable for prosecutorial fallibilities. The normative position articulated recognizes that prosecutorial decision-making—whether undertaken by state officials or private actors—must be subject to clear guidelines, institutional transparency, and robust checks and balances. These safeguards are essential to ensuring the legitimacy, fairness, and democratic accountability of the criminal legal process, regardless of the prosecutor.

This framework acknowledges its own limitations and does not presume that making decisions in accordance with a public interest rooted in substantive equality is straightforward or uncontentious. For instance, decision-making reasoning relating to the prosecution of domestic violence can be very complex, particularly when social injustices that are rooted in gender-based and intersectional inequities are at play.[13] However, in contrast to prevailing conceptions of the public interest—which often remain vague, abstract, or undefined—it contends that prosecutorial decision-making should include an explicit commitment to incorporating empirical evidence and experiential knowledge brought forward by the citizen-victims who advance substantive equality responses. In this sense, social context must be considered on a case-by-case basis, ensuring that responses are appropriately contextualized and attentive to the power dynamics at play. By doing so, the framework encourages more transparent, reasoned, and inclusive deliberations about what constitutes the public interest in specific contexts.

Rooting the victim's role within a public democratic framework—one that recognizes victims as citizens capable of holding and advancing public interests, rather than merely as bearers of possessive individual rights—recasts victim participation as a civic duty owed to the polity. This reconceptualization legitimizes the victim's involvement in addressing a range of state failures, including individual prosecutorial errors, misinterpretations of evidence, decisions that diverge from the public interest, and systemic injustices rooted in racism, ableism, and other entrenched power structures.

These duties may vary according to social context. Some victims may be excluded, disenfranchised, or reluctant to engage with accountability mechanisms due to systemic barriers or a lack of confidence in the legal system. Accordingly, it is important to tailor civic duties to account for social context so that victims are not encumbered with unrealistic or inequitable civic duties. Importantly, the civic duty of holding the state to account need not fall solely on the direct victim. Members of the polity, including advocacy organizations and NGOs, may also be well-positioned to identify and challenge state failures.

Although recognizing state failures and accountability may initially seem to threaten the legitimacy of state authority, the existence of robust accountability mechanisms can, in fact, strengthen that legitimacy by fostering transparency, trust, and procedural fairness. For this reason, acknowledging the role of victims as agents of state accountability is of critical value as it enhances the legitimacy of the criminal justice system by supporting a more accurate and just attribution of responsibility in instances of potential wrongdoing.

The proposed framework also challenges the prevailing assumption that victim participation is inherently punitive or incompatible with the rights

[13] Dempsey (n 3).

of the accused. Instead, it reframes victims' involvement as a form of democratic engagement—where they contribute to the accountability of the state, particularly when prosecutorial decisions undermine legal norms or substantive equality. In fact, it can often align with the broader interests of communities and accused persons alike—particularly where transparency and accurate communication of responsibility are mutually desired outcomes. By enabling victims to participate as civic actors concerned with both individual and relational responsibility,[14] this model promotes a more accurate ascription of criminal responsibility as part of prosecutorial decision-making.

To date, broader conversations about recognizing state failures as part of an accurate ascription of criminal responsibility remain limited and contentious in most common law jurisdictions, particularly in the assessment of prosecutorial decision-making. These discussions challenge the traditional role of the state as a neutral or victimized party, and instead suggest that the state itself can engage in criminogenic conduct or errors that ought to be acknowledged and addressed within prosecutorial assessments as part of the criminal justice process.

Accordingly, mechanisms of accountability should not be treated as peripheral or external to the public criminal process, but rather as integral to its operation—particularly insofar as they support a more accurate and communicative approach to prosecution. Within this framework, the role of victims as agents of state accountability extends beyond merely fulfilling red light functions, which conceive of state errors as isolated anomalies to be corrected. Instead, it contributes to advancing green light functions rooted in deliberative democratic ideals. These ideals envision the state and its institutions—including prosecutorial bodies—as reflexive and responsive, engaged in a continuous communicative process of self-examination, transparency, and improvement. Such a dynamic model supports prosecutorial decision-making that is more transparent, inclusive, and aligned with a public interest that can be understood through the lens of substantive equality.

4. Broader Contributions and Future Research

While the legal analysis in this monograph has primarily focused on mechanisms available in England and Wales as well as the United States, the normative

[14] Marie Manikis, 'Recognising State Blame in Sentencing: A Communicative and Relational Framework' (2022) 81(2) CLJ 294.

framework might be of interest to other common law jurisdictions that are similarly rooted in English legal tradition. These jurisdictions may also seek to develop prosecutorial accountability mechanisms that recognize victims as potential holders of public interests. More broadly, across the common law, this framework can serve as a valuable resource for scholars, citizens, policymakers, legal professionals, as well as activists committed to promoting and strengthening prosecutorial accountability within the criminal legal process. For instance, such an expansion would also provide an opportunity to develop policies that recognize the role of victims in holding the prosecutorial state accountable in contexts of charges and prosecutorial agreements—such as plea bargains or DPAs. Although prosecutors in many common law jurisdictions, including Canada and Australia, increasingly engage in these negotiated resolutions, victims have not been recognized as legitimate actors capable of holding the prosecutorial state accountable in these processes. Consequently, the role of victims in such proceedings remains underdeveloped.

Future research may build on this analysis and normative framework by expanding the comparative inquiry into victim participation in prosecutorial state accountability mechanisms. In particular, it would be valuable to examine how the role of victims as agents of state accountability has developed—and is implemented—in civil law traditions. Such inquiry could explore how victim interests are conceptualized within those legal systems and whether these conceptualizations give rise to distinct forms of accountability. For example, comparative analysis of the *partie civile* in France and the *Nebenklage* in Germany—both of which enable victim participation in the prosecutorial process, within the prosecutorial process—may offer important insights into how victims can hold prosecuting authorities to account in jurisdictions that depart from the adversarial common law model. The interdisciplinary and normative frameworks developed in this monograph may prove useful in assessing how victim interests are constructed, and how accountability mechanisms position and portray victims within varying institutional, legal, and cultural settings.

While the present study has focused primarily on the victim's role in holding the prosecutorial state accountable for failures in charging and related decision-making, recognizing victims as potential bearers of public interests may have broader implications across other stages of the criminal legal process. These include, most notably, trial and sentencing, which merit separate and sustained examination.

Finally, as outlined in this monograph, conceptualizing the victim as a potential holder of public interests may have important repercussions for other forms of legal participation beyond accountability. Future work could explore these broader implications and examine whether—and under what conditions—victim participation in the criminal process might be deepened or diversified in ways that are consistent with democratic values, substantive equality, and the public interest.

Bibliography

Aaronson D, 'New Rights and Remedies: The Federal Crime Victims' Rights Act of 2004' (2008) 28 Pace L Rev 623

Ailes E, 'Claims I Had Sexsomnia Destroyed my Rape Case' (*BBC News*, 5 October 2022) https://www.bbc.com/news/uk-63116989 accessed 5 February 2023

Aiyer S and others, 'Exposure to Violence Predicting Cortisol Response During Adolescence and Early Adulthood: Understanding Moderate Factors' (2014) 43(7) J Youth Adolesc 1066

Alexander M, *The New Jim Crow: Mass Incarceration in the Age of Colorblindness* (The New Press 2010)

Allen CK, *The Queen's Peace* (Stevens and Sons Ltd 1953)

Arnstein S, *A Ladder of Citizen Participation in the USA* (Royal Town Planning Institute 1971)

Aronson M, 'The Growth of Substantive Review: The Changes, Their Causes and Their Consequences' in Jason NE Varuhas and others (eds), *Public Law Adjudication in Common Law Systems: Process and Substance* (Hart Publishing 2016)

Ashworth A, *The Criminal Process* (OUP 1998)

Ashworth A and Redmayne M, *The Criminal Process* (4th edn, OUP 2010)

Bamforth N, 'Accountability of and to the Legislature' in Nicholas Bamforth and Peter Leyland (eds), *Accountability in the Contemporary Constitution* (OUP 2013)

Barth J, 'Criminal Prosecution in American History: Private or Public' (2002) 67 S D L Rev 119

BBC News, 'CPS Grants Lord Janner Review' (*BBC*, 16 May 2015) <www.bbc.com/news/uk-32757978> accessed 4 February 2024

BBC News, 'RSPCA Prosecution Powers "To be Examined by MPs"' (*BBC*, 22 September 2015) <https://www.bbc.com/news/uk-34314004> accessed 7 June 2023

BBC News, 'Post Office Scandal: Government Rejects Call to Extend Inquiry' (*BBC*, 27 April 2021) <https://www.bbc.com/news/business-56905442> accessed 7 June 2023

Beal SS and others, *Grand Jury Law and Practice § 4:2, 2nd edn., & Annual Supplements 1998–2021* (Thomson Reuters 1997)

Beale SS, 'Rethinking the Identity and Role of United States Attorneys' (2005) 6 Ohio St J Crim L 369

Bellot HHL, 'Origin of the Attorney-General' (1909) 25(4) L Q Rev 400

Beloof D, 'The Third Wave of Crime Victims' Rights: Standing, Remedy, and Review' (2005) 2 BYU L Rev 255

Beloof D, Cassell PG, and Twist SJ, *Victims in Criminal Procedure* (3rd edn, Carolina Academic Press 2010)

Beloof D, Cassell PG, and Twist SJ, *Victims in Criminal Procedure* (4th edn, Carolina Academic Press 2018)

Beloof D, Cassell PG, and Twist SJ, *Victims in Criminal Procedure* (5th edn, Carolina Academic Press 2024)

Berger B, 'Mental Disorder and the Instability of Blame in the Criminal Law' in Francois Tanguay-Renaud and J Stribopoulos (eds), *Rethinking Criminal Law Theory* (OUP 2012)

Bessler J, 'The Public Interest and the Unconstitutionality of Private Prosecutors' (1994) 47 Ark L Rev 511

Bingham TH, 'Should Public Law Remedies Be Discretionary?' (1991) PL 64

Blondel E, 'Victims' Rights in an Adversary System' (2008) 58 Duke LJ 237

Bovens M, 'Analysing and Assessing Public Accountability: A Conceptual Model' (European Governance Papers (EUROGOV) C-06-01, 16 January 2006)

Bovens M, 'Analysing and Assessing Accountability: A Conceptual Framework' (2007) 13(4) Eur LJ 447

Bovens M, Schillemans T, and Hart PT, 'Does Public Accountability Work? An Assessment Tool' (2008) 86(1) Public Admin 225

Bovens M, Goodin R, and Schillemans T (eds), *The Oxford Handbook of Public Accountability* (OUP 2014)

Bremner JD, 'Traumatic Stress: Effects on the Brain' (2006) 8(4) Dialogues Clin Neurosci 445

Brinkerhoff DW and Wetterberg A, 'Gauging the Effects of Social Accountability on Services, Governance, and Citizen Empowerment' (2016) 76(2) Public Admin Rev 274

Brown B, 'The Constitutional Validity of Pennsylvania Rule of Criminal Procedure 113 (b)(2) and the Traditional Role of the Pennsylvania Courts in the Prosecution Function' (1990) 52 U Pitt L Rev 269

Buchanan M, 'Voyeur Sentenced After Woman's Five-Year Campaign' (*BBC News*, 4 September 2020) <https://www.bbc.com/news/uk-england-london-54027088> accessed 13 June 2023

Buchhandler-Raphael M, 'Underprosecution Too' (2022) 56 U Rich L Rev 409

Burns P, 'Private Prosecutions in Canada: The Law and a Proposal for Change' (1975) 21 McGill LJ 269

Burton M, 'Reviewing Crown Prosecution Service Decisions Not to Prosecute' [2001] Crim LR 374

Button M and others, 'Confronting the "Fraud Bottleneck": Private Sanctions for Fraud and Their Implications for Justice' (2015) 1(3) J Crim Res Policy Pract 159

Calaico JA, *James Fitzjames Stephen and the Crisis of Victorian Thought* (Palgrave Macmillan 1983)

Capers B, 'Against Prosecutors' (2020) 105 Cornell L Rev 1561

Cassell PG, 'Protecting Crime Victims in Federal Appellate Courts: The Need to Broadly Construe the Crime Victims' Rights Act's Mandamus Provisions' (2010) 87 Denv U L Rev 599

Cassell PG, 'The Crime Victims' Rights Movement: Historical Foundations, Modern Ascendancy, and Future Aspirations' (2025) 56 U Pac L Rev 387

Cassell PG and Joffee S, 'The Crime Victim's Expanding Role in a System of Public Prosecution: A Response to the Critics of the Crime Victims' Rights Act' (2011) 105 Nw UL Rev 164

Cassell PG, Edwards BJ, and Peck J, 'Circumventing the Crime Victims' Rights Act: A Critical Analysis of the Eleventh Circuit's Decision Upholding Jeffrey Epstein's Secret Non-Prosecution Agreement' (2021) 211 Mich St L Rev 211

Cassell PG, Mitchell NJ, and Edwards BJ, 'Crime Victims' Rights During Criminal Investigations? Applying the Crime Victims' Rights Act Before Criminal Charges are Filed' (2014) 104 J Crim L & Criminol 59

Chitty J, *A Practical Treatise on the Criminal Law*, vol 1 (A J Valpy 1816)

Clifford Law Office, 'Victims' Families of MAX8 Crashes Files Motion to Oppose DOJ New Non-Prosecution Agreement with Boeing' (18 June 2025) <https://www.cliffordlaw.

com/victims-families-of-max8-crashes-file-motion-to-oppose-doj-new-non-prosecution-agreement-with-boeing/> accessed 24 June 2025

Cohen J, 'Deliberation and Democratic Legitimacy' in James Bohman and William Rehg (eds), *Deliberative Democracy: Essays on Reason and Politics* (MIT Press 1997)

Collins PH, *Black Feminist Thought: Knowledge, Consciousness and the Politics of Empowerment* (Routledge 2019)

Colman S, 'A Comparison of the Implementation of the Victims' Right to Review in England and Wales, Scotland and Northern Ireland' (2018) 5 Crim LR 365

Colman SJ, *'Evaluating Challenges to Decisions Not to Prosecute: Do the Victims' Rights to Review, Judicial Review and Private Prosecution Provide a Coherent and Principled Framework?'* (DPhil thesis, University of East Anglia 2020)

Conway O, 'Are There Stories Prosecutors Shouldn't Tell?: The Duty to Avoid Racialized Trial Narratives' (2021) 98 Denv L Rev 457

Coppola F, *The Emotional Brain and the Guilty Mind: Novel Paradigms of Culpability and Punishment* (Hart Publishing 2021)

CPS, 'Appeals: Judicial Review of CPS Prosecuting Decisions' (*CPS*, September 2019) <https://www.cps.gov.uk/legal-guidance/appeals-judicial-review-cps-prosecuting-decisions>

Craig P, *Administrative Law* (9th edn, OUP 2021)

Crenshaw K, 'Mapping the Margins: Intersectionality, Identity Politics, and Violence Against Women of Color' (1991) 43 Stanford L Rev 1241

Crown Prosecution Service, 'Appeals: Judicial Review of CPS Prosecuting Decisions' (*CPS*, September 2019) <https://www.cps.gov.uk/legal-guidance/appeals-judicial-review-cps-prosecuting-decisions> (version of 16 December 2020, updated 27 May 2021) accessed 27 May 2022

Crown Prosecution Service, 'Victims' Right to Review Data' (*CPS*, May 2021) <https://www.cps.gov.uk/publication/victims-right-review-data> (version of 16 December 2020, updated 27 May 2021) accessed January 2024

Crown Prosecution Service, 'Victims' Right to Review Scheme' (*CPS*, May 2021) <https://www.cps.gov.uk/legal-guidance/victims-right-review-scheme> (version of 16 December 2020, updated 27 May 2021) accessed 24 June 2023

Crown Prosecution Service, 'Victims' Right to Review Scheme' (*CPS*, 2025) <https://www.cps.gov.uk/legal-guidance/victims-right-review-scheme> (version of 16 December 2020, updated 27 May 2021) accessed 24 June 2023

Crown Prosecution Service, *The Code for Crown Prosecutors* (*CPS*, 2018) <https://www.cps.gov.uk/publication/code-crown-prosecutors> accessed 17 May 2023

Dangel S, 'Is Prosecution a Core Executive Function? Morrison v. Olsen and the Framers' Intent' (1990) 99 Yale LJ 1069

Davis AJ, *Arbitrary Justice: The Power of the American Prosecutor* (OUP 2007)

Davis AJ, 'The Perils of Private Prosecutions' (2022) 13(7) Calif L Rev 7

Davis PL, 'Rodney King and the Decriminalization of Police Brutality in America: Direct and Judicial Access to the Grand Jury as Remedies for Victims of Police Brutality When the Prosecutor Declines to Prosecute' (1994) 53 Md L Rev 263

Dawson M and Maricut-Akbik A, 'Procedural vs Substantive Accountability in EMU Governance: Between Payoffs and Trade-offs' (2021) 28(11) J Eur Public Policy 1707

Day P and Klein R, *Accountabilities: Five Public Services* (Tavistock 1987)

Dempsey MM, *Prosecuting Domestic Violence* (OUP 2009)

Devlin P, *The Criminal Prosecution in England* (Yale UP 1958)

Devlin P, *The Criminal Prosecution in England* (OUP 1960)

Dickens BM, 'Control of Prosecutions in the United Kingdom' (1973) 22 ICLQ 1
Doak J, 'The Victim and the Criminal Process: An Analysis of Recent Trends in Regional and International Tribunals' (2003) 23 LS 1
Doak J, *Victims' Rights, Human Rights and Criminal Justice: Reconceiving the Role of Third Parties* (Hart Publishing 2008)
Dubnick MJ, 'Accountability and the Promise of Performance: In Search of the Mechanisms' (2005) 28(3) Public Perfor & Manag Rev 376
Dubnick MJ and Frederickson HG, 'Accountable Agents: Federal Performance Measurement and Third-Party Government' (2011) 40(2) J Public Adm Res Theory 437
Duff RA, 'Law, Language, and Community: Some Preconditions of Criminal Liability' (1988) 18 OJLS 189
Duff RA, *Answering for Crime* (Hart Publishing 2007)
Duff RA, 'Blame, Moral Standing, and the Legitimacy of the Criminal Trial' (2010) 23 Ratio 123
Duff RA, *The Criminal Process* (OUP 2018)
Duff RA, 'When Should We Plead Guilty' in Julian V Roberts and Jesper Ryberg (eds), *Pleading Guilty: Ethical Perspectives on Sentencing the Self-Convicted* (Hart Publishing 2023)
Duff RA and Marshall SE, 'Communicative Punishment and the Role of the Victim' (2004) 23(2) Crim Just Ethics 39
Dworkin R, *A Matter of Principle* (Harvard UP 1986)
Edmonds T and Jugnarain D, 'Private Prosecutions: A Potential Anticorruption Tool in English Law' (Open Society Foundations 2014)
Edwards I, 'An Ambiguous Participant: The Crime Victim and Criminal Justice Decision-Making' (2004) 44(6) Br J Criminol 967
Edwards JLJ, *The Law Officers of the Crown* (Sweet & Maxwell 1964)
English Collective of Prostitutes, 'Successful Private Prosecution of Serial Rapist—R v Davies' (*English Collective of Prostitutes*, 1 January 1996) <https://prostitutescollective.net/private-prosecution/> accessed 24 June 2023
Erez E, 'Victim Participation in Sentencing: And the Debate Goes On . . . ' (1994) 3 IRV 17
Erez E, 'Who's Afraid of the Big Bad Victim? Victim Impact Statements as Victim Empowerment and Enhancement of Justice' (1999) Crim LR 545
Fairfax RA Jr, 'Outsourcing Criminal Prosecution: The Limits of Criminal Justice Privatization' [2010] U Chi Legal F 265, pt III
Farmer L, 'Criminal Law as an Institution: Rethinking Theoretical Approaches to Criminalization' in RA Duff and others (eds), *Criminalization: The Political Morality of the Criminal Law* (OUP 2014)
Feintuck M, *'The Public Interest' in Regulation* (OUP 2004)
Fenwick H, 'Rights of Victims in the Criminal Justice System: Rhetoric or Reality?' (1995) Crim LR 843
Fenwick H, 'Procedural "Rights" of Victims of Crime: Public or Private Ordering of the Criminal Justice Process?' (1997) 60 MLR 317
Ferguson C, 'Actualizing Justice: Private Prosecution Regimes for Modern Social Movements' (2023) 54(4) Colum J L & Soc Probs 578
Fionda J, *Public Prosecutors and Discretion* (Clarendon Press 1995)
Fricker M, *Epistemic Injustice: Power and the Ethics of Knowing* (OUP 2007)
Gardner J, 'Criminals in Uniform' in RA Duff and others (eds), *The Constitution of the Criminal Law* (OUP 2013)
Gavison R, 'Feminism and the Public/Private Distinction' (1992) 45 Stan L Rev 1

Gifford DG, 'Equal Protection and the Prosecutor's Charging Decision: Enforcing an Ideal' (1981) 9 Geo Wash L Rev 659
Gittler J, 'Expanding the Role of the Victim in a Criminal Action: An Overview of Issues and Problems' (1984) 11 Pepp L Rev 117
Goldsmith Chambers, 'Changing the Legal Landscape for Abuse Victims' (*Goldsmith Chambers*, 27 May 2022) <https://www.goldsmithchambers.com/changing-the-legal-landscape-for-abuse-victims/> accessed 7 June 2023
Graham DA, '"Probable Cause" in the Killing of Tamir Rice' (*The Atlantic*, 11 June 2015) <https://www.theatlantic.com/politics/archive/2015/06/tamir-rice-case-cleveland/395420/> accessed August 2023
Grear A, 'Theorizing the Rainbow? The Puzzle of the Public-Private Divide' (2003) 9 Res Publica 169
Green BA, 'Why Should Prosecutors "Seek Justice"?' (1999) 26(3) Fordham Urb LJ 607
Green BA and Roiphe R, 'Rethinking Prosecutors' Conflicts of Interest' (2017) 58 BCL Rev 463
Green BA and Ruben BP, 'Should Victims' Views Influence Prosecutors' Decisions?' (2022) 87 Brook L Rev 1127
Green L, 'Two Views of Collective Rights' (1991) 4 CJLJ 315
Gutmann A and Thompson D, *Why Deliberative Democracy?* (Princeton UP 2004)
Hagan J, *Victims Before the Law: The Organizational Domination of Criminal Law* (Butterworths 1983)
Haklay M, 'What Is Citizen Science? The Challenges of Definition' in Silke Vohland and others (eds), *The Science of Citizen Science* (Springer 2021)
Hall DJ, 'Victims' Voices in Criminal Court: The Need for Restraint' (1991) 28 Am Crim L Rev 233
Hall M, *Victims and Policy Making: A Comparative Perspective* (Willan Publishing 2010)
Harlow C, *Accountability in the European Union* (OUP 2002)
Harlow C and Rawlings R, *Law and Administration* (2nd edn, Butterworths 1997)
Harlow C and Rawlings R, *Law and Administration* (3rd edn, CUP 2009)
Hay D, 'Controlling the English Prosecutor' (1983) 21(2) Osgoode Hall LJ 165
Hay D and Snyder F (eds), *Policing and Prosecution in Britain 1750–1850* (Clarendon Press 1989)
Held V, *The Public Interest and Individual Interests* (Basic Books 1970)
Higgins T, 'Reviving the Public/Private Distinction in Feminist Theorizing' (2000) 75 Chicago-Kent L Rev 847
Hilson C, 'Discretion to Prosecute and Judicial Review' [1993] Crim LR 739
Hobbes T, *Leviathan* (first published 1651, EP Dutton & Co 1947)
Holder R, *Just Interests: Victims, Citizens, and the Potential for Justice* (Elgar 2018)
Iliadis M and Flynn A, 'Providing a Check on Prosecutorial Decision-Making: An Analysis of the Victims' Right to Review Reform' (2018) 58(3) Br J Criminol 550
Jones P, 'Group Rights' in Edward N Zalta (ed), *The Stanford Encyclopedia of Philosophy* (Stanford 2016)
Joshi A and Houtzager PP, 'Widgets or Watchdogs?: Conceptual Explorations in Social Accountability' (2012) 14(2) Public Manag Rev 145
Justice Committee, *Private Prosecutions: Safeguards* (2019–2021, HC 495)
Kaufman E, 'The Past and Persistence of Private Prosecution' (2024) 173(1) U Pa L Rev 89
Kendall P, 'A Prosecutor Says No to a Rape Charge, So a College Student Calls Her Own Grand Jury' (*Washington Post*, 19 May 2021) <https://www.washingtonpost.com/natio

nal/a-prosecutor-says-no-to-a-rape-charge-so-a-college-student-calls-her-own-grand-jury/2021/05/18/2ea9a130-b766-11eb-a5fe-bb49dc89a248_story.html> accessed August 2023

Kendall P, 'A College Student Who Called Her Own Grand Jury Doesn't Get the Rape Charge She Sought for Her Attacker' (*Washington Post*, 3 November 2021) <https://www.washingtonpost.com/nation/2021/11/03/college-student-who-called-her-owngrand-jury-doesnt-get-rape-charge-she-sought-her-attacker/> accessed 11 February 2025

Kennedy J, 'The Citizen Victim: Reconciling the Public and Private in Criminal Sentencing' (2019) 13(1) Crim L & Phil 83

Kennedy J, 'Beyond Judicial Solitude: Listening in the Politics of Criminal Sentencing' (2024) 43(3) Crim Just Ethics 225

Kilpatrick DG and Otto RK, 'Constitutionally Guaranteed Participation in Criminal Proceedings for Victims: Potential Effects of Psychological Functioning' (1987) 34 Wayne L Rev 7

Kohler-Hausmann I, *Misdemeanorland: Criminal Courts and Social Control in an Age of Broken Windows Policing* (Princeton UP 2018)

Krauss C and Wallace G, 'DOJ Drops Boeing Criminal Charge over 737 Max Crashes' (*CNN*, 30 May 2025) <https://www.cnn.com/2025/05/30/business/boeing-criminal-charge-dropped> accessed 28 June 2025

Lacey N, 'Criminal Justice and Social In(Justice)' (LSE International Inequalities Institute Working Paper No 84, October 2022)

Lacey N, 'Criminal Justice and Social (In)Justice', in Virginia Mantouvalou and Jonathan Wolff (eds), *Structural Injustice and the Law* (UCL Press 2024)

Langbein JH, *Prosecuting Crime in the Renaissance: England, Germany, France* (Harvard UP 1974)

Langbein JH, 'The Criminal Trial Before the Lawyers' (1978) 45 U Chi L Rev 263

Le T, 'Data, Anecdotes, Anecdotal Data: Feminist Data Activism Against Gendered Violence Post #Metoo' (2024) 11(4) Big Data Soc 1

Lernestedt C, 'Victim and Society: Sharing Wrongs, but in Which Roles?' (2014) 8 Crim L & Phil 187

Levine D, 'Public Wrongs and Private Rights: Limiting the Victim's Role in a System of Public Prosecution' (2010) 104(1) Nw UL Rev 335

Lippke R, 'Chronic Temptation, Reasonable Firmness, and the Criminal Law' (2014) 34(1) OJLS 75

Liston M, 'Expanding the Parameters of Participatory Public Law: A Democratic Right to Public Participation and the State's Duty of Public Consultation' (2017) 63 McGill LJ 375

Littleton, 'Jamie Susskind Acts in Landmark High Court Case Over Non-Prosecution of Neo-Nazi' (*Littleton Chambers*, nd) <https://littletonchambers.com/jamie-susskind-acts-in-landmark-high-court-case-over-non-prosecution-of-neo-nazi/> accessed 13 June 2023

Lonsway KA and Archambault J, 'The "Justice Gap" for Sexual Assault Cases: Future Directions for Research and Reform' (2012) 18 Violence Against Women 145

Loughlin M, *Public Law and Political Theory* (OUP 1992)

Luther King Jr M, 'Three Views of Violence' in Clayborne Carson (ed), *The Papers of Martin Luther King, Jr: Volume V, Threshold of a New Decade, January 1959–December 1960* (University of California Press 2005)

MacCormick N, *Institutions of Law: An Essay in Legal Theory* (OUP 2007)

MacKinnon C, 'Substantive Equality: A Perspective' (2011) 96 Minn L Rev 1

MacKinnon C, 'Substantive Equality Revisited: A Reply to Sandra Fredman' (2016) 14(3) Int'l J Const L 739

Macpherson C, *The Political Theory of Possessive Individualism: Hobbes to Locke* (OUP 2010)

MacPherson W, *The Stephen Lawrence Inquiry* (Cm 4262-I 1999)

Maitland FW, *Justice and Police* (MacMillan and Co 1885)

Malena C, Forster R, and Singh J, 'Social Accountability: An Introduction to the Concept and Emerging Practice' (Social Development Papers: Participation and Civic Engagement, Paper No 76, The World Bank 2004)

Manikis M, 'Recognizing Victims' Role and Rights During Plea Bargaining: A Fair Deal for Victims of Crime' (2012) 58(3) Crim LQ 411

Manikis M, 'Victim Impact Statements at Sentencing: Towards a Clearer Understanding of Their Aims' (2015) 65 UTLJ 85

Manikis M, 'Expanding Participation: Victims as Agents of Accountability in the Criminal Justice Process' (2017) 1 PL 63

Manikis M, 'A New Model of the Criminal Justice Process: Victims' Rights as Advancing Penal Parsimony and Moderation' (2019) 30(2) Crim L Forum 201

Manikis M, 'Conceptualizing the Victim within Criminal Justice Processes in Common Law Tradition' in Darryl K Brown, Jenia I Turner, and Bettina Weisser (eds), *The Oxford Handbook of Criminal Process* (OUP 2019)

Manikis M, 'Conceptualising the Victim in England and Wales and the United States within a Spectrum of Public and Private Interests' (2021) 41(1) OJLS 219

Manikis M, 'Recognising State Blame in Sentencing: A Communicative and Relational Framework' (2022) 81(2) CLJ 294

Manikis M, 'Victim-related Assumptions Underlying Plea-based Sentence Reductions: A Communicative and Experiential Framework' in Julian V Roberts and Jesper Ryberg (eds), *Pleading Guilty: Ethical Perspectives on Sentencing the Self-Convicted* (Hart Publishing 2023)

Manikis M and Iliadis M, 'Analysing the Victim Review Scheme of Decisions Not to Prosecute in England and Wales and Within Comparative Jurisdictions' in Pamela Cox and Sandra Walklate (eds), *Victims' Access to Justice: Historical and Comparative Perspectives* (Routledge 2022)

Marshall S, 'It Isn't Just About You' Victims of Crime, Their Associated Duties, and Public Wrongs' in RA Duff and others (eds), *Criminalization: The Political Morality of the Criminal Law* (OUP 2015)

Marshall SE, 'Victims of Crime: Their Station and Its Duties' (2004) 7(2) CRISPP 104

Marshall SE and Duff RA, 'Criminalization and Sharing Wrongs' (1998) 11 Can J L Juris 7

Mayson SG, 'Bias In, Bias Out' (2019) 128 Yale LJ 2218

McIntyre S, 'Deference and Dominance: Equality Without Substance' in Sheila McIntyre and Sanda Rodgers (eds), *Diminishing Returns: Inequality and the Canadian Charter of Rights and Freedoms* (LexisNexis 2006) 95

McIntyre S, 'Answering the Siren Call of Abstract Formalism with the Subjects and Verbs of Domination' in Fay Faraday, Margaret Ann Denike, and M Kate Stephenson (eds), *Making Equality Rights Real: Securing Substantive Equality under the Charter* (Irwin Law 2009)

McKee D, 'The Public/Private Distinction in Roncarelli v. Duplessis' (2010) 55 McGill LJ 461

Mervyn J and Ashton S, 'Trauma-Informed Neurobiology and Criminal Behaviour' in Shereen Hassan, Dan Lett, and Leah Ballantyne (eds), *Introduction to Criminology* (KPU Press 2023)

Ministry of Justice, *Consultation on the Oversight and Regulation of Private Prosecutors in the Criminal Justice System* (CPd 43/2025, March 2025) <https://assets.publishing.service.gov.uk/media/67c57c4f72e83aab48866ce8/oversight-regulation-private-prosecutors-consultation.pdf> accessed 7 June 2025

Morabito MS, Williams LM, and Pattavina A, *Decision Making in Sexual Assault Cases: Replication Research on Sexual Violence Case Attrition in the United States* (National Criminal Justice Reference Service 2019)

Morse SJ, 'Diminished Rationality, Diminished Responsibility' (2002) 1 Ohio St J Crim L 289

Motivans M, *Federal Justice Statistics 2012—Statistical Tables, DOJ NCJ 248470* (Bureau of Justice Statistics 2015)

Mulgan R, *Holding Power to Account: Accountability in Modern Democracies* (Palgrave 2003)

Natapoff A, *Punishment Without Crime: How Our Massive Misdemeanor System Traps the Innocent and Makes America More Unequal* (Basic Book 2018)

National Crime Victim Institute, Fifty States, and D.C., *Survey of Laws that Authorize or Recognize Private-Citizen Initiated Investigation and/or Prosecution of Criminal Offenses* (2015)

National Research Council, *The Growth of Incarceration in the United States: Exploring Causes and Consequences* (The National Academies Press 2014)

Nelken D, *Comparative Criminal Justice: Making Sense of Difference* (Sage 2010)

Nussbaum MC, 'The Weakness of the Furies' (*Boston Review*, 17 October 2023) <https://www.bostonreview.net/articles/the-weakness-of-the-furies/> accessed 3 July 2025

O'Hara EA, 'Victim Participation in the Criminal Process' (2005) 13 JL & Pol'y 229

Oliver D, *Common Values and the Public/Private Divide* (Butterworths 1999)

Onuche EI, 'Attorney General's Power of Nolle Prosequi: A Relic of Colonialism or a Burden to Rule of Law?' (2021) 5(2) AJLHR 55

O'Reilly L, 'Property Firm Owner Jailed After Failing to Grant Wife Jewish Religious Divorce' (*Independent*, 1 April 2022) <https://www.independent.co.uk/news/uk/crime/jewish-cps-southwark-crown-court-salford-b2048991.html> accessed 24 June 2023

Orfield LB, 'The Federal Grand Jury' (1958) 22 FRD 343

Ozymy J and Jarrell ML, 'Of Sex Crimes and Fencelines: How Recognition of Environmental Justice Communities as Crime Victims Under State and Federal Law Can Help Secure Environmental Justice' (2020) 38(1) Pace Environ L Rev 109

Padover S, *The Complete Jefferson* (Tudor Publishing Company 1943)

Pollock F and Maitland FW, *History of English Law* (2nd edn, CUP 1968)

Pooler M and Croft J, 'Bankruptcy, Jail, Ruined Lives: Inside the Post Office Scandal' (*Financial Times*, 11 September 2020) <https://www.ft.com/content/0138cd7d-9673-436b-86a1-33704b29eb60> accessed 7 June 2023

Riley S, 'The Public-Private Divide: Which Side is Criminal Justice On?' in Malcolm Cowburn and others (eds), *Values in Criminology and Community Justice* (Policy Press 2013)

Roach K, *Due Process and Victims' Rights: The New Law and Politics of Criminal Justice* (UP of Toronto 1999)

Roach K, 'Four Models of the Criminal Process' (1999) 89(2) J Crim L & Criminology 671

Roberts JV and Erez E, 'Communication in Sentencing: Exploring the Expressive Function of Victim Impact Statements' (2004) 10 IRV 223

Robinson P, 'Should the Victims' Rights Movement Have Influence Over Criminal Law Formulation and Adjudication?' (2002) 33 McGeorge L Rev 749

Rock E, 'Fault and Accountability in Public Law' in Michael Elliot, Jason Varuhas, and Shona W Stark (eds), *The Unity of Public Law* (Hart Publishing 2018)

Rock E, *Making Sense of the Public Law/Private Law Divide* (Federation Press 2020)

Rocker S, 'Jailed Businessman Was Not a "Get Refuser", Beth Din Said' (*The Jewish Chronicle*, 19 April 2022) <https://www.thejc.com/news/news/jailed-businessman-was-not-a-get-refuser-beth-din-said-6anQOzSjcchNbfKaWfRvhb> accessed 7 June 2023

Rogers J, 'A Human Rights Perspective on the Evidential Test for Bringing Prosecutions' (2017) 9 Crim LR 678

Ross T, 'Thomas Ross QC on the Private Prosecution of David Goodwillie and David Robertson' (*Scottish Legal News*, 21 February 2022) <https://www.scottishlegal.com/articles/thomas-ross-qc-on-private-prosecution-of-david-goodwillie-and-david-robertson> accessed 14 June 2023

RSPCA, 'We're Reviewing Our Prosecutor Role to Focus on Frontline Cruelty' (*RSPCA*, 28 June 2021) <https://www.rspca.org.uk/-/news-reviewing-prosecutor-role-to-focus-on-frontline-cruelty#:~:text=We've%20announced%20we're,for%20animals%20and%20investigating%20cruelty> accessed 7 June 2023

Savage M, 'Plans to Reform Private Prosecutions After Post Office Horizon Scandal' (*The Guardian*, 13 January 2024)

Schafer S, *Victimology: The Victim and His Criminal* (Reston Publishing Company 1977)

Serious Fraud Office and Crown Prosecution Service, *Deferred Prosecution Agreements Code of Practice* (2014)

Shelby T, 'Justice, Deviance, and the Dark Ghetto' (2007) 35 Phil & Pub Aff 126

Shelby T, *Dark Ghettos, Injustice, Dissent, and Reform* (Harvard UP 2016)

Sheppard C, 'Contester la discrimination systémique au Canada: Droit et changement organisationnel' (2018) 14 La Revue des droits de l'homme <https://doi.org/10.4000/revdh.4161>

Sheppard C, 'Litigating Structural Inequality: Micro, Meso and Macro Dynamics' in Cheryl Milne and Sophia Moreau (eds), *Litigating Equality* (Lexis Nexis 2024)

Shubber K, 'The British Private Investigator Taking Criminals to Court When the State Won't' (*Financial Times*, 19 May 2023) <https://www.ft.com/content/135ab383-5df7-4824-bed5-1199e60a8597> accessed 7 June 2023

Sidman A, 'The Outmoded Concept of Private Prosecution' (1976) 25 Am U L Rev 754

Simmons AJ, *The Lockean Theory of Rights* (Princeton UP 1992)

Sklansky JA, 'The Nature and Function of Prosecutorial Power' (2016) 106(3) J Crim L Criminol 473

Smith RJ and Levinson JD, 'The Impact of Implicit Racial Bias on the Exercise of Prosecutorial Discretion' (2012) 35 Seattle UL Rev 795

Stark F, 'The Demise of the Private Prosecution?' (2013) 72(1) CLJ 7

Starmer K, 'Finality in Criminal Justice: When Should the CPS Reopen a Case?' (2012) 7 Crim LR 526

Starr JW, Flack BL, and Foley AD, 'A New Intersection: Environmental Crimes and Victims' Rights' (2009) 23(3) Nat Resources & Env't 41

Steinberg A, *The Transformation of Criminal Justice: Philadelphia 1800–1890* (University of North Carolina Press 1989)

Stenning PC, *Appearing for the Crown: A Legal and Historical Review of Criminal Prosecutorial Authority in Canada* (Brown Legal Publications 1986)

Summers RS, 'Evaluating and Improving Legal Processes: A Plea for "Process Values"' (1974) 60(1) Cornell L Rev 1

Taggart M, 'Proportionality, Deference, Wednesbury' (2008) 18 New Zealand L Rev 423

Teubner G, 'After Privatisation: The Many Autonomies of Private Law' (1998) 51 CLP 393

'The Post Office Prosecutions', (*Publications Parliament UK*, 2 October 2020) <https://publications.parliament.uk/pa/cm5801/cmselect/cmjust/497/49704.htm#footnote-135> accessed 24 June 2023

'The State of Private Prosecutions', (*Publications Parliament UK*, 2 October 2020) <https://publications.parliament.uk/pa/cm5801/cmselect/cmjust/497/49705.htm#footnote-108-backlink> accessed 24 June 2023

Tomkins A, 'In Defence of the Political Constitution' (2002) 22 OJLS 157

Tuerkheimer D, 'Incredible Women: Sexual Violence and the Credibility Discount' (2017) 160 U Pa L Rev 1

Turner JI, 'Victims as a Check on Prosecutors: A Comparative Assessment' (2022) 13 Calif L Rev 72

Tyler TR, 'Procedural Justice and the Courts' (2003) 44(4) Court Review 26

US Department of Justice, *Justice Manual* (2018)

US Department of Justice, 'Federal Judge Sentences Three Men Convicted of Racially Motivated Hate Crimes in Connection with the Killing of Ahmaud Arbery in Georgia' (8 August 2022) <https://www.justice.gov/archives/opa/pr/federal-judge-sentences-three-men-convicted-racially-motivated-hate-crimes-connection-killing> accessed 24 September 2024

Varuhas JNE, 'Against Unification' in Hanna Wilberg and Mark Elliott (eds), *The Scope and Intensity of Substantive Review* (Hart Publishing 2015) 91

Varuhas JNE, *Damages and Human Rights* (Hart Publishing 2016)

Vasanthakumar A, 'Epistemic Privilege and Victims' Duties to Resist their Oppression' (2018) 35(3) J Appl Philos 465

Vogel ME, 'The Social Origins of Plea Bargaining: Conflict and the Law in the Emergence of Plea Bargaining, 1830–1860' (1999) 33 L & Soc'y Rev 161

Vogel ME, 'Plea Bargaining Under the Common Law' in Darryl K. Brown, Jenia Iontcheva Turner, and Bettina Weisser (eds), *Oxford Handbook of Criminal Process* (OUP 2018)

Walklate S and Fitz-Gibbon K, 'The Evolving Place of Victims within the Penal Landscape: The Case of England and Wales' (2019) 28(2) Soc & Leg Stud 181

Weiss EB, 'Bottom Up Accountability' (2007) 37 Environ Policy L 259

Wemmers JAM, 'Victims' Rights Are Human Rights: The Importance of Recognizing Victims as Persons' (2012) 19(2) Temida 71

Wilberg H and Elliott M (eds), *The Scope and Intensity of Substantive Review: Traversing Taggart's Rainbow* (Hart Publishing 2015)

Wooler S, *The Independent Review of the Prosecution Activity of the Royal Society for the Prevention of Cruelty to Animals* (2014)

Worrall JL, 'Prosecution in America: A Historical and Comparative Account' in John L Worrall and M Elaine Nugent-Borakove (eds), *The Changing Role of the American Prosecutor* (State University of New York Press 2008) 5–6

Yarwood L, *State Accountability under International Law: Holding States Accountable for Breach of Jus Cogens Norms* (Routledge 2011)

Younger RD, *The People's Panel: The Grand Jury in the United States (1631–1941)* (Brown UP 1963)

Zedner L, 'Pre-crime and Post-criminology?' (2007) 11 Theor Criminol 261

Index

For the benefit of digital users, indexed terms that span two pages (e.g., 52–53) may, on occasion, appear on only one of those pages.